The son of the test pilot for the Gloster Meteor, the RAF's first fighter jet, **Mike Daunt** was educated at Rugby School before being dragged screaming by his short and curlies to ~~the R~~ ... every drill sergeant to ~~a nervo~~ commissioned into the Royal Green Jackets and ~~after~~ ... years of mutual incompetence left to start his own highly successful fish and game business. This was entirely based on sex, and he eventually sold it (the company, not the sex; this he has always been happy to give away free to any woman so down on her luck as to want him). He then became a Spey-casting instructor to the stars. Among his clients are: Chris Tarrant, Ronnie Corbett, Jeremy Paxman, Eric Clapton, Guy Ritchie and Fiona Armstrong. He has shown a large amount of foolish optimism by being married three times. He has three very loved sons and an adored daughter, and lives near Hungerford in Berkshire. His previous book, *Endangered Species: The Bart and the Bounder's Countryside Year*, written with his cousin, Sir Richard Heygate, Bt, was published in 2007; the pair had featured in a BBC2 documentary, *The Bart and the Bounder*, first broadcast in 2006.

the riotous true-life adventures of a bon viveur

THE BOUNDER

MIKE DAUNT

WITH A FOREWORD BY CHRIS TARRANT

JOHN BLAKE

First published by
John Blake Publishing Limited
3 Bramber Court, 2 Bramber Road
London W14 9PB

www.johnblakebooks.com

www.facebook.com/johnblakebooks ⓕ
twitter.com/jblakebooks ⓔ

First published in paperback in 2016

ISBN: 978-1-78418-770-5

British Library Cataloguing-in-Publication Data:

A catalogue record for this book is available from the British Library.

Design by www.envydesign.co.uk

Printed in Great Britain by CPI Group (UK) Ltd

1 3 5 7 9 10 8 6 4 2

The lines from T. S. Eliot's 'The Journey of the Magi' on p.43, and 'The Love
Song of J. Alfred Prufrock' on p.238, are reproduced by kind permission
of the Eliot Estate and Faber and Faber Ltd.

The right of Michael Daunt to be identified as the author of this work has been
asserted by him in accordance with the Copyright, Designs and Patents Act 1988.

Papers used by John Blake Publishing are natural, recyclable products made from
wood grown in sustainable forests. The manufacturing processes conform to the
environmental regulations of the country of origin.

Every attempt has been made to contact the relevant copyright-holders,
but some were unobtainable. We would be grateful if the
appropriate people would contact us.

Contents

For Ros (1946–2013)
I was far too young when I married you to appreciate
what a gem I had, and for
Jonny Ducat-Hamersley (1945–2009)
the greatest friend that anyone could ever ask for.

Foreword

Michael Daunt is the most annoying, most foul-mouthed man I have ever met. He is also the most sweetly descriptive, articulate and intelligent man on earth. He is appallingly coarse, often pig-headed and plain stupid, deeply sensitive and highly intelligent. He is, above all, one of the kindest men you'll ever be lucky enough to encounter.

I have fished with Daunty a lot, in places as far apart as Somerset for pike, and the extreme north of Russia for huge salmon. Without exception it's always been a nightmare. He is a brilliant caster of a salmon fly and teaches people with more money than sense how to do it. He once tried to teach some captain of industry, or similar sort of grandee, how to cast, but gave up exasperated after several hours, gave him his money back and told him to go forth and multiply, something no one else had ever dared to do. 'He drove me mad,' said Daunty, 'the arrogant sod just wouldn't listen,' Even knowing this, I too once booked a lesson. I have never been so ruthlessly cajoled or had my inadequacies so brutally and loudly exposed in my life! – and this as a more than handsomely paying customer. I must admit, though, that by the end of the day my casting was improved 100 per cent, but my ears bled for several days.

A few of us once took him to the River Wye to catch his first barbel. The barbel is an immensely powerful fish and its bite famously savage. We put the very excited Michael in a prime spot and the rest of us took bets on how soon after his first bite he would blaspheme. Mine was easily the lowest bet – I said 5 seconds. I won, but was 4½ seconds over in my estimate. The moment his rod slammed over towards the water he uttered the loudest, most vile oath any of us had ever heard, completely missed the bite and landed in a quivering heap.

What I love about Daunt is that although he must have been fishing literally tens of thousands of times, he still gets so extraordinarily excited, and actually doesn't sleep the night before a fishing trip. He has this wonderful infectious enthusiasm like a little boy, even though he's been fishing since some time before the Battle of Hastings.

This book is an often-bawdy romp through just some of his adventures, from a deeply unhappy childhood to the raddled septuagenarian scribe, bon viveur and lecher that he is today.

The chapters are as complex as the man himself. Occasionally hugely funny, sometimes deeply shocking, and once in a while very sad. His clear dislike of his father, his pain at being cruelly kept apart from his mother, his, at best, ambivalence towards Dirk Bogarde, and his on-off/off-on but always passionate relationships with the many, many women in his life are just a part of the great adventure that has been Michael Daunt's shameless life so far. I stress *so far*, because I see no sign of him slowing up. I fear there are many more atrocities to come.

A word of warning. I would not offer his description of the day his father chose to try to teach the young Daunt the 'facts of life' to anyone of a squeamish nature; to less sensitive souls among you, however, I cannot recommend these pages highly enough. It is an absolute hoot, like Daunty himself.

CHRIS TARRANT

Prologue

So why on earth should you read a book by Mike Daunt, of whom you have probably never heard? Because I am a very ordinary person who *so far* has had an amazing and 'unordinary' life. A few years ago now, Adam Edwards, a freelance journalist, wanted to interview me for the *Daily Telegraph* 'Weekend' section. Every journalist is always looking for a new angle to a story or a good quote, so I told Adam that I had never done a day's work in my life. Anyone who hears this immediately assumes that I am lucky enough to have a vast private income and am essentially a playboy. Nothing could be further from the truth. I have never had any private means and yet somehow I have travelled to some of the most exciting places on earth, and stayed with, laughed with and enjoyed the company of some of the most famous and interesting people. I haven't engineered any of this. It has just happened because everything I have done I have hugely enjoyed – yes, even the army.

In this book I have intentionally not told the stories of my wives, and there have been three, nor my children, of which I have four, and no father could either love his children more, or be closer to them. They are my adored friends as well as my children. We always have such fun together with an enormous warmth of laughter (there's a new collective noun for you).

I have also been so rich in friends, one of whom, Toby Buchan, has been my editor for this book. In fact, without Toby, it would never have been written. He and I met occasionally for wonderful laughing lunches when we put the world to rights, discussed books and poetry and blissfully drank far too much nourishing wine. At one of these Bacchanalian booze-ups I told Toby that I had the urge to write a book. I had some ideas for a novel but these never came to fruition and Toby eventually said: 'Why don't you write about you?' Initially I thought this was ridiculous as I was sure that no one would be interested. However, I scribbled a few memories, and was amazed when I was then told to write it all down and lovely lucre was thrust into my very willing hands. Thank you so much, Toby, for being a tower of knowledge and encouragement.

I also want to thank *The Field* magazine, for which I so enjoy writing and which has been kind enough to publish so much of my work, some of which I have included here. I would say to Jonathan Young, the editor, ''Tis a lovely man ye are', as would be said in my ancestral country.

Not long ago, a sailing friend of mine found himself in

one of the most insalubrious and rough areas of Portsmouth.
(Why he was there, I have no idea and I felt it rude to enquire.)
He had had a most enjoyable lunch, which had consisted
mostly of oysters. Suddenly, as can happen to anyone, he
knew that he had to get to a lavatory and very fast. Luckily
for him, his pride and his laundry bill, there was a very scruffy
council loo just across the road. Here he hurried and was
sitting in joyful relief when he noticed that the lavatory door
was covered in the usual sordid scribblings. All of us enjoy
reading graffiti, particularly when there is nothing else to do,
but among the crude invitations, the pornographic drawings
and the pathetic boasts, he found this gem. Knowing my
passion for poetry he kindly memorised it as follows:

I shall acknowledge age when the call of far, wild seas
No longer stirs my blood.
When I cannot see,
As a boy would see,
Homebound ships harbouring on the flood.

Only then will I sit in the lea of harbour walls
Conjuring dreams from the river's mist;
Only then will I weep an old man's tears
For ships which I might have sailed;
For girls I have left unkissed.

I have no idea who wrote it and, despite much searching,
I cannot find out but, whoever it was, was a man after my
own heart.

THE BOUNDER

For me, Hilaire Belloc really summed it all up so well when he wrote:

From quiet homes and first beginning,
Out to the undiscovered ends,
There's nothing worth the wear of winning,
But laughter and the love of friends.

MIKE DAUNT

ONE

The Actress

The moment I set eyes on her I thought her the loveliest woman I had ever seen. She had a figure of which any girl of twenty would have been proud, the high cheekbones of the truly beautiful, eyes robin-bright, a very determined set to her chin and Titian hair that fell like a waterfall to her slim shoulders. She was dressed in motorbike leathers, the masculinity of which only emphasised her sexiness and femininity. She was with a very good-looking man, one of the regulars in the pub where I was drinking and whom I knew to be Britt Ekland's then manager. She looked like a film star, which was not surprising as she was one, and her legs were insured for a million dollars.

I was in The Nelson in Montpelier Square, Knightsbridge, having a quiet drink with some of the other regulars. The Nelson was one of those pubs where one of the bars was

1

almost a club. (I write 'was' because, sadly, it no longer exists, having fallen prey to the ever-rising value of property in London. It is now a multi-million-pound private house.) It had two bars: a large public one and a tiny saloon, which was the 'club'. It was run by an ex-Indian Army major who spent all his time in the saloon bar with his cronies and left the running of both bars to various very pretty girls. This was a happy situation as everyone loved the girls and he was a fund of amusing stories and, against all the gambling laws, encouraged the playing of backgammon and poker dice for very liberal stakes. It was here that I was standing, supping my beer, when I saw 'The Vision'. No, I am not going to tell you her name as I hate shag-and-sneak stories. She will be known as 'L.', for reasons that I shan't explain.

I immediately greeted her companion and asked to be introduced before buying them both a drink. I then joyfully spent the next hour chatting up the star, to the fury of her friend. Eventually he could stand it no longer and whisked her outside where he had parked his motorbike, onto which she climbed with an obvious lack of experience. I noticed that she wasn't wearing a crash helmet, which was against every law in the land. Much later I asked her why. Her reply was typical of her: 'Because I like looking beautiful and it is impossible in one of those awful things.' There was a bellow of engine, a puff of exhaust smoke and a flowing of red hair in the wind and L. disappeared into the distance. But I had her phone number.

I rang her the next day and suggested dinner, which was joyfully accepted and, after I had picked her up in my ancient

1955 MG TF 1500 from her Belgravia house, we drove to a well-known Chinese restaurant in South Kensington in which Patrick Lichfield had a share. We then sat at our table and I just stared with cow-like eyes at this beautiful woman opposite me. I suddenly realised that I was enormously sexually excited. I wriggled uncomfortably in my seat. 'What's the matter?' said L., so I told her the truth. In fact I was so overcome with lust that I could think of nothing else to say to her – and then suddenly realised that she felt the same. We rubbed ankles over the delicious food and I found I could eat nothing. My stomach was churning so hard that it could not have digested anything. There is no doubt that this was the quickest dinner I have ever had. Suddenly, neither of us could stand it any longer. I called a waiter over, paid the bill and we both rushed out. At the door the manager enquired solicitously if there was anything wrong. 'Nothing,' said L., 'we're just in rather a hurry.'

We jumped into my car and set off. The traffic lights at the junction of Sloane Avenue and Brompton Road stopped us and I leant across and kissed her. We were still kissing after the lights had changed twice, and only stopped when the driver of the car behind us tapped me on the shoulder and, with a huge smile, suggested that I drive on as there was now a jam as far back as Harrods. What was so extraordinary about it all was that we weren't a pair of star-struck teenagers, but fortyish-year-old adults, and we were totally powerless to stop. The feeling of intense sexual attraction combined with a cornucopia of chemistry was an almost religious experience. It had never happened to me before and it has never happened since, and I think that I am very lucky to have found it even once in my lifetime.

Somehow we drove back to Graham Terrace in Belgravia, where she lived. She ran up the steps and fumbled hopelessly with her keys and I nearly kicked the door down. Eventually we got in and rushed up the stairs to the first-floor bedroom. She was undressed and in bed in seconds and I, determined not be outdone, ripped my clothes off, too. On the chest of drawers I noticed a picture of Tyrone Power who, I later discovered, was an ex-lover. However, at the time, I was certain that he would have been able to undress faster than I and this spurred me on. With complete abandon and determined to look like the Mr Atlas that I wasn't, I ripped off my shirt and trousers and hurled them across the room; straight into the dog's bowl of water, something I am certain Mr Power would not have done. And thus started an affair that lasted off and on for nine years.

Because we were both strong characters there were inevitably huge rows, one of which was the most farcical that I have ever known. L. had been out to a 'theatre drinks party'. This is a get-together, organised by one of the profession, at which everyone sniffs around everyone else to see what's going on. Managers and agents push their clients with directors, directors talk to producers, and actors and actresses, however well-known or even famous, make themselves pleasant to one and all. Not surprisingly I was not invited, nor did I wish to be there, for the sight of everyone at their most vulnerable and sycophantic is not a pretty one. However, L. seemed to enjoy it and returned saying that she had met 'a truly wonderful couple, darling, who are dying to meet you'. I took this with a huge pinch of salt as she was still in the party mode of pleasing all. The next evening the promised phone call came and we were bidden to dinner. Two days later, we set forth for Hampstead in L.'s beautiful white open-topped two-seater Mercedes, which I drove because she loved being driven.

I don't know why I had a bad feeling about the whole thing, but I did. I think it was something to do with the fact that the couple in question were a husband-and-wife agent team, and that L. already had a really lovely agent who did his best for her and cared for her. I asked if this pair were after her professionally and was told in no uncertain fashion that they were just new friends with no ulterior motives whatsoever. At last we arrived at an expensive North London address. A man with dyed hair answered the door with his wife hovering behind him. They introduced themselves to me as Tarquin and Rosebud and offered us drinks. 'I'd love a gin and tonic, please,' I said.

'What sort of gin?' asked Tarquin. 'We've got everything,' he added proudly.

'I really couldn't care less,' I said. He gave me a withering look and I quickly realised two things: firstly that they were both unbelievably pretentious, and secondly that I, not being in the entertainment world, was regarded as a pretty low form of life.

After some name-dropping and 'Do you know So-and-So?' Tarquin declared proudly, 'We had Larry to dinner last week. Of course, his son has the same name as I do.'

'Who's Larry?' I asked, before anyone else could reply. I knew that it would cause misery and I knew that he meant Laurence Olivier, but I simply couldn't resist it.

'You know perfectly well, darling,' said L., trying to defuse the situation.

'No,' I said. 'I've no idea. Larry the Lamb?'

There was a horrified silence, into which Rosebud announced, 'Shall we go in to dinner?' As we followed our host and hostess into the dining room, L. gave me a filthy look and mouthed, '*Behave*'. I pretended not to notice. We sat down, whereupon Tarquin and Rosebud disappeared into the kitchen.

'We're leaving,' I said to L. in a stage whisper.

'What do you mean?' she demanded.

'Just watch and take your cue from me,' I said.

As our host and hostess returned carrying the starter I was seen to be rolling around on my chair, clutching my stomach and groaning. 'I'm sorry,' I muttered through terrible convulsions, 'I'm afraid we've got to leave. A touch of amoebic dysentery. Picked it up in Malaya.' Of course I shouldn't have done it but I knew that if we stayed I was likely to say something truly awful, and anyway, why waste a beautiful summer's evening? Tarquin and Rosebud were too amazed to say anything much as we both hustled ourselves to the door, with me bent double and L. following in my wake. I staggered into the driving seat of her car and drove away.

'How dare you treat my friends so fucking badly!' screamed L., as soon as we were out of earshot.

'How dare you have such fucking awful friends,' I replied.

'And,' L. continued, 'it was an appalling piece of acting.' The Ultimate Insult.

We drove on in vituperative silence until we were passing the Hyde Park Hotel. 'I want a drink,' demanded L. I carefully parked the car and we went into the down-stairs bar.

'What would you like?' I asked frostily.

'A champagne cocktail,' she replied, ordering the most expensive thing possible.

'Two of those,' I said to the barman, not to be outdone. L. was, as always, looking unbelievably beautiful. She was dressed in a purple silk trouser suit from Hong Kong that showed off her red locks to their ultimate. Of course, everyone in the bar recognised her and there was much nudging and pointing among the rest of the throng. We sat at our table in silence until I asked tactlessly, 'What on earth do you see in those two? They really are awful.'

'Don't you *dare* criticise me,' she shouted and, picking up her glass, she threw the contents straight in my face, rose imperiously from her chair and stalked from the bar. I stared, dripping, at her gorgeous back, which was as straight as a Roman road, as she pushed through the swing doors. There was silence in the bar. Everyone goggled. This was much better than *Coronation Street*. I sat and dripped until a thoughtful barman brought me a cloth. 'Could you bring me another one of those, please?' I asked, indicating my glass. I had decided to let L. hail a taxi, get home, which was only half a mile away, and calm down before I followed her.

At last I finished my drink, paid the outlandish bill and left. Once outside the hotel I realised that it had started to rain and I hurried to where I had parked the car. By this time it was pouring down and I drove slowly to Graham Terrace and let myself in. The house was empty. Miserably I rang two of L.'s friends to try to find her, but eventually, unhappy, tired and worried, I went to bed. I had hardly been there for more than two minutes when the front-door bell rang. I went to the window and peered down into the street. Standing on the doorstep, her fabulous purple trouser suit clinging to her wonderful figure and her hair hanging saturated around her face, was L. I rushed downstairs and let her in.

'All my keys and money are in my handbag which is in the car,' she shouted. 'Well, I've had enough. You can fuck off.' And rushing upstairs with tears streaming down her cheeks, she went to the wardrobe, grabbed handfuls of shirts and hurled them out of the window into the piss-pouring night in a great dramatic gesture.

I knew that L. was now playing Martha in *Who's Afraid of Virginia Woolf?* It is essential if you live with an actress (or actor, for that matter) to know when they are on stage, and when genuine. I grabbed her and kissed her and seconds later we were in bed. Later, much later, I said, 'Darling, I've got to go and get my shirts.' She was nearly asleep but murmured, 'I know.' I put on a dressing gown, went downstairs and let myself out into the soaking night. By now the shirts were in an interesting state. Cars had run over them, people had trodden them into the gutter and dogs had crapped on them. I scooped them up into a soggy mess and carried them upstairs to our bedroom. L. was asleep. I shook her gently. I wanted her to see them. She came half awake and murmured, 'Chuck them in the bath, we'll sort them out in the morning.'

'No, my darling,' I said with a hand on her shoulder to waken her fully, 'I want you to see them now.' Her eyes opened wide and she started to answer crossly, then stared at the shirts and began to laugh. Soon she was convulsed with laughter. They were her shirts.

Most evenings at around 6 p.m. there were drinks at Graham Terrace, and people from all walks of life, provided they were interesting, would drop in. One of the regulars, and a man who very obviously had a creative and intelligent brain, was a struggling actor who had worked with L. in a West End play. His name was Julian Fellowes. I like Julian. He is original, amusing, kind and very 'un-actorish'.

He is a precise person and, in many ways, rather old-fashioned in his speech, dress and manner. He is an extremely social man and was always to be seen at every possible gathering or party. One evening, as L. and I were having a drink together, Julian dropped in. L. had been to Lots Road Auctions and had bought a very lovely mirror, which now hung over the fireplace. Julian immediately noticed it.

'What a beautiful looking glass,' he said, rather pompously and pretentiously I thought.

'It's not a fucking looking glass, Julian,' I said. 'It's a mirror. You're behaving like Nancy Mitford.'

'You're wrong,' remarked Julian, scathingly. 'Saying mirror is like referring to a lavatory as a toilet.' We looked it up in a dictionary not, as Julian remarked, that the compilers of *Chambers Dictionary*, would have any idea what form of speech was socially acceptable and what wasn't. Of course he was right, but in *Chambers* a looking glass is defined as 'noun, old use a mirror'. It was a classic argument between two people who love the English language and it was very satisfying to find out that we were both correct.

One weekend Julian kindly invited L. and me to stay the weekend with him at his beautiful country house, Chiddinghurst, near Lewes. We arrived on the Saturday evening at drinks time to find that also in the party was an 'angel'. (Note: an angel, in theatrical parlance, is someone who puts money into a production. They are essential to the survival of the theatre.) This angel's name was Nancy McLarty and she turned out to be an old friend of L.'s. We had a delicious dinner because Julian is an excellent host and then returned to the drawing room for brandy and coffee. It was the month of April and the Snooker World Championships were being played. I am a very keen follower of snooker and therefore asked if we could possibly turn on the television so that I could see what the score was.

Julian was horrified. 'Certainly not,' he said and, as it was his house and he was my host, I was just about to back down when Nancy chimed in. 'Oh yes please,' she said, 'I love the snooker. Do let's see what's happening.' Of course Julian couldn't refuse her, so with a face like thunder, and a filthy look at me, he turned on the television.

However, he is not a man to bear grudges and we went out for a pub crawl in London the following week. Nonetheless, his most telling remark was at one of L.'s dinner parties. A fellow guest, seated next to him, invited him for kitchen supper, as she put it, the following week. She was a rather gushing woman and I could see that Julian wasn't totally enamoured with her, to put it at its best.

'Don't dress up,' she said, 'just come casual.' Julian looked at her and paused.

'I am not a casual person,' he said. And that was the end of that.

Since those faraway days Julian has achieved an enormous amount and is the most famous screenwriter in Britain, firstly with *Gosford Park*, which was an enormous box-office success, and secondly with his hugely popular television series, *Downton Abbey*. Recently, he was the guest speaker at my youngest son's boarding school, Milton Abbey. I wondered if this incredible success had changed him. After he had spoken, I talked to him and was so pleased to find that it hadn't, and that he is still the warm, kind and interesting person he has always been.

To me Kenya is the most beautiful country on our lovely planet (except England in the middle two weeks of May, when it is breathtaking in its glory). The moment I arrive at Jomo Kenyatta airport in Nairobi, and smell the heat and the dust, all my senses come awake and I feel hugely alive. I always try to go in February, which is the dreariest month of the English winter and the difference between the two countries is at its greatest. I had been lent a car by a friend and drove through Tsavo game reserve to the coast. There

I turned right, missing Mombasa, which I hate as it is now a Kenya Blackpool only a great deal more expensive, and headed for the Tanzania border. Here there is a tiny village called Shimoni where there is the best big-game fishing in Kenya and arguably in all Africa, at the Pemba Channel Fishing Club. It was then run by an old Kenya family, Pat and Mia Hemphill, with their son, Simon. In 1986 the accommodation was comfortable but basic and the food classic English. It was cooked by Mia and consisted of such old favourites as steak and kidney pudding and shepherd's pie. These were always perfectly well prepared but somehow completely alien to Kenya's climate. What one was desperate for was a delicious lobster or prawn salad, and there was an abundance of raw material, but Mia always saw fit to produce food more suited to an English February than a Kenya one. However, the fishing was always wonderful. There were three big-game boats and these were skippered by Pat, Simon and Kadi Nahoda, a local Kenyan.

L. wasn't with me when I first arrived there as she was filming in London, but was going to fly out in three days' time. She had never been to Kenya and was hugely looking forward to it. We had a friend, Sam Redhead, who owned a house a short way down the coast. She let it for most of the year but was there for the worst of the English winter. She had agreed to collect L. from Mombasa airport, as I would be out fishing. I would then drive over and pick up L. from Sam and maybe have dinner there in the evening.

In the meantime, I joyously fished with Simon as the skipper until L. arrived. I always like to fish alone or with a close friend. I hate sharing the boat with strangers, and was thus horrified when Pat asked me on my return after the first day if I would mind taking out someone else in my boat on the following day. 'He has just turned up out of the blue,' said Pat. 'He's a friend of one of my best clients and so I really don't want to turn him down. Please help me out and I'll knock 5 per cent off your bill.' Even with that incentive I was loath to do it. 'What does he know about fishing?' I asked, 'I have no idea,' replied Pat. 'I know nothing about him.'

'What nationality?' I asked.

'German,' replied Pat.

'Oh God!' I said, 'I really don't want to, but you and I have caught a lot of marlin together over the years so, for free beer for the rest of my stay and a bottle of wine each evening for L. when she arrives, I'll do it. And it's for one day only,' I added forcefully.

'Done,' said Pat.

Later that evening I was introduced to Adolf, who turned out to be entirely typical of some of his race: blond, blue-eyed and humourless. He spoke very little English and I thought to myself, 'Tomorrow isn't going to be a riot but at least I'll have Simon to keep me company.'

The next morning we set off, as usual, at 6 a.m. The routine is that the boat trolls for bonito, on the way out to the deep water where the marlin and sailfish are found. These are then used as bait for the big boys. After we had caught a bucketful of bait fish, we were heading for the fishing grounds when Simon spotted a tiger shark basking on the surface and, quite rightly, doing his job, he pointed it out to me and Adolf. Now normally, and certainly when I was fishing, the boat would not bother with tiger shark as it wastes valuable and expensive time which could better be spent catching marlin. However, when I had told Simon to pass it, which he was expecting, I was surprised, and somewhat annoyed, to hear Adolf say that he wanted to have a go for it.

'Let's leave it,' I said. 'We're after marlin, not shark.' Adolf's face flushed with anger (and I hadn't even mentioned the war!).

'I vish to fish for ze shark,' he shouted, 'I pay half zis boat und I vant to catch ze shark.'

'Anything for a peaceful life,' I thought, and turning to Simon said, 'Okay, let's do it.' Simon reeled in all the rods and re-rigged one of them with a wire trace and a big bonito. He then winked at me, which I didn't understand, and we went after the fish. This involved doing a circle of the shark with the bait and then manoeuvring the boat so that the bonito would come as close as possible to the tiger. With great skill this was accomplished. There was an enormous splash as the shark grabbed the bait and it was well and truly hooked. Adolf was already in the fighting chair and the reel straps were in place. 'Now tighten on it hard,' said Simon. Adolf reeled in and struck. For a moment everything went solid and then the line slackened and trailed loosely in the sea. Adolf swore a great many Teutonic oaths and reeled up. At the end of the wire was a tiny bend.

'Oh dear,' said Simon, 'The trace must have had a kink in it. What a shame.' He turned away and again winked at me

14

and I suddenly realised that he had intentionally put a kink into the wire when he organised the rod. I swore to at least double his tip.

We re-baited and now had two rods on outriggers and two with flat lines. Adolf remained sulking in the fighting chair and Simon and I went into the cabin for a very well-deserved beer and breakfast. We were just opening a second bottle each when, from out on deck, there came a terrible scream. It was the shriek of a man in mortal agony and I hope I never hear the like again. Simon and I dropped our beers and rushed out on to the deck to find Adolf standing near the fighting chair, still screaming and clutching his right hand from which blood was squirting like a water pistol. What had happened, we later discovered, was this: Adolf, the inexperienced, bloody fool, had wrapped one of the flat lines around his index finger and had been pulling the jig back and forth in the belief that it would attract more fish. He had been right, and a 30-pound yellow fin tuna (as we later discovered when we wound in the rod) had grabbed the lure, which had resulted in the 80-pound test line cutting through Adolf's index finger as easily as a wire through cheese.

There was blood everywhere and Simon, with great presence of mind, put a tourniquet below the middle joint where it had been severed. I, meanwhile, had found the cut-off bit lying beside the fighting chair and had put it into a glass that I had filled with ice and then stored in the boat's fridge. This I hoped, somewhat optimistically, would allow the finger to be reattached. Of course that was the end of the fishing for the day and we turned around and made the fastest speed possible for the club. Luckily, it was a calm day and therefore we could go virtually flat out. We radioed ahead to say what had happened and there was a car ready and waiting to take Adolf to Mombasa and the nearest hospital. The last I heard of the whole sad affair was that, of course, the finger I had put into a beer glass was well past repair, but we got the glass back and Adolf was charged the full amount for the day's fishing.

The next evening L. was due to arrive and, the moment we returned from the sea, I couldn't wait to drive to Sam Redhead's house and collect her. It is a beautiful house set on top of a small cliff above the delphinium blue of the Indian Ocean. There is a walkway down to the sea and a swimming pool and tennis court next to the house. I rang the doorbell and walked in. The room was full of Sam's friends, all with huge drinks in their hands. Sam gave me a hug and then held me away. 'I've got bad news,' she said, 'L. wasn't on the 'plane.' My heart fell a hundred feet and my face must have shown my feelings, and then suddenly L. was walking towards me looking more beautiful than ever and was in my arms and I couldn't stop kissing her. 'When did you two last see each other,' enquired some wag enviously. 'Five days ago,' I replied, 'far too long.'

'Give the man a drink,' said Sam turning to the questioner. He hastened to obey and proceeded to pour me a rather weak gin and tonic. 'That's not a drink,' shouted Sam, 'that's a sweaty glass.'

After the wonderfully strong, re-made drink I grabbed L. and we drove back to Shimoni. We had turned down

Sam's kind offer of dinner because I hate driving on the pot-holed Kenya roads at night and also because we wanted to be alone. After a blissfully unsuitable Mia dinner of Irish stew and our free bottle of wine, we went to our hut, which, with its hard twin beds (we cuddled into one), beaten earth floor and thatched roof, could not have felt more fitting or romantic for L.'s first night in Africa. Neither of us would have swapped it for Claridge's.

The next day we had Pat Hemphill as our skipper. I am sure this was because he wanted to get to know L. and had thus usurped his son. He it was who had started The Pemba Channel Fishing Club and he had built the whole place, a great deal of it with his own hands. It was a tremendous achievement. No one had fished there before and he'd had to work out everything from scratch. He had begun with only one boat, *White Otter*, and had slowly bought the other two, one of which is a twin hull, and there are three boats to this day. L.'s first day big-game fishing was a warm, beautiful one with a soft onshore wind. It wasn't too hot by Kenya standards, there was a slight swell and everything felt right. The first marlin to hit the trailed bonito was a 457-pound blue, which took me over an hour-and-a-half to bring to the gaff. L. was fascinated and asked if she could have a go.

'These conditions are really good,' demurred Pat, 'and if she hooks a record I don't want to lose it because she has to give the rod to you.' (For record purposes, only one person can handle a fish.)

'Okay,' I said, 'if I hook another marlin we'll look at it first and, if it's a small one, I'll let her play it.'

Ten minutes later there was a cry from the lookout: 'Stripey behind the bait.' Striped marlin are the smallest of the marlin species and rarely go bigger than 200 pounds. Both L. and I watched in fascination as the sickle fin followed the bait. The marlin had 'lit up' now and we could see it vividly. 'Drop it back towards him and then pull it away,' said Pat. 'With any luck that'll drive him mad and he'll grab it.' I did as I was told and sure enough, the fish couldn't eat the bonito quickly enough. I waited and let the spool run until I was sure it had the bait well inside its mouth, slammed in the clutch and struck. The fish jumped immediately, showing that it was no record breaker, but a striped marlin of about 150 pounds. Pat fitted L. with the fighting harness, put her into the chair, and I gave her the rod. It was soon very obvious that L. was no match for the fish. It was simply too strong for her. She tried to pump it as I had shown her but very nearly fell out of the chair with the effort.

'Wind, woman, wind!' shouted Pat pompously.

'What the fuck do you think I'm trying to do,' L. yelled back and Pat retired hurt. No one had ever spoken to him like that before, and especially not a woman. Although completely exhausted, L. stuck to her task and eventually landed her first marlin.

We left Shimoni the next day under a slight cloud and drove back through Tsavo, stopping the night in the park so that L. could see some of the game there, among which there was an ostrich. 'Oh what a wonderful sight,' she cried, 'it looks just like Denise Kilmarnock, so endearingly stupid.' (The Lady Kilmarnock, now sadly dead, was an acquaintance of L.'s and part of the London social scene. It was a viciously accurate description.) We drove on to Nairobi and the Norfolk Hotel, one of the great hotels of the world and the building around which modern Nairobi was founded. Here I had arranged to meet Dave Allen. Dave, in those days, was a legend in Kenya. He was a pilot of matchless skill but also, in true 'Happy Valley' tradition, had a girlfriend near every airstrip in the whole country. Not for him a lonely night in a chilly sleeping bag on the hard earth but a soft bed and voluptuous body to keep him warm. I had met him several times before and had always liked him as he was amusing and interesting. His knowledge of the country was enormous and there was no one that he didn't know. I always let him choose where to take me and I had never been disappointed, staying in some of the most unusual and wildest places on earth.

It was immediately obvious that he had taken a great shine to L., which, as he was a connoisseur of beautiful women, was not surprising.

'So where are you going to take me this time?' I asked.

He looked at me hard. 'When you told me that you had L. with you,' he said, 'I immediately realised that this had to be somewhere very special.' He turned to L. and with typical Allen charm remarked, 'I have always been a great fan of yours and loved your work, so this really is a one-off and wonderful.' We both waited to hear where we were going. 'I'm going to take you to Kora, *Kampi ya Simba* [Camp of the Lions],' he said. My eyes lit up. It was somewhere I had wanted to visit for a long time, but I could see that it meant nothing to L.

'It's where George Adamson lives,' I explained. 'It's the place upon which the film *Born Free* was based. George was married to Joy and they were played in the film by Bill Travers and Virginia McKenna.'

'Of course I know all about it,' replied L., her face animated. 'Oh, how wonderful. I can't wait. When are we going?'

'How about this afternoon?' said Dave.

We had an early lunch and, leaving our car at the Norfolk, we went with Dave to the tiny private Nairobi aerodrome where he kept his plane. We put in our sparse luggage and, with me in the front seat and L. in the back because she was nervous of small aircraft, we started to taxi to the runway. I looked at the instrument panel and suddenly, to my horror, noticed that the fuel gauge was showing virtually empty.

'Dave,' I shouted above the roar of the engine, 'we are terribly low on fuel,' and I pointed at the control panel.

'Don't worry about that,' said Dave, 'the gauge doesn't work but I put a stick in the tank this morning and we've plenty.' This was classic Kenya, where there are no such boring and bourgeois rules as health-and-safety regulations. Luckily L. couldn't hear this exchange or I think she might have left.

Kora is approximately 200 miles north-east of Nairobi, so the flight was just under two hours. After we had been in the air for about half an hour, Dave turned around to where L. was sitting and said, 'Hold the joystick a moment could you, please, I want to light a cigarette,' and before L. could begin to explain that she had never flown a plane in her life, he had turned away and was soon puffing happily. Despite this interesting interlude we flew on, unperturbed, towards Kora. At last I saw a collection of huts in the distance and these we buzzed as a signal for someone to drive from the camp and collect us. Sure enough, after a bumpy touchdown on the earth airstrip, a Land Rover was waiting. 'Hi, I'm Tony Fitzjohn,' said a handsome man of about forty, dressed in nothing but torn khaki shorts and sandals. 'I'm George's assistant.' I had heard of Fitzjohn. He was a wild child who had the extraordinary gift of being able to communicate with lions and other big cats. He was a genuine big-cat whisperer. It was also obvious that he was drunk and it was a sad truth, that at that time, this was his normal condition. Several years later he dried out and became a very big man in the conservation of the wild animals of Africa, for which he was, quite rightly, awarded the OBE. (Read his book, *Born Wild*.)

The camp was about a mile-and-a-half from the airstrip and was in the depths of a wilderness. It consisted of merely a few sleeping huts, a mess hut and a lavatory. The latter was the best loo I have ever had the joy of having a crap upon. It was a small enclosure of rattan in the centre of which were the bones of the lower jaw of an elephant but with the teeth removed. This made an ideal seat and I have often wondered why no one has ever produced a replica commercially. The whole camp was surrounded by a ten-foot high wire fence, presumably so that the lions couldn't get in, although, as L. remarked to me, it was such a weak fence that it wouldn't have kept a domestic cat out, let alone a lion.

We were introduced to George Adamson and I was thrilled to meet him. For years, like Denys Watkins-Pitchford, he had been one of my heroes. He was a good-looking man of average size and, at that time, in his early eighties. He still had a full head of hair, a moustache and a short white goatee beard. Like everyone else in the camp he wore nothing except shorts and sandals. His skin was deeply tanned and wrinkled by the sun but he looked the picture of good health. He welcomed us to the camp with old-fashioned courtesy, but it was obvious that he was in a hurry. We had arrived late in the afternoon and Dave had brought some big containers in the aeroplane, which George couldn't wait to open.

'I'm so sorry to rush you,' he said, 'but it's feeding time. Come with me and I'll show you where you can watch, but please sit completely still and don't move.' We were led out of the wire enclosure to where some chairs had been placed. We sat in these while George walked forward and sat in another chair a short distance from us. He had taken with him one of the containers which had been brought in with us on the plane. The African night was just beginning to draw in and suddenly, across the hard, sun-bleached earth, came a pair of impala and a dik-dik. These were antelope that George had reared and released into the wild. They happily approached him and fed out of a bucket in his hand. All was peace in the African evening, the air throbbed with dying heat and the sky had begun to turn the purple of dusk. Then, with no urgency, the antelope ceased feeding and moved slowly back into the bush. They had sensed, long before anything was visible, the arrival of something else.

George stood up from his chair. 'Time to go in,' he said and motioned us to return to the enclosure and close the gate in the wire. He himself stayed outside, seated in his chair with the container beside him, which he now opened. We all sat completely still and in total silence as the fast dusk of the African night set in. Suddenly, they were there and I felt the hairs creep up on the back of my neck. There had been no sound, no breaking of twigs or rustling of undergrowth as the three lions approached. They had just quietly padded up and now stood only ten feet from George. He reached into the container and pulled out huge chunks of raw meat, which he threw to them. The lions fed contentedly. There was no squabbling over the food. George was careful, I noticed, to throw pieces to individuals. However, he held on to one piece and the biggest lion came up to his chair and took the meat from his hand and allowed him to ruffle its mane. But then that was only natural because George had reared all of them from cubs before releasing them into the wild. It is only when you see a lion as close as that to a man that you realise how huge they are. Man is a weak chunk of food beside a lion and that is why it was so miraculous for George to be there with them. Eventually the lions finished feeding and slowly departed as silently as they had arrived.

We stayed in Kora for a week before flying back to Nairobi and the Norfolk Hotel. Here we had arranged to meet some old friends, Jim and Shirley Deterding, before flying with Dave up to Lake Turkana, which is famous for its huge Nile perch. Jim and Shirley owned a beautiful estate on the north coast of Norfolk and L. and I had stayed with them many times, and I had shot some fast and high pheasants and partridges there. They are a brilliantly unconventional couple which is why they were such good friends of ours. Shirley is a talented professional artist and paints the cold, bleak landscape that surrounds the estate. I have several of her pictures and looking at her oils of mallard and teal about to land on a reed-girt broad, or greylag geese flighting under a bitter, January moon, I can almost feel the icy wind howling in from a raging North Sea.

Lake Turkana, previously called Lake Rudolf, is in Northern Kenya and is the world's largest alkaline lake. This makes it fecund with fish and it is the home to some giant Nile perch. This was the main reason for our visit to the lake as we wanted to catch some of these almost mythical creatures which can grow up to 250 pounds. It is at least three days' drive from Nairobi along rough and deserted roads. The climate is very hot and dry and the surrounding countryside is mainly volcanic with dried-up lava flows. It has few inhabitants and almost no tourists.

We flew into South Island and Dave managed a perfect landing on the tiny airstrip in the middle of the island. 'Go and look around,' he said, 'while I put up the camp, but, whatever you do, however hot you are, don't go swimming in the lake. It is full of Nile crocodiles.' I unpacked a fly rod, which I had carefully brought with me. This was not for the vast Nile perch but for tilapia which I intended to use as live bait. There was a very strong wind blowing, and after borrowing a bucket from Dave we set off for a shore with the wind behind us. We used ordinary loch trout flies and very soon had three or four small tilapia swimming in the bucket. I had also brought a salmon spinning rod with me, some pike snap tackle with large treble hooks and a packet of condoms. L. stared at these in amazement, 'You're not using those vile things on me, I hope,' she said. 'Nor me,' repeated Shirley. 'And certainly not me,' said Jim before we all collapsed laughing. 'It's for a float,' I explained, 'I couldn't find any balloons in Nairobi so I bought these instead.' And so saying I blew one up until it was the size of a football and attached it to the line. I then put a tilapia on the trebles and put everything into the shallows at the shore of the lake. The tackle was far too heavy for my light spinning rod to cast and so I had to rely on the wind to blow it away from us with the condom acting as a sail. It was a strong live bait and the 'float' kept on bobbing under and coming up again – and then suddenly it didn't reappear. It was just like fishing for pike, and so I waited and when the line started to run off the spool I struck. And nothing happened; the bait had obviously entangled itself in a rock. The line was totally solid. I put on more pressure and suddenly the 'rock' shot out into the lake at speed. The first run of the fish must have been a good one hundred yards and I thanked God that I had plenty of line. However, Nile perch don't really fight that much for their size, certainly nothing like a salmon, and after two or three much shorter runs the fish was on its side and I managed to bring it up the sloping beach. It was vast. Dave had brought some scales and it turned these to just over 80 pounds, certainly the largest freshwater fish that I had ever caught. We killed it and gave it to the local tribesmen, who dried it in the sun. It would feed the whole village and so was a welcome present.

Jim and Shirley tossed up between them to decide who should next have the rod as we only had one between us. Jim won and a new tilapia was attached to the hooks and sent sailing out into the waves. The lake is full of huge, hungry Nile perch and thus the tackle had not gone far when again the condom disappeared. Jim waited and struck. The fish surged out into the lake leaving an enormous bow wave but, like mine and about the same size, it soon gave up and Jim towed it on its side towards the shore. Suddenly, when it was only ten yards or so from the bank, a crocodile some twelve feet long grabbed it and started the twisting motion that crocs do with their prey. We all stared in horror and then, thank God, the line went slack and Jim sadly wound it in. And that was the end of our live-baiting because, foolishly, that was the only set of pike snap tackle that I had brought with me.

We stayed on South Island for another couple of days and explored Lake Turkana in the collapsible boat that Dave had brought on the plane. We caught more Nile perch using spinners but there was nothing which came near the one that I had caught on a live bait. At last we said goodbye to Turkana and flew back to Nairobi, and then on to London.

Two years after we'd been there, in 1989, George was murdered by Somali bandits, known as *shifta*. He had asked one of the women, who worked in the camp, to take a Land Rover to the airstrip and meet a plane which was bringing in visitors. The woman, Inge Ledersteill, took one of the long-term camp employees with her, Osman Bitacha. The Land Rover was ambushed, Osman and Inge dragged from it and money and valuables demanded from them. Back at the camp, George had heard shooting. He gathered four camp employees and, armed only with his old revolver, set off to the rescue. He arrived at the ambush in time to see Inge being dragged into the bush screaming for her life. Osman was lying in the road with a smashed thigh, which the *shifta* leader had deliberately broken with a crowbar. Two of the rescuers jumped out but George didn't hesitate and, drawing his pistol, he bravely accelerated and with the other two drove directly at the five *shifta*. He died with his two companions, his revolver in his hand, charging at his enemies like an old lion, as the *shifta* opened fire with every weapon that they had and riddled the Land Rover and its occupants with bullets. Then, like the cowards that they were, they ran away. George was eighty-three years of age. Inge survived and so did Osman, albeit with a broken thigh.

L. and I both feel incredibly lucky to have stayed at Kora and deeply honoured to have known George, even for such a short time. It is unquestionably one of the highlights of both our lives.

L. has a son, by a previous marriage who, for the purpose of this book I shall call Jack. He is, to this day, a close friend of mine and, while L. and I were together, he was like a son to me. He is a man with a great sense of humour, hugely kind and very loyal to his friends, three traits which I consider the most important of all. He is also a completely unique and individual person who does not in any way conform to the general trend. This is not surprising considering his parentage, for his father is another well-known actor.

When he was a boy, Jack managed to get himself a job as an aide to a rock superstar and I can think of no more exciting occupation for a young lad, especially as they travelled the world. Thus, when L. and I returned from Kenya and Jack was working in Paris, I was not particularly surprised when she said that she wanted to go there for the weekend to see her son.

'It'll be terrific fun, darling,' she said. 'I'll find a cheap hotel for us for a couple of nights and we can go to the gig and see Jack during the day. I'm sure that he will be able to take a few hours off to see his mum.' We rang Jack, told him where we were staying, and he said that he would sort out tickets for the show.

When we arrived at our hotel we were handed a letter. It was from Jack with all the arrangements, including an invitation to the Paris Ritz after the show for a drink. We had the best possible seats, next to the front-of-house desk, and it was a brilliant performance.

After the show we drove to the Ritz and were collected from reception by Jack, who led us up to the star's suite and introduced us. We were made very welcome there, and a bottle of delicious vintage champagne was immediately opened. Suddenly a small packet was produced out of which five generous lines of coke were poured. Now, I had never had coke before but I am all for trying anything once and I felt that if I was going to lose my hard-drug virginity it might as well be with a rock star. A 100-franc note was rolled up and offered to me. And here was a small problem: I hadn't the slightest idea what to do with it. 'Put it up your nose,' said L. kindly, immediately realising my dilemma. This I did, and then blew. There was a horrified pause and L. explained, 'He's never done it before' as, like a snowstorm, clouds of coke flew everywhere. Everyone was shaking with laughter and I felt a complete fool. Some more lines were poured and I tried again. After that I took to it like a monk to prayer, although it is not something of which I make a habit.

'I've let Graham Terrace for a month,' said L. 'It doesn't matter because we'll live in the flat in Ebury Street as it's in between lets.' L. was very canny with property. Over the years, she had bought several flats and houses in fashionable areas of London and had a very good income from letting them. The one in Ebury Street, because of its location, was extremely popular and nearly always occupied. This was mainly because she had a brilliant agent who found visiting American actors who either wanted to have a holiday in London or who were working and didn't feel like staying in a hotel. However, by luck, it was empty.

'To whom have you let it this time?' I asked.

'Lee Marvin,' she replied, looking very pleased with herself. 'He moves in next week, so this Saturday you can take me to Brighton for a seriously dirty weekend.'

'What a great idea,' I said. 'But why Brighton?'

'Tradition,' replied L.

That Saturday found us driving out of London to the

Grand Hotel on the Brighton seafront. I had decided that we might as well stay somewhere seriously comfortable and do the whole thing in style. We checked in and then decided to go out for dinner at one of the fish restaurants for which Brighton is famous. We had a delicious meal and went to bed in our hotel relatively early. The next morning we rose late, had a superb lunch and drove at a leisurely pace back to London, thus finishing a very ordinary weekend break, which we both thoroughly enjoyed. This was the beginning of October 1984. On the twelfth of that month, in the early hours of the morning, the IRA attempted to kill Margaret Thatcher and most of her Cabinet, all of whom were staying in the Grand for the Conservative Party Conference. The terrorists set off a long-delay time bomb in the hotel, precisely where we had been staying. Mrs Thatcher survived, but five other people died, with others badly injured, and it would be nearly two years before the refurbished Grand reopened.

Both L. and I were horrified at this, particularly as the bomb had been planted three weeks earlier behind a bath panel in room 629. The following Monday, five days before we were due to move out of Graham Terrace, we were woken up at 6 a.m. by the insistent ringing of the doorbell. 'Try and go back to sleep, my darling,' I said. 'I'll sort it out, whatever it is.' I put on a dressing gown and went downstairs. When I answered the door I was confronted by two uniformed policemen and a third, very heavy, plain-clothes man with his hand under his jacket. 'Are you Mister Daunt?' Plain Clothes asked. 'Mister Michael Daunt?'

'Yes,' I replied, by now terrified. What the hell had I done? This couldn't be another parking ticket.

'Were you in Brighton on Saturday, sixth October?'

'I'm not sure,' I replied. 'Yes, yes I think so, but how do you know and what have I done that you wake me up at six in the morning?'

The detective ignored my questions and continued: 'Did you stay at the Grand Hotel?'

And suddenly it all started to fall into place.

'You signed in to the hotel and in the register, under nationality, you put Irish,' Plain Clothes said.

Now, I am very proud of my Irish ancestry on my father's side and, possibly foolishly, always put my nationality as Irish in hotel registers. This is, strictly speaking, not entirely true as my mother was Welsh.

'Yes, I may well have done,' I replied, 'but I wouldn't have done so if I was a member of the IRA and going to plant a bomb, now would I?'

'You can never tell with the Irish,' said Plain Clothes, darkly. 'I am afraid we are going to have to ask you to accompany us to the police station for further questioning.'

My heart sank as I realised that, although completely innocent of anything, this could take hours and I had work to do that morning.

At this point L., who had been listening to these exchanges from the bedroom, decided to take a hand. She exploded on to the landing at the top of the stairs and shouted down into the hall, 'You stupid Welsh twit, what the hell did you think you were doing signing yourself as Irish?' The police stared

31

up at her and I was immediately forgotten, firstly because they recognised her instantly, and secondly because she was stark naked. Quickly, as journalists from the more vulgar tabloids do, they made their excuses and left.

Later that week we moved out to Ebury Street. However, before we left and without telling L., I carefully planted a book on the coffee table in the drawing room. This was *Big Fish and Blue Water* by Peter Goadby, which in those days was the defining work on big-game fishing. I knew that Lee Marvin was mad about the sport and this would give me an excuse to go back to the house and meet him. Thus I could talk marlin, sailfish and swordfish with someone I knew to be an expert and who, as an actor, had always fascinated me.

I duly arrived two days after Lee had taken up residence and rang the doorbell, hoping that he would answer it. To my disappointment a woman, whom I presumed to be his wife, appeared and so I explained who I was and, with deep apologies, said that I had left a book behind 'by mistake' which I was halfway through reading. Before she could answer me, a well-known gravelly voice called from the drawing room, 'If that's the guy who owns the big-game fishing book send him down.' I went downstairs to the drawing room, which filled the whole basement of the house, and there was the man himself, and looking exactly as I would have expected. He could not have been nicer to me and I spent a happy hour, I think to his wife's boredom, talking marlin. The only marlin fishing I had done was at Shimoni. I told Lee about the last time I had been there with L. and what she had said to Pat Hemphill. Lee was thrilled to hear this tale and told me, 'I've been there myself. It's very well-run but he can be a pompous asshole and will only do things his way.'

We continued to talk fishing, and then Lee suggested I take him on a tour of London pubs – 'You know, the ones that aren't on the tourist trail, where all you locals drink.' We made a date for the next night and I was shown out of the house by his wife, who I discovered was called Pamela.

'Don't take him out and get him drunk,' she hissed at me. 'He's here to work and I don't want him pissed and hung-over.' It was obvious that she was not pleased to see that Lee had found a potential drinking buddy.

I collected Lee in the MG the following evening and decided to take him on a tour of my favourite Chelsea and Knightsbridge pubs, finishing in The Nelson in Montpelier Square, where I had first met L. Lee had visited London several times before but had never been taken on a trip round the pubs. 'Boy, am I looking forward to this,' he said as he squeezed his long body into the tiny MG. Firstly, I took him to The Australian in Milner Street, where he was immediately welcomed by the locals and the landlord, Ted Saunders. Here, he proceeded to sink several pints of Heineken. This pattern was repeated in The Admiral Codrington just up the road in Mossop Street, The Surprise in Christchurch Square, the Nag's Head in Kinnerton Street and finally in The Nelson, where I had arranged to meet L. She was greatly looking forward to meeting Lee as they had never met or worked together. I knew he would appreciate her, for he loved beautiful women.

When we arrived, we were both in that happy state of

finding the world a wonderful place and laughing loudly at each other's silliest jokes. I was reminded of the piece of doggerel that runs:

The wonderful love of a beautiful maid,
And the love of a staunch true man,
And the love of a baby, unafraid,
Have existed since life began.
But the greatest love – the love of all loves,
Even greater than that of a mother –
Is the tender, passionate, infinite love
Of one drunken sod for another.

Lee was still drinking endless amounts of Heineken and, as we went into the saloon bar, I noticed that Alan Stickland, the ex-Indian Army major who was the landlord, was playing liar dice surrounded by a small crowd. I introduced Lee to Alan. 'Please hang on a moment and I'll greet you properly, but I am in the final stages of removing money from this kind gentleman,' Alan said, pointing to the man opposite him. Now Alan was very good at liar dice and used to supplement his income from the pub by playing for high stakes against anyone who was foolish enough to take him on. I explained the game to Lee, who looked fascinated and said that he had played a little on various film sets while waiting to be called.

When Alan had won his money he turned to Lee and welcomed him properly, before saying, 'Feel like a game?' I saw Lee's eyes light up.

'You bet your ass,' he said.

'Want a little bet?' enquired Alan hopefully.

'Sure,' said Lee. 'How about five hundred pounds on the game?'

This was very big money for those days, but Alan didn't blink. 'No problem,' he said. They started playing and their table was soon surrounded by locals; even drinkers from the public bar came in to see this high-stakes match. The tiny saloon bar was at bursting point and people were standing on chairs to get a better view. The game swung to and fro with first Alan in the lead and then Lee. It soon became very apparent that Lee had played a great deal and knew precisely what he was doing. I am sure that Alan had initially thought that here was another mug whom he could fleece for a few bob, and had been thrilled to play for such big stakes. Now I noticed that the facetious remarks and glib comments had ceased, and that he was concentrating on every hand. At the climax, Lee laid out three aces on the table. 'Bait,' he said, 'throwing two.' The dice rattled in the cup and Lee inspected his hand. A smile spread over his face and he looked hard at Alan. 'Four aces,' he called.

'Taken,' said Alan.

'I haven't finished,' said Lee.

'Well hurry up,' replied Alan irritably. The stakes were beginning to get to him. Lee regarded him and then slowly placed the fourth ace on the table. 'And a queen,' he said, and I knew that he had it. There was something so positive about his voice that no one was in any doubt, including Alan. He had to take it or admit defeat.

Alan leant across. 'I believe you,' he said, 'but let's see

anyway,' and he lifted the cup. The green queen winked from the table. Alan was now visibly sweating while Lee was leaning back in his chair with a cheroot gripped between his teeth.

'I'll throw it open,' said Alan, 'Either it's there or it's not and you won't believe me if I throw it closed.' He picked up the single dice and there was total silence in the pub. He rolled it on the table and a red king smiled up at him. A great cheer went up from the surrounding throng and a happy smile spread across Alan's face. He *must* have won. Lee had only a one-in-six chance of throwing an ace.

Again there was silence as Lee held the dice in his hand. Then, suddenly, into the throng walked L. I leapt from my chair and brought her into the circle near Lee, who was on his feet with an expectant smile on his rugged face. I introduced them and, while Alan ground his teeth with impatience, Lee insisted on pushing his way to the bar and buying her a drink. He explained what was happening. 'You couldn't have arrived at a better or more exciting moment,' he said. Then he addressed the crowd about the table. 'I'm going to make this a one-off,' he growled and turned to me. 'Hold the door open for me. I'll go into the other bar and throw the dice the whole length of the pub onto this table.' And he strode into the completely empty public bar.

Everyone watched as the big man stood completely still ten yards from the crowd. Slowly he drew his arm back for an underarm throw, then suddenly brought it forward and the dice arced glittering in a slow parabola. On it flew towards the packed crowd round the table, which had moved to one side so that the dice could fly the length of the pub. And, at that moment, L. held her full vodka and tonic out in the long glass and caught it. Lee ran to her side as the dice slowly sank to the bottom. With the certainty of fate it fell, and the single ace blinked up at the throng like Cyclops.

Lee rang me the next day. 'Listen buddy,' he said, 'I've got to work for the rest of the time I'm here but give me a call in the States when I get home and we'll make a date to fish together for marlin. I've got a boat in Cairns, Australia and that's where the biggest marlin in the world live.'

Because of pressure of work and various other reasons, I foolishly didn't ring Lee for three years and then, in February of 1987, I decided that I must take him up on his offer. I rang him and we arranged to fish the following November. I bought my air ticket and was greatly looking forward to the trip.

In August, Lee Marvin's secretary rang to tell me that he had suffered a huge heart attack and died.

'Try and get back from work early today,' said L. 'I've got some friends dropping in for a drink and I think that you'd like to meet them.'

'Who?' I asked.

'I'm not telling you,' she replied. 'Just wait and see.'

Overcome with curiosity, I hurried home and arrived at Graham Terrace at teatime. Letting myself in I went downstairs to the drawing room and walked straight into Dirk Bogarde. He and L. had been friends for many years and he was, I discovered, Jack's godfather. I had my black Labrador,

Rosie, with me, and Dirk seemed more pleased to meet my dog than me; I later discovered that he had always been hugely jealous of all L.'s lovers. With him was a good looking man to whom I took an instant liking. He was as warm and welcoming as Dirk was distant. We were introduced and I discovered that this was Tony Forward, or 'Tote' as he was called by everyone. He had been Dirk's manager as well as his lover for many years. It was, I discovered, an extremely happy 'marriage', indeed much happier than many heterosexual ones. Tote, in his early sixties, looked ten years younger and had weathered life well. His face had character written all over it and there was also kindness and naughtiness there in equal proportions.

I have to admit that I was thrilled to meet Dirk. He had been one of my favourite actors for many years and I also loved his books. I found that meeting him in the flesh was something of a disappointment because of his lack of warmth, and it became very obvious that, for a long time, he had been having a passionate love affair with only one person – himself. However, in fairness, for L.'s sake we both made a great effort to like each other and Dirk nicknamed me 'The Vet' because of my dog and the ferrets I kept on the roof terrace. The evening was an interesting one as, provided we kept to the subject of Dirk and his work, he was fascinating and amusing. I enjoyed enormously listening to him recounting his tales of world-famous names. Before he and Tote left for the Connaught, which was their London home, he issued an invitation for both of us to come and spend a few days at Le Haut Clermont, their house in the olive groves above Cannes in the South of France. He invited us for the second half of May – 'before it's too hot and pre hoi polloi season', as Dirk put it, being an appalling snob. We arranged that L. would stay for a week and that I would be there for three days only. The reason for this was that it was the height of the mayfly season and I was determined not to miss the best time of the trout-fishing calendar. It is also the moment when nowhere in the world is as lovely as England. The countryside is at its most fresh and green and the rivers are running with the sparkle of incipient summer. It was obvious that Dirk was very put out about this. I mean, how could anyone turn down an invitation to stay with the great Dirk Bogarde? The situation wasn't helped by Tote, who said that he wished he could fish with me and that he had very happy memories of the mayfly season.

Eventually, the time for us to go and stay with Dirk arrived and we flew to Cannes and hired a car. Finding Le Haut Clermont was a nightmare as it really was in the middle of nowhere. However, L. somehow remembered the way and we arrived in time for drinks before dinner. These consisted almost entirely of champagne, L.'s favourite tipple. The house itself was incredibly beautiful. It had been a very run-down old farmhouse dating from 1641 when Dirk bought it in January 1970, and he and Tote had turned it into something very lovely. They had not 'improved' it at all but had insisted on keeping its old character, light being of the greatest importance. The view from the terrace was breathtaking, looking for miles over Provence. Inside, Dirk and Tote had knocked three rooms into one and this had become the world famous Long Room, exquisite in its furniture, colours and paintings, one of which was an original Picasso.

I remember waking on that first morning, with L. sleeping gently next to me and the sun streaming through a tiny crack in the curtains and finding it all hard to believe. Here was I staying in the unbelievably lovely home of one of the world's most famous film actors. Admittedly he and I didn't really like each other greatly, but it was still an enormous privilege to be there and I was determined to make the most of it. I wandered downstairs to the kitchen where I found Dirk and Tote having coffee and croissants. 'What a beautiful place,' I remarked. 'And I mean both the house and the location.'

'Please feel free to go anywhere you wish,' said Dirk, 'but,' he added waspishly, 'don't take photographs if you're going to sell them.' As I discovered later when I discussed him with L.'s ex-husband, he was known as the Black Widow by anyone who knew him well. He could be very charming on first meeting him, but then turn and be viciously unkind the next minute. He seemed unable to help himself and was even cruel to his beloved Tote on occasions, referring to him as 'my useless bloody manager'. However, he and L. were obviously very close and I watched their interplay over the next few days with interest and amusement. They both had a very similar sense of humour and attitude to life and I am certain that had Dirk been heterosexual, L. would have set her cap at him in a big way. There was no question but that Dirk was hugely jealous of my relationship with her, as I gathered he had been of her former husband too. It seemed that, because of his sexuality, he knew that he could never have her but greatly resented her relationship with a heterosexual man. I was a guest in his house, however, and we both observed the niceties this demanded with great diligence.

I soon found that Dirk was at his most fascinating in the evenings over dinner when, with little prompting, he would regale us with stories of the world's most famous actors and actresses. He and Tote had also had Princess Alexandra to stay.

'Why?' I asked. 'Is she a friend?'

'No,' replied Tote. 'She was a fan of Dirk's and when she was staying in the area, her secretary rang to say that she *so* wanted to meet him and please could it be arranged. And so we invited her for dinner and on the night I managed to drop my cock deeply in the custard.'

Both L. and I roared with laughter. Tote had so much love of life, and always relished a bit of wickedness.

'What did you do?' demanded L.

'Well,' continued Tote, 'I was just serving the first course for dinner, which was a truly magnificent soufflé, when the telephone rang. "Get rid of them quickly," Dirk said, "or the soufflé will collapse." So I put the soufflé down and answered the phone. Carrying the portable handset through to the princess I said, "Darling, it's your bloody husband," and I have no doubt that Sir Angus James Bruce Ogilvy, KCVO, heard every word. And also I should not have called The Princess Alexandra "*Darling*".'

'And what happened then?' I asked when I had stopped laughing.

41

'The Very Darling Princess told hubby to bugger off or the soufflé would be ruined,' said Tote happily.

It was a strange three days and I have to say that I heaved a sigh of relief when I boarded the flight back to London. And yet I would not have missed it for anything, for it was a fascinating peek into the world of a cinema legend, and I still regard myself as incredibly lucky to have stayed in that incomparably beautiful house with its complicated, intelligent and ridiculously talented owner.

I didn't see Dirk again for many years. When I did he had sold Le Haut Clermont and he and Tote had moved to London. Tote was suffering from liver cancer and they both wanted him to be in England to receive the best possible care, but Tote also felt that, if he was going to die, he wanted to do so in his home country. Eventually, the cancer killed him and Dirk was left alone in his flat in Cadogan Gardens.

About a year later, I asked the editor of the *Mail on Sunday*, for whom I wrote a fishing column, if I could interview Dirk. I was given the go-ahead and rang him to make an appointment. We fixed a date and, I have to admit, I was greatly looking forward to interviewing him. It would be fascinating to see how this, essentially, lone wolf would be coping alone. I arrived on a spring morning feeling happy in body and soul. It took Dirk precisely five minutes to reduce me to a miserable wreck. He was at his most introspective and morose. 'I'm sorry Vet dear,' he said, 'but I don't want to do this interview. I simply don't feel up to it. I can see the end of the tunnel and it's dark and terrifying. And there's something else too,' he continued. 'When everyone came down and stayed with me at Le Haut Clermont I thought that you were all *my* friends and that you all came to visit me, particularly because I was the Great Big Star. But you didn't, did you? None of you really liked me at all. You all came because of the house and, more than anything else, you came to see Tote because he was such fun.'

Of course I denied it hotly. But it was completely true.

The tragedy of L. and me was that, essentially, we were made for each other. We both had the same sense of humour and a huge feeling for the ridiculous. We both loved the arts, beautiful things, restaurants and good food. And we were incredible in bed together. More important than anything, we loved each other passionately. But there were also huge problems. I am at heart a countryman, loving fishing, shooting and everything to do with the countryside. L. hates it and is really only content within 'a short walk from Harrods', as Dirk so aptly titled one of his books.

As T.S. Eliot wrote in his wonderful poem 'The Journey of the Magi':

All this was a long time ago, I remember,
And I would do it again, but set down
This set down
This...

Thus, I am going to go back to the child that made the man, and the man that made the lover.

TWO

Childhood

I cannot understand why my parents married, or even went out together. I am sure they would have been brilliant at a one-night stand, when very little actual talking takes place, but not in any form of relationship. The only two things that could possibly have attracted them to each other were that they were both very good looking and my mother was relatively rich. They had nothing in common whatsoever. Mum was artistic, bohemian and came from a family who were much the same. Her friends were all actors, writers and artists. She was part of the Bloomsbury set. My father was a classic philistine. He read almost nothing and thought poetry was for poofs (his words). He did, nevertheless, compose a most romantic little ditty for my mother, which he gave her on Valentine's Day 1941. It went as follows:

THE BOUNDER

A pint or three she will not shirk
Because it makes her bowels work.

He was highly suspicious and denigrating of all my mother's friends, and couldn't tell a Manet from a Mozart. He played a great deal of rugger both for Marlborough, his public school, and for Cambridge University before he was sent down for doing no work. He had a trial for Ireland and played for London Irish as a wing three-quarter. However, his greatest achievement was that he was an outstanding and enormously brave pilot who flew the first British jet, the Gloster Whittle E28/39, and later the Gloster Meteor, the first jet fighter to enter RAF service. As chief test pilot of the Gloster Aircraft Company he was a very glamorous figure.

His crashes were many and dangerous and how he wasn't killed is amazing. In those early days of jet flight, the pilot was just about in touch with the ground by radio, except when the plane went through a dead spot, and those on the ground would issue such terrifying commands as: 'See what happens when you turn sharp left.' The answer was quite often that the aircraft went out of control and had to be righted – if there was time. In one of his crashes, when he had been asked to try to loop the plane, most of the tail fell off and he quickly headed towards a field to try to land. He was approaching far too fast and at the end of the field was a Cotswold stone wall, which spelt death. However, in the middle of the field were two trees. My father managed to steer the stricken jet between the trees and thus took the wings off and slowed it down so that it stopped before the wall. He suffered a broken collarbone, broken arm and concussion.

The field had potatoes planted in it, which meant there were King Edwards virtually going in one end of the jet engine and chips coming out of the other. It was owned by two old ladies, sisters of gentle birth, who were not, however, gifted with any great intellect. Instead of doing anything sensible, like sending for the emergency services, they called on their friend the vicar. They had seen my father arrive, somewhat precipitously, in their field and, not possessing a telephone, had walked to the vicarage. The parson had had the common sense to summon an ambulance before walking to what was left of the aeroplane to see if he could be of assistance. At the same time, the ambulance arrived and two stretcher-bearers took my father to hospital.

Later, when Dad was in hospital, my mother went to see the vicar to thank him for his help. 'When you arrived at the cockpit, did you speak to my husband?' she asked.

'Yes,' replied the vicar, 'and I think he must have been uttering some sort of university rugger cry. He kept on saying what sounded like "foo me, foo me".'

At some stage Mum, I suspect driven mad by endless talk of nothing but aircraft and rugger, and permanently in a state of terror because of my father's exploits, had an affair to give her comfort.

My father also practised playing the trumpet while sitting on the loo in the morning, and this in a tiny flat with only one loo. I, personally, feel that anyone who behaves like that deserves to be cuckolded. Of course my father found out and, instead of playing his trumpet, he played the wronged husband to the hilt. He insisted on a divorce, despite Mum begging him not to. I was two at the time but, because Mum, in the eyes of a misogynistic judge, was 'a Scarlet Woman' and therefore obviously unfit to bring up a child, I was given into my father's custody and not very tender hands. When, in her defence, my mother mentioned the sounds from the lavatory in the mornings, the judge got the wrong end of the stick as to where the noises originated, and was then heard to remark that no lady would ever comment on her husband's private habits.

During his career at Gloster he and my mother (plus his mother, her sister and a nanny!) were living in a rented flat in Cheltenham, near the airfield where my father did most of his flying. This is where I was born. My father then had one crash too many and lost his nerve. I believe absolutely that there is a well of courage inside each of us and that when that well has run dry there is nothing that can be done to refill it. He retired from Gloster, my grandmother bought a beautiful Georgian house in the village of Pyrton at the foot of the Chiltern Hills, and everyone went to live there. It had seven bedrooms, one bathroom and two lavatories. There were three acres of gardens, a ten-acre paddock and an orchard.

My father rented a farm near by, and this he ran incompetently for three years before going bankrupt. During this time he married a woman called Monica and had two more children by her. He then disappeared from Pyrton, trailing

Monica and his two new offspring, to seek his fortune else-where. I, thank God, was left behind.

I can remember little of this period of my life and my earliest memories are of the household consisting of my grandmother (my father's mother), her sister (my spinster great-aunt), a woman called Betty Moore and Nanny. There were also three other servants and a cook who came in daily. In the garden was Newbold, a man in his late twenties whose wife was one of the daily helpers in the house.

Betty was a friend of my grandmother's on whom she had taken pity when her husband died just after the war. Almost my very first memory is of Betty. I cannot remember what she looked like, but I vividly recall her standing by an open sewer outside the back door and weeping before two men in white coats arrived and took her away. She was never seen again. I asked Nanny what had happened and was told to go to my room. Later that night I crept downstairs to the drawing room and listened outside the door. Apparently Betty had gone completely mad and had been attacked by a fit of guilt because, since her husband had died, she was extremely rich. She wanted to give it all to the poor but had been strongly dissuaded by my grandmother. There had been a terrible row and Betty had stormed out, drawn a hundred pounds from the bank (a large sum of money in those days) and then disappeared into one of the two lavatories. She had eventually emerged and defiantly told my grandmother that she had wiped her arse with the large white five-pound notes of the era and then flushed them down the loo. My grandmother, a practical woman, had summoned Newbold,

the gardener, and made him fish them out of the sewer before
calling a doctor and having poor Betty Moore certified and
removed to a mental home. Years later I was told that eighty-
five pounds of the hundred was found. (I have often wondered
whether Newbold, in revenge for such a vile task, sensibly
nicked the other fifteen pounds.) What my grandmother
did with this money, history does not relate, but I am pretty
certain that she would have regarded it as 'finders keepers'.

The next memory I have is of one of my father's few visits.
He had arrived with Monica and taken me out to lunch at the
nearby Stonor Arms. To get to Stonor from Pyrton you have
to go up Howe Hill, which runs up the side of the Chilterns
and is very steep. On the return journey we reached the top
of the hill and here we stopped. I was in the back of the
car and vividly remember seeing my father's wide shoulders
shaking. He turned to Monica. 'I can't do it,' he said. 'I can't
drive down the hill.' He got out, Monica took over and we
met him at the bottom. That's what I mean by the well of
courage, and my poor father's was empty.

Opposite our house was the drive to Pyrton Manor, a
classic Elizabethan house of great beauty, and this was the
domain of the Ducat-Hamersley family. They had lived
there for 250 years and owned a great deal of the village.
They were the quintessential English squires, a responsibility
which they had always taken very seriously, with the result
that the village adored them. At the head of the family was
Colonel Jack; tall and slim, gentle and kind, he became the
father I never had. He was a great naturalist and taught me
about the countryside, its inhabitants and their habits. He

also, essentially, taught me how to fish: the greatest gift I have ever been given and one which has been my passion all my life. His wife, Tara, was intelligent, kind and very beautiful. She had an enormous sense of the ridiculous and was a stand-in mother to me.

There were three children. Hugh, who was the eldest, was just three months younger than me. Then came Jonny, his younger brother by two years. Hugh greatly resembled his father in character whereas Jonny had his mother's brains and humour. He and I quickly became friends and he was my closest chum until he died sixty years later. Hugh was mad about horses and Jonny and I hated them. Jonny and I were devoted to fishing and spent nearly all our spare time indulging in the sport. Then, as so often happens in families, there came a later child, a daughter named Anthea. I don't think that I have ever heard her called by her correct name. She was, and still is, called Scrute by one and all. The origin of this name is rather interesting. Not surprisingly she grew up as a total tomboy and longed to be like her two brothers. She was a great horsewoman, a keen shot and an average fisherwoman. She was also extremely beautiful. One day she appeared at breakfast having been reading *Robinson Crusoe*. 'I want to be called Crusoe,' she announced determinedly, and 'Scrute' was born. As her father remarked, 'Thank God she didn't want to be Man Friday.' A few years later a doting aunt decided to give her some scent for Christmas and enquired as to her favourite smell. 'Used cartridge cases,' said Scrute positively.

In front and to one side of the manor was an S-shaped lake

which, for reasons nobody understood, was called 'The Moat'. It did not resemble a moat in any way. It didn't surround any house and never had done, but that was its name, and always had been for as long as anyone could remember.

One morning Uncle Jack (for so I called the colonel, although he was no relation whatsoever) confronted Jonny and me and said, 'Tomorrow I'm going to teach you both how to fish.' I suppose I was probably about seven and Jonny was five. The moment he said it, even though I had never held a rod in my life, I knew with complete certainty that this was something that would always be very important to me and which I would love. 'Now Mike,' he said, 'have you got a fishing rod, because if you haven't I'll lend you one.' By sheer luck I had been given a rod while I was still in my mother's womb. This had been a present from my godfather, the country writer John Moore. It was an eight-foot six-inch fly rod made of greenheart, but I had no reel to accompany it. 'It doesn't matter,' said Uncle Jack. 'We'll tie a bit of line to the tip of your rod and put a cast, a float and hook on it and you'll be fine.'

That night, I was so excited I could hardly sleep and the next morning I gobbled my breakfast, grabbed the rod, which Nanny had found in the attic, and ran across to the manor. Jonny and his father were in the huge kitchen and we were shown how to make dough for bait. All we had to do was to mix flour and water into a stiff ball. We made one between us, which we could share. Then we were shown how to put up the rods and fix the porcupine-quill floats to the cast. Lastly, we were taught which knot to use to tie on the tiny hook.

'There are three sorts of fish in the moat,' said Uncle Jack. 'Pike, chub and roach. The most numerous by far are the roach and that's what we're after today. I'll show you how to catch the chub and pike another time.' We went to the moat and, without putting any bait on, Uncle Jack showed us how to flick the float out into the water with an easy underarm swing of the rod. We put some dough on our hooks and both of us cast out into the moat. 'Watch the floats,' said Uncle Jack 'and if they move, you strike, which means you give the rod a quick jerk upwards to set the hook.'

We both stood gripping our rods as tightly as our small hands could manage with our eyes glued to the floats. Suddenly Jonny's moved sideways in the water. He pulled upwards immediately and a small silver fish flew through the air and landed on the bank. Jonny threw his rod down and rushed towards it and I, forgetting everything, did the same. 'Mike, stop!' shouted Uncle Jack, 'look at your float.' I turned and looked but it was nowhere to be seen, and then I noticed that the line was moving away. I grabbed the rod and heaved upwards and another silver fish flew over my head and into the stinging nettles behind. Not caring about being stung, I retrieved my roach and looked at it in awe. It was incredibly beautiful. It had a dark back, red fins, a white belly and bright silver scales on its side. Jonny and I compared our fish and they were like two peas in a pod, and suddenly we both realised that we were shaking with excitement. Two fishermen were born and we both decided that we wanted to eat our roach for lunch.

'They'll taste disgusting,' said Uncle Jack, 'but if you like a combination of mud and cotton wool I'll show you how to gut them and then you can give them to Maggie to cook. Every fisherman worthy of the name must be able to prepare his catch so that it can be cooked.' Jonny and I wanted to continue fishing but Uncle Jack marched us to the kitchen, laid one of the roach on the table and showed us how to ready it. Then we carefully did the other, taking it in turns with the knife to gut and then de-scale it. We insisted that poor Maggie should cook it immediately and this, grumbling to herself, she did. It tasted perfectly foul but Uncle Jack insisted that we finish every tiny piece. 'You either eat fish or you return them to the water,' he explained. 'What you don't do is waste them.' We never tried to eat another roach.

Thus I grew up, the luckiest little boy in the world. I could so easily have been a lonely small person in a huge house surrounded by servants, a nanny and two old ladies. Instead, because of the Ducat-Hamersleys, I had 700 acres of beautiful Oxfordshire countryside and a lake to play in. I also had a friend who was more like a brother and with whom I played every day. Of course we fished in the moat a lot of the time but we also learnt, through Uncle Jack, how to set snares for rabbits, how to trap moles and make gloves out of their skins, how to trap foxes and even how to follow a wasp to its nest and then destroy it. We also learnt how to catch worms. This may sound a strange pastime but there is a great skill to it and it is almost a sport in its own right. The lobworm, aka the common earthworm (*Lumbricus terrestris*), is our largest land worm and makes wonderful bait for numerous fish.

What is needed for their capture is a summer night and a

well-mown lawn which has just been soaked in rain. Then is the time for the hopeful worm catcher to sally forth. In his hand is a torch. Very gently he must tiptoe across the lawn, for there must be not the slightest vibration, because lobworms will disappear at the smallest tremor. At night they lie out upon wet grass but always keep their tails rooted in the ground. The worm catcher shines his torch upon the lawn and, if he sees a worm, he instantly moves the torch away so that the worm is on the outermost periphery of the beam. They are very sensitive, and again, will disappear instantly if they feel too much light upon them. Very stealthily he creeps forward, sees where the worm has its tail in the ground, and like lightning presses the worm down where tail and earth meet so it cannot reverse into its hole. Then he holds the worm tightly and gently pulls (if he heaves too hard the worm will break and what is left will disappear). He will feel the worm contracting and trying to reverse into its hole but, after a short time, it will suddenly relax and he will be able to draw it out of its burrow. Jonny and I became very adept at this pastime and collected huge quantities of worms from both our home lawns. These we sold on a regular basis to the local fishing-tackle shop in Oxford for pocket money. We also used them for fishing.

Once every three months, I went to visit my mother. The divorce-court judge, who must have been not only a misogynist but a raging latent homosexual too, had ordered that I be allowed to see my mother for two days every three months. However, this unknowing and uncaring idiot had stipulated, as my mother had been found to be 'the guilty party' and thus a Scarlet Woman, I must always be accompanied on these visits by Nanny to ensure that my mother did not influence me badly. Thus, each quarter year, Nanny and I caught a train and, by various routes arrived at Granny Lloyd's beautiful home, which was another large Georgian house called Cleavers in Welford-on-Avon.

My mother lived in one of the cottages attached to Cleavers, but we always went over to the main house for our meals. My mother's family were the Lloyds of Birmingham and in 1765, Sampson Lloyd had started Lloyds Bank. I am proud to say that, mainly through fast women and slow horses, there is now almost none of the original fortune left. Here, when I was born, my father, who at that time was still talking to my mother, had dropped a note from an aeroplane he flew over Cleavers. It was the day of my birth and the note read:

We welcome here this afternoon
A little baby Daunt typhoon.
Safely delivered, bless his heart,
Guess what? – with little undercart.

Looking back on those years, I can think of nothing more dreadful than for a mother to be deprived of her firstborn in such a way. I can remember always weeping when the short visit was over and silently swearing that one day I would go and live with her. After the divorce, my mother had several lovers, among whom were Henry Williamson, the writer, whose most famous work, *Tarka the Otter*, I have always loved, and the actor Robert Newton, whom I remember with great affection because of his all-enveloping kindness towards me.

During the summer holidays from my prep. school I was allowed a whole week with Mum (although, of course, accompanied by Nanny) and we nearly always went to Lyme Regis, where her sister Gwyneth had a cottage. I still remember Lyme with great affection as Gwyneth always had her children, George and Richard, with her. Gwyneth had recently become divorced from their father, Sir John Heygate, so the two sisters were in a similar situation to me, although Gwyneth had been given custody of her children. Richard and I were great friends and spent large amounts of time at the end of the Cobb with drop nets catching prawns that we ate for tea with freshly baked bread and farmyard butter. Bobby Newton usually came with us on these expeditions, but he always had a bottle with him and I remember wondering why he was so thirsty. 'Can I have some please?' I once asked, thinking it was Lucozade. 'With pleasure,' replied kind 'Uncle Bobby' and handed me the bottle. I took a long pull and of course hated it, as it was virtually neat whisky. Sadly, Uncle Bobby was a chronic alcoholic. He died, aged just fifty, after making his final film *Around the World in 80 Days*. But to me he was a kind and gentle man who loved prawning.

Both my mother and Gwyneth were beautiful women, both were unconventional and both were strong characters. With these similarities it would have seemed natural for them to compete in every way. Yet nothing could have been further from the truth, and all their lives they were the closest of friends.

Mum particularly loved Lyme Regis as she and Bobby Newton had often trysted there. He was once playing a minor part in pantomime at the Marine Theatre in Lyme and, as he did not appear until the second act, my mother and he disappeared to the nearest pub for refreshment. At last they decided to make their way back to the theatre, by this time much the worse for wear. They stumbled to the back of the stalls, arriving just in time to witness a terrifying silence from the stage. Swaying gently and with a beatific smile, Bobby turned to my mother and slurred, 'You're going to like this bit. It's where I come in.'

Such tales have become part of family fable. When the two sisters were well into their seventies they decided to take a trip down memory lane and rented a cottage in Lyme Regis. I went down for a weekend and the three of us visited the same pub that had caused Bobby's downfall all those years ago. After they had been there for a short time my mother, pink with pleasure and whisky, turned to her sister and asked her a question which had obviously been brewing for half a lifetime. 'Did you ever, with Bobby? – well, you know,' she said, hesitating with embarrassment. 'Yes I did,' replied my aunt, and the subject was never mentioned again.

Mum always gave me wonderful presents for both my birthday and Christmas and, for my eighth birthday she gave me a .177 airgun. This was, without doubt, the most marvellous present I had ever been given. I had told Mum that I wanted one because both Hugh and Jonny Ducat-Hamersley had airguns so, of course, I wanted one too. I already possessed a catapult, which had been made for me by Newbold, our gardener. He had taught me how to aim and fire and which were the best pebbles to use. Several times I had seen him shoot an unwary pigeon out of the huge cedar tree that grew beside the house. I had tried myself but always missed. It didn't matter whether Newbold hit them in the body or the head, they always fell out of the tree. 'But,' said Newbold, 'if you hits 'em in the body them's only winded and you have to grab them quickly.'

When Jonny wasn't about, Newbold was my greatest companion and friend. He was a man in his late twenties with the weather-beaten face of the true countryman. I am sure he recognised in me, child though I was, the hunter-gatherer instinct I had in profusion. Together with Uncle Jack, he taught me all about country lore. I had mentioned Newbold to Uncle Jack but had met with a stony silence. Years later I discovered that Newbold was our gardener in the daytime but in 'the season of the year' he was the local poacher at night, and I'm sure had garnered more than a few of his employer's pheasants. Jack Ducat-Hamersley was the local magistrate and told me that several times Newbold had been in front of him for poaching, although he had never been caught on his land.

The first bird I ever shot with my new air rifle was a sparrow. These obliging birds sat in their hundreds on the roofs of the farm buildings and were an ideal target for a young lad with an airgun. However, it wasn't the first *thing* I ever shot. That was Nanny's bottom. She was bending over a laundry basket below the clothes line and I couldn't resist. Luckily, it was a cold day and she was wearing a thick tweed skirt and it was a long shot from my bedroom window, so the pellet didn't penetrate, but it did make her leap, most satisfactorily, in the air. She warmed my bum considerably with the back of a hairbrush, but a far worse punishment than that was the confiscation of the beloved airgun for a week, a tremendous lecture from Uncle Jack on the use of firearms and the banning of me fishing in the moat for seven days on top. It utterly served me right and I have been very careful of gun lore ever since.

One day, at the farm buildings after I'd had my rifle returned, Jonny and I were after sparrows again and had shot three or four when one of the feral pigeons flew over my head. It was irresistible and I swung up the airgun and fired. To both Jonny's and my amazement it collapsed. Of course, it wasn't dead as, by great good fortune, I had hit it in the wing and broken it, but it was my first flying bird. That same day I took Jonny to my home and showed him a wood pigeon's nest in one of the trees in a small wood at the back of the house. Pigeons' nests are built of a ramshackle of twigs, which are a pretty certain defence against an airgun pellet. Despite this, Jonny optimistically aimed at the centre of the nest and I stood ready to have a shot as the pigeon flew away. However, by an unbelievable stroke of luck, Jonny hit the pigeon in the head and it fell out of the nest stone dead.

Unquestionably our 'dread of the week' was riding lessons. Jonny and I both hated riding and were terrified of horses. It was, however, considered a skill that we must master and we were put into the untender hands of a woman with a pronounced moustache called Biddy O'Sullivan. This harridan, who was unquestionably a sadist, took great pleasure in putting Jonny and me on the most difficult horses in her stable, which would run away with us, buck or suddenly swerve. We always fell off and lay weeping on the ground until made to remount. 'Don't just lie there crying, boy, get up,' Biddy would shout unsympathetically.

One day we were in our paddock on our horses and Biddy was lecturing us on the importance of being in control of the horse. 'Always ensure that it is you who is the master and not the horse,' she was saying. 'It is vital that you sit straight in the saddle, grip with your knees and hold the reins correctly.' She was just starting on more of this drivel when, with no warning, her horse reared up on its hind legs and, to our joy, Biddy was deposited on her large backside on the hard ground where, for a moment, she lay stunned while we sniggered joyfully. Much later, when Biddy had gone, Jonny and I saw Newbold digging in the garden. He signalled to us to come over. 'Bloody good shot that, weren't it?' he said, and pulled the catapult out of his pocket. Suddenly, we realised that he had shot Biddy's horse in the arse and this is what had made it rear. 'I carrn't abide that woman,' he said. 'Bossy bitch, an' thinks 'erself all 'igh and moighty.'

When I was eight, I was sent away from home to my prep. school, Hurst Court, near Hastings in Sussex. Set in a huge old house with beautiful grounds and wonderful playing fields, it was run by an outstanding headmaster called Richard Curtis. This splendid man had a glass eye that was very unstable in its socket so that it never synchronised with its natural counterpart. When he taught geography, which was his subject, he sat at the desk and chain-smoked. This irritated the glass eye and so this great man used to take it out and clean it, much to the joy of his pupils.

There were about seventy boys in the school ranging in age from seven to thirteen, when they went on to their public school. There was a teaching staff of seven, two matrons, three gardeners, four kitchen staff, three cleaners and a man called Len who taught carpentry. I have no idea what the fees were, but with twenty employees, I cannot imagine that the school made a profit. However, I think it must have done since it had been going for at least fifty years before I arrived. In fact, my father had been there too.

The staff were all outstanding people with the exception of the assistant headmaster, Cecil Robson. I have no idea what his real Christian name was but with hindsight he was unquestionably a screaming homosexual and probably a paedophile as well. I state this with certainty as he always somehow managed to supervise the showers and I was threatened with a beating for shouting out, 'Here comes Robbo, cock-spotting.' It was only stopped at the last moment by Richard Curtis, who made me do extra Latin instead which, luckily, I thoroughly enjoyed. I am sure that Curtis decided that Robson was a mistake because the following term he wasn't there.

My favourite master was a tall, gangling man of about

thirty, with a shock of unruly red hair, called John Farrar. His subjects were history, English and games. He was a natural teacher and I was extraordinarily lucky to have been taught by him. He had a gift, for which any teacher would be grateful, of noticing what talents a pupil had even before that pupil knew he had them. In my case, he saw, hidden beneath layers of childish shyness and reticence, a love of English words and especially poetry. He was a great countryman and knew all about butterflies, moths and wild flowers. I, at that time, was just beginning to collect butterflies and his encouragement gave me a lifetime's interest in them.

John's passion was the sport of the school. He had played cricket for Sussex 2nd XI, and trained us hard in bowling and batting so that we rarely lost a match. We played football in the winter term and rugger in the spring. John was madly keen on both games and, for all members of the football eleven and the rugger fifteen, there was compulsory skipping before breakfast in the gym each morning. Most small boys would have hated this but John made it such fun, and led it so well, that everyone vied to be a member of both teams.

With his skill at recognising talent he formed a small poetry society of six of us, which met once a week in his study. John would then give us ten poems to read during the week and the next time we met we were asked to read out our two favourites and give the reasons why we liked them so much. None of us was made to attend these sessions, we were invited, but, so great was John's enthusiasm, and such fun were the lessons, that all of us enjoyed and attended every one. The poems ranged through time and history from Beowulf, through Chaucer to Wilfred Owen and even to a poet who was increasingly making a name for himself: John Betjeman. At the weekly sessions John never criticised our choice of poem and would ask the other members of his 'coven', as he called us, to comment. It was all such *fun*, which is why I went on to study history and English at A-level.

The only real problem at Hurst Court was the food, which I remember, even from all those years ago, as being utterly disgusting. Even allowing for the fact that this was 1950 and just after the war, it was difficult to produce such filth. The porridge was thick, the soup thin, the tea cold and the water warm, the eggs hard and the toast soft and soggy. But the cook saved her true inspiration for the stew. This was a grey mess of congealing gristle, and to swallow this witches' brew it was necessary to drink gallons of water and gulp it down like pills. It should have been served to Oliver Twist, who would certainly never have asked for more. So why did we have to eat this miasma of muck? Because if you didn't you were made to take your plate and stand at the windowsill. The dining room of the school was enormous and in it there were long tables where we all ate together. The staff and headmaster mingled with the boys and were also subjected to the same swill. When he spotted a child weeping, standing at the side with his plate, Richard Curtis, the headmaster, would bang a spoon upon the wooden table until there was silence.

'Why are you standing at the side, boy?' he would bellow.

'Because I don't like my stew, sir,' would be the mumbled reply.

'You have exactly one minute to clean your plate or else you will be beaten,' said the head.

Somehow, with a great deal of gagging and retching, the unfortunate child got it down. Nowadays, every time I see contestants on *I'm a Celebrity... Get Me Out of Here!* having difficulty chewing a goat's raw testicle or some other choice cut, I feel that compared to my prep. school's food, they are eating a delicacy.

When we first arrived at Hurst Court, as very small boys aged eight, we were put in the lowest possible form where we were taught by a kind and gentle woman with the wonderful name of Mavis Gopp. Miss Gopp was in her early twenties, with dark, frizzy hair and an enormous sense of humour. She was also a very good teacher, and every newly arrived, frightened little boy who had suddenly been cruelly torn from his mother's arms was comforted and cared for by Miss Gopp.

One day, while collecting butterflies in one of the farthest corners of the school grounds, I saw, coming towards me, John Farrar and Mavis Gopp and *they were holding hands*. They leapt apart as soon as they saw me and John had a look at my killing jar to see what I had caught. 'Ah,' he said, 'a comma and a holly blue, well done,' and then they wandered off into the fields. I was seriously overexcited and rushed back to the main school. 'Mr Farrar and Miss Gopp are going to mate, Mr Farrar and Miss Gopp are going to mate.' I shouted the glad tidings until stopped by Mr Marshall, my Latin teacher.

'What on earth are you talking about, Daunt?' he asked.

'I've just seen Mr Farrar and Miss Gopp holding hands,' I exclaimed excitedly. 'Our gardener, Newbold, says that when animals touch each other closely that they're going to mate. He says we're just like animals too and that when animals mate they have babies. So Mr Farrar and Miss Gopp will probably have a baby soon,' I added knowledgeably. I was, I think, eleven at the time and Newbold had just explained 'the Facts of Life' to me by taking me to watch badgers mating. The sad thing about all this was that none of my contemporaries either understood what I was talking about or cared, but I would have loved to have seen the happy couple's faces when Dick Marshall told them about my deductions. Much later, John Farrar married Mavis Gopp and went on to become headmaster of Claremont School, just down the road from Hurst Court, which is why I sent my eldest son there. Thus John Farrar and Mavis Gopp educated two generations of Daunts.

Before I left the school to go on to Rugby, Mr Curtis had all the leavers into his study for their farewell talk. As we trooped into the room he was pacing up and down with a worried frown upon his face. Then he stood still and faced us. His glass eye was looking out of the window while the real one stared up at the ceiling. There was a long silence.

'When you arrive at your public schools,' he said momentously, clasping his lapels and standing full square with his legs apart, 'you will find that there are older boys who will want to talk to you.' He paused to let this shocking announcement sink in. 'Now, these are bad boys,' he finished. None of us had the slightest idea what he was talking about.

To this day I love pike fishing. They are such beautiful fish, with their bodies built for speed and their big heads full of teeth. The first time that Jonny and I were introduced to them was at the end of the summer holidays. We had been fishing for roach as usual when suddenly, just as I was bringing one splashing across the surface to the bank, it was grabbed by something heavy which, one moment was on the end of the line and then was gone. When I lifted out my float there was no hook. I told Uncle Jack about this. 'Pike,' he said succinctly. 'It bit through your line. You need wire for pike. Next holidays I'll teach you both how to catch them. They're best caught in the winter and it'll give you both something to look forward to.'

True to his word, Jonny's father did so on the first day of the winter holidays. We used salmon spinning rods, a big spring salmon fly hook tied to a wire trace and a wine cork as a float. We had old centrepin reels and pulled the thick line off onto the ground, from where, if we were lucky and it didn't catch on something, it flew out across the water when it was cast. We used a roach, freshly caught, as live bait.

'I put a pair of pike into the moat just after I returned from the war,' said Uncle Jack. 'They were small, under one pound. I caught them on a fly spoon in the River Thame at Stadhampton and brought them back here in a bucket. By luck they were male and female, and they've done well and spawned because I've seen them or their progeny striking at the roach. The original pair must be about twelve to fifteen pounds by now, although the hens are always bigger than the cocks. They've never been fished for so you should have some fun.' Jonny and I couldn't believe our ears. We had only caught small roach and to us, therefore, the pike was a true leviathan.

The first day of the holidays was cloudy and overcast with a warm south-westerly wind, which is always perfect for any type of fishing. Jonny and I sat together on the banks of the moat. We had cast out our roach and now our wine corks bobbed, optimistically, two feet apart on the black waters. It was, we had decided, much more fun to fish close together as we could share each other's happenings. The floats quite often went under the surface, but, as Uncle Jack had explained, this was just the live bait swimming about. 'You'll know all about it if a pike takes,' he'd told us. 'It'll go down fast and suddenly and you must not strike. Leave it while you count to thirty, SLOWLY,' he said, looking hard at both of us. 'And then strike. If you catch a pike I want it put back as I don't know how many there are in the moat.'

For a long time nothing happened. Our floats moved gently across the surface, still close together, until suddenly mine began to move fast, bobbing and dipping as it went. 'I think there's something after it,' I said hopefully. All at once Jonny's bait appeared on its side on the surface (we weren't using any weights) and then, with an almighty splash, everything disappeared. 'Wind yours in,' shouted Jonny. 'We don't want to muddle the lines.' Then, completely forgetting his father's instructions to count slowly to thirty, he picked up his rod and gave it an enormous heave. The old reel started to scream and a huge bow wave appeared on the surface as the pike charged across the moat, turned and headed straight back again with Jonny winding as fast as his young hands would allow. Everything held and, after several runs, eventually the pike was wallowing on its side close to the bank. We could both see the single hook, by a total stroke of luck, firmly embedded in the corner of the fish's mouth. And the pike looked huge.

Of course we had no landing net and even if we had had I doubt it would have been big enough. We looked at each other, and the pike chose this moment to right itself and lunge forward. The water was about two feet below us down a steep bank. What were we to do? I think we both realised that this called for drastic measures. Jonny laid his rod on the ground, knelt down and put his hand under the pike's chin and tried to lift it, but it was too heavy for him. 'Wait,' I said, 'just hold it there and don't let go.' And I slid down into the cold water that came up to my waist. Then, with me shoving from below and Jonny heaving from above, the pike was pushed and pulled onto the bank. I clambered out and we both knelt beside the fish and stared at it. It was enormous. 'Stay and make sure it doesn't slip back in,' said Jonny. 'I'll go and get a keepnet, which we'll put it in so we can show Dad before we put it back.' Soon he returned with the net and we slipped the pike into it. It was so large that, with its head in the bottom, its tail stuck out of the top. Then we both ran to find Jonny's father.

He was in his study writing letters. We burst in. 'Jonny's

caught the fifteen-pounder, Jonny's caught the fifteen-pounder,' we chorused. 'Let's see this amazing creature,' said Uncle Jack, no doubt thinking to himself that it would be half that size. However, he carefully went to the fishing cabinet and picked out a salmon spring balance. Then we returned to the keepnet and slid the pike onto the grass and even Uncle Jack stared at it in amazement. 'My God,' he said, 'that's more than fifteen pounds. It's more like twenty.' And, putting the hook of the balance under its jaw, he held it up. 'Twenty and a quarter pounds,' he pronounced. 'You lucky little boy. Grown men go a lifetime and don't catch a pike that size.'

'Shouldn't we put it back now before it dies?' said Jonny.

'That's not going back,' said Uncle Jack. 'That's going to be set up.'

And to this day that pike is in a glass case with the inscription: 'Caught by J R Ducat-Hamersley aged nine, Pyrton Manor, Pike 20lb 4oz.'

'Your father's coming here to see you tomorrow,' said my grandmother at breakfast one August morning of the summer holidays. 'Now, please try not to annoy him and make it a pleasant visit.'

I looked down at my porridge. 'Why's he coming?' I asked.

'Well, just to see you,' she replied brightly.

I didn't deign to answer and my grandmother sighed audibly. There was always a reason for my father's visits and rarely was it a pleasant one as far as I was concerned. His appearances were few and far between and I seldom saw him since he had disappeared to God knows where, trailing my stepmother, Monica, and their two progeny. However, I had some inkling of what was afoot as the last time he had come I had overheard him talking to my grandmother and saying that he felt it was time for 'The boy to learn about babies', as he put it. I thus had a whole day to plan mischief, but I needed the help of my stepmother, and this I plotted carefully.

He arrived, with Monica mid-morning, and for once, I greeted her like a long-lost friend. I rushed up, threw my arms around her and hugged her. She, despite being somewhat surprised by this previously never shown affection, responded well and kissed me. My father hustled me towards the drawing room.

'I need to have a word with you in private,' he said.

'I want Monica to come too,' I replied, clinging on to her hand. Since I had previously only been rude to my stepmother, they both regarded this as a big jump forward and immediately complied.

Once in the drawing room, they sat on the uncomfortable Queen Anne sofa and I was put into a hard chair facing them. My father cleared his throat nervously. 'Now,' he said, 'I'm going to talk to you about how babies are made or in other words "The Facts of Life". You're twelve years old now and starting at Rugby next month and you should know about these things before you go.'

This was exactly what I had hoped for, as I was sure it would deeply embarrass Monica. I already knew the facts of life anyway, but was certainly not going to admit to it. Being a country lad I had seen them all around me from an early age with the sheep and the cattle on the farm and the dogs and cats in the house, and one night, Newbold had taken me to a badgers' sett at full moon and I had watched those beautiful creatures mate by moonlight. He had told me that all animals mated like that, including humans, and thus I had learnt in the most natural way possible.

In the drawing room, Monica shuffled and stared at the floor and I could see that she was longing to leave. All her dreary respectability shone to the fore. However, it was obvious that she felt she had to stay and support my father, and I also knew she was hoping to improve her dismal relationship with me. It was exactly what I had planned for and why I had given her a hug. I had never been able to stand her self-satisfied and smug manner, and in me, a natural rebel, she brought out the worst. She hated swearing and therefore, at every opportunity, I would say the filthiest words I knew, and when she complained I would gleefully taunt her with, 'Daddy says it, don't you Dad?'

My father cleared his throat again and it was obvious that he wished with all his might Monica would leave the room, but there she sat with a martyred expression upon her face, determined to see it through. Thus I had somehow managed the best of both worlds.

'Now,' he said, 'in order to reproduce we have to go through a certain act. Now I'm going to use the Latin names for the parts of the body concerned but I'll try and explain what I mean as we go along.' He adjusted his tie and shuffled his feet again. 'A man has a penis and a woman has a vagina,' he said, 'and to make a baby the man has to insert his penis inside the woman's vagina.'

He looked at the ceiling and I glanced up at Monica. She was puce in the face and gripping her hands into tight fists. My father looked down at me.

'Do you understand?' he asked. This was the moment I had been waiting for and for which I had plotted. I put on my most innocent expression.

'I think so,' I said. 'Do you mean the man sticks his cock into the woman's cunt?'

The result was deeply satisfactory. Monica gave a little shriek, burst into tears and ran out of the room, quickly followed by my father. Shortly afterwards, I heard the front door slam and the car leave. 'Oh, dear,' said Nanny, appearing with tea and biscuits on a tray, 'has Master Niall left already?' (My father had been christened Niall Michael, but was invariably known as Mike – except by Nanny.)

In the Michaelmas term of 1955, I went to Rugby.

THREE

Boyhood

'What the bloody hell's going on here?' came the stentorian shout from the duty master, Mr Browne. It was just what my roommate and I didn't need. We were engaged in a lucrative venture, but it was certainly not one of which the school would approve and we were likely to be expelled, and certainly beaten, if we were caught.

I had been sent to Rugby in the Midlands, because the then headmaster, Sir Arthur fforde, was a distant cousin of the family and I am sure that my father received a discount on the fees. I did not enjoy it at all as, being a country boy, I felt claustrophobic in this essentially industrial town. However, there were moments of joy. When I arrived back for my third year, I found that I had been put into a room in The Towers, which was a small enclave of peace, far from the milling scrum of the rest of the house dormitories and at the top of one of the hideous, battlemented Victorian towers that had been added on to the main building. It was a delightful place to be and there were twelve of us in six cubicles of two. There was also a staff bedroom, which was normally occupied by a junior master. This adjoined the room I shared with a chap called Harry Gather-Angreigh, who was of vile demeanour with angry spots all over his face and unruly hair that he never brushed. Like me, he specialised in Latin and English, but at scholarship level. He also had a very naughty sense of humour. All the cubicles and the staffroom were separated by walls of pine planking, rather like a shooting lodge in Scotland.

When we arrived back at the beginning of the Michaelmas term we soon discovered that, oh joy of joys, a beautiful under-matron, by the name of Miss Broadbent, had been allotted the staff bedroom next door to Harry and me. She had long, chestnut hair, an exquisite figure and radiated calm and peace, which was incredibly sexy. It was an agony for all of us in The Towers to know that this beautiful girl slept next door to us, and each night we listened for her to come up to bed. We had to have our lights out at 10.30 p.m. and her footfall could usually be heard climbing the stairs about half an hour later. Then her light would appear under her door and we could hear an erotic rustling as she undressed. Her close presence greatly encouraged the sin of Onan, and I certainly had her in mind most nights.

It says a great deal for the times in which we lived that neither Harry nor I, by now fifteen, had ever seen a naked woman, apart from a few pictures in a book which I had found in my father's sock drawer during one of the rare times I stayed with him. This I smuggled back to school and charged a Mars bar to anyone who wanted to borrow it for twenty-four hours. All went well with this commercial enterprise until a junior was caught looking at it in a chemistry class. The junior was asked where he got it from and instead of saying that he had found it in a dustbin (or some such nonsense) he said that he had been given it. Unfortunately, it had my father's name in it and I was duly beaten and the book confiscated.

However, pictures in a well-thumbed book are no substitute for the real thing and Harry and I were determined to find a way of seeing Miss Broadbent in all her naked glory. Harry was rather keen on carpentry, which I suppose was natural for someone whose family made their fortune from wood mills in Borneo or some other far-flung place, and went to woodwork classes twice a week. One day he came back with a small drill that he said would be the perfect size for a peephole. That night Harry and I drilled through the pine partition. We were worried about leaving telltale sawdust in Miss Broadbent's room and so Harry drilled and every so often I sucked out the sawdust. I considered it worth the discomfort and foul taste because of the hoped-for visions to come.

At last, Harry broke through, but it was a bitter disappointment as we had obviously drilled the hole behind the dressing-table mirror. Another hole was drilled and I had another mouthful of pine dust, but on looking through this one we could see her room in every detail. Our hole was in exactly the right place, just to the left of her bed, and I knew that we would have a perfect view. All this was done at about 9 p.m., when we first went to bed, and thus we had two long hours to wait before Miss Broadbent appeared. At 10.30, we turned out our lights and lay there in the dark in an agony of suspense. At last we heard click, click, click as her high heels came up the linoleum-covered stairs. Into her bedroom she went and turned on the light. A small beam appeared through the peephole. Harry, as instigator of the scheme, was to have first look. He knelt on my bed, which was next to the partition, and peered through.

'What's she doing?' I whispered after a while.

'Nothing,' he said. 'She's sitting on her bed having a cigarette.'

After some five minutes of kneeling on the bed Harry said, 'She's taken off her jumper. She's standing facing me in her bra. Now she's taken off her bra. Jesus, they're huge.'

'Let's have a look,' I hissed at him.

'Not bloody likely,' he said. 'I want to see all this.'

'Bastard!' I said.

'Now she's taken off her skirt and shoes. She's standing in only knickers, stockings and suspenders. Christ! She's taken off her suspenders and is rolling down her stockings. Her legs are wonderful. Now she's just standing in her knickers. She's taking them down. I can see the whole thing. Its enormous and black and staring me straight in the eye.'

I had had enough. Throwing all caution to the winds I pulled Harry away from the hole. He fought back hard and we both fell off the bed with a thump. Before he could get up I had lunged to the hole and glued my eye to it. I was too late. Miss Broadbent had pulled on a long nightdress and was calmly doing her hair.

The next night I did see the whole thing, and it was well worth waiting for, but then I had an idea.

'Harry,' I said, 'if everyone will pay a Mars bar to see those pictures in my father's book, just think what they will pay for a view of the real thing.'

'My God,' he said, 'you're right. Let's start off with only the occupants of this Tower and see how we get on. We can charge them at least a shilling a look.' [Note: This, the equivalent of 5 pence today, was an exorbitant sum for those days as most boys would have had pocket money of no more than a shilling a week. It would be equivalent to charging £2 a peep nowadays.]

We casually spread the word around The Tower and, although there was some demurring at our price, the next night found almost everyone crowded into our cubicle when 'lights out' was called. At exactly 11 p.m. Miss Broadbent came to bed. We allowed her five minutes for her cigarette and then the first person had his peep. It was at this point we realised that we had a problem. There just wasn't the time for everyone to see the show before she put on her nightdress. We had to give some of the money back and rethink our enterprise.

'The answer,' said Harry, 'is quite simple. We need to drill more holes. How many punters can we fit on your bed at any one time?' He paused, then added, 'And remember we have to avoid the dressing-table mirror.'

'I reckon,' I said, 'that with a gap for the mirror we can get four on the bed. These can be considered the stalls because they have the best view and we will charge a shilling for them. We can drill two more holes at the end of the bed and two at the head, which will be the equivalent of the gallery. The view will not be so close and they will have to kneel on the floor. For this we will charge sixpence. That means that we can have a total of eight at each performance, which will give us an income of six shillings a night if we have packed houses.'

'That's two guineas a week,' said Harry.

'I know,' I said. 'One guinea a week *each*.' Harry is pretty sharp and I wanted to establish our contract at an early stage. Eight weeks, I thought, only eight weeks and I'll be able to buy myself a new Hardy trout fly rod. [Note: a guinea was 21 shillings, or £1.05 today.]

Carefully, Harry and I drilled seven more holes in the partition, each with a good view. I was worried that Miss Broadbent would see them, but until it was time for a performance we kept them blocked up with chewing gum so that the light would not show through. Although I say it myself, our opening night was a huge success. Harry had stolen some bottles of beer from the masters' common room and these we served between 'lights out' and the beginning of the performance. No one asked for their money back and we, in fact, had several repeat bookings. We decided to extend our publicity to the rest of the house.

All went well for the first two nights and then disaster struck. The head of house was a tall, creepy horror called Dixon with a lisp and a limp wrist. He was very into religion and junior fags! [Note: The Very Reverend Claud Dixon went from Rugby to Sandhurst, from which he was asked to 'retire' under a cloud. He then joined the Church, eventually becoming a bishop until the famous 'Bonking Bishop' scandal, involving a choirboy, a verger and the organist. This was revealed with banner headlines in the *News of the World*.] As I was finishing supper, I felt a tap on my shoulder.

'Daunt, Gather-Angreigh – in my study, now!' said the awful Dixon

'Bit old for you, aren't we,' I said.

'Just you two wait until you hear what I have to say,' he snarled sadistically. 'I know what you've been up to and I'm going to get to the bottom of it.'

'So, what's new?' drawled Harry.

Dixon didn't deign to reply but hurried us into his study.

'Now,' he said with a vicious smile on his face, 'I know all about your little racket with Miss Broadbent's room. What do you both have to say for yourselves?'

There was no point in denying it. He had obviously been told by some toady who had seen the show and he was now hell-bent on puritanical vengeance. We both stood and looked at him in silence.

'Right,' he said, 'either I go straight to the headmaster, in which case you will both be flogged or expelled and, with any luck, both. Or I get fifty per cent of the profits paid daily. That's three shillings a day,' he added to show that he really did know all about it. 'This money will be sent to The Reclamation Fund for Fallen Women in Africa,' he gloated sanctimoniously.

'All right,' said Harry grudgingly. Dixon looked at him in surprise, obviously expecting resistance. He seemed disappointed that there was none and growled venomously, 'First payment tomorrow morning. Now get out.'

We left. 'Why the hell did you give in so easily?' I demanded.

'Because he had us over a barrel. We couldn't win,' said Harry, 'but we can still beat him.'

'How?'

'By drilling more holes!' said Harry. 'Look! At the moment we have four in the stalls on the bed and we have four kneeling on the floor in the gallery at either end of the bed. We fit in eight more.'

'Eight!' I said.

'Eight,' said Harry. 'We drill four more holes above those on the bed and two more above the ones at either end. The people looking through those will have to stand and lean over those kneeling. We charge them fourpence each and put up the price of the gallery to eightpence each. We can't charge more for the stalls because one shilling is all that anyone can possibly afford. That way we take a total of nine and four pence per night, which will cover Dixon's money and also give us an extra fourpence.' I blinked and slowly worked it out. Harry was right.

'But bloody Dixon will find out,' I said.

'Yes, he probably will,' said Harry 'and we'll have proof that he's as bent as a donkey's dangler and threaten to drop him in it too if he tries anything.'

That night we stuck to our normal full house of eight

and the next morning dutifully handed over three shillings to a surprised Dixon. 'I knew you two would see sense,' he gloated and went on his way laughing. During break that morning we drilled another eight holes above the original eight. When we had finished I spat a mouthful of sawdust out of the window and viewed our handiwork. Well covered with chewing gum the holes hardly showed. 'I think all we need to do now is spread the glad tidings,' said Harry.

At 10.30 our cubicle had a queue outside the door as sixteen boys tried to squash into it. Eventually, just in time, we had them all either kneeling or standing, according to their pockets, and at 11 p.m. Miss Broadbent made her appearance centre stage. We had a little trouble with one boy who was playing with himself and whom we had to ask to leave, but generally all went well. In fact, for a week, we played to full houses. Miss Broadbent put on a marvellous show each night and everyone was satisfied. After the third night Dixon found out and demanded more money but was threatened with exposure and backed off, content with three shillings, particularly as I reminded him that I had seen him coming out of a lavatory with a spectacularly good-looking junior.

It was when we were well into our second week that we became greedy.

'How about sharing a peep hole?' I suggested to Harry one evening after games. 'If we charge one and six to share the stalls, then everyone will benefit. We make more money, and if the four stalls share their kneeling position with a friend, they will get a one-shilling show for ninepence. Sometimes

Miss Broadbent stands for quite a long time naked before she puts on her nightie. She even does her hair starkers on occasions, although you can't see quite as much when she's in front of the mirror.'

'A very good idea,' he replied. 'And if we aim our sharing-stalls market at the juniors they'll be small enough to fit in and it will show them that there are far greater pleasures than Dixon.'

It was unfortunate that the night we decided to launch our new 'Share the Sights for 1/6' (as we had advertised it) a man newly down from Oxford was duty master. He was the beak who had the misery of trying to teach me chemistry. His name was Mr Browne, but it should have been Mr Grey. He was a drab man, old before his time in both body and mind, with dandruff on his collar, pebble glasses and a distinct lack of humour. He taught the sciences, to which I have a deep aversion. The joys of English and Latin are embedded in my heart, but chemistry, and particularly physics, leave me cold. He also took himself and his newly found authority very seriously. He and I shared a natural dislike of each other, so that when he suddenly appeared in The Towers and found me trying to usher twenty people into position for the show he was naturally suspicious.

'What the bloody hell do you think you're doing?' he bellowed. 'It's well past "lights out" and why are all these boys in your cubicle?'

There was, of course, chaos. People were kneeling on the bed and on the floor while others were standing behind them pushing forward. Two juniors fought over who should have first peep. With great aplomb Harry spoke up: 'Sir,' he said, 'we are practising for the gymnastics display competition and we are doing it at this time of night so that no one may be able to guess precisely the form our entry will take. These boys,' he continued, pointing at the juniors, 'will stand on the seniors' backs and form a double arch, preparatory to performing a triple crescendo somersault as a finale.' I had never heard such supreme, spontaneous, lying drivel in my life. It was sublime and, as fiction, worthy of the Nobel Prize in Literature.

'Get to bed all of you,' shouted the master. 'You two, Daunt and Gather-Angreigh, downstairs now to the housemaster's study.' And of course, yet again, we were given six of the best from the housemaster's strong right arm. On the whole, however, I believe it was worth it. We made very good money in a short space of time so that I could afford to buy myself some new fishing tackle. The glories of the female form were opened up to us and I feel that we may have saved some of the juniors from a career of sodomy with Dixon.

Later, we were marched in front of the headmaster himself, the newly appointed Walter Hamilton. He was a classicist who taught me Latin. He was also no fool.

'If, for one moment,' he said, 'you expect me to believe that bunkum about a gymnastics competition you are badly mistaken. You seem to have destroyed the wall in your cubicle and the cost of its repairs will be deducted from your pocket money. I have also moved Miss Broadbent while these repairs are being carried out and Mr Browne will sleep there in her place. Any more behaviour like this from either of you and you will be expelled. Do I make myself clear?'

But as we left I could see a tiny twinkle in his eye.

After the debacle of the Peep Show I kept my head well down for the next two terms but, come the summer term, I decided to look for somewhere to go fishing. I therefore contacted Denys Watkins-Pitchford, who wrote under the pseudonym of 'BB', to ask his advice. He had always been a hero of mine and wrote enthralling, and much acclaimed, country books about fishing and wildfowling, among them *Confessions of a Carp Fisher* and *Dark Estuary*. He illustrated all his books with his own wonderful scraperboards. His writing is so descriptive that you can smell the dank depths of the carp pond and hear the wind murmuring in the reeds. You can feel the bitter cold of a morning flight for the greylag geese and hear their plaintive calling. One of my very prized possessions, which hangs above my desk as I write, is an original scraperboard by 'BB' of Redmire Pool where in 1952 Richard Walker caught his record carp of 44 pounds. It has a letter from him on the back to his publisher, Tony Witherby, who kindly gave these to me. 'BB' was art master at Rugby from 1930 until 1947 and I therefore felt that if anyone knew where there was a good place to fish it would be him. He replied to my letter by return post and described a lake called the Dark Pool, which was within cycling distance of the school and apparently full of carp. He gave me directions on how to get to it and also said that he had no idea who owned it and that he had never seen anyone fishing there.

He had caught myriad carp there, some of them around the 20-pound mark. He also wished me luck and said that he had spent many happy days there.

I, of course, could not wait to take his advice, and a week later, I skipped off cricket practice at the nets and followed his directions. Immediately after Chapel I set off on my bicycle with an old greenheart salmon fly rod tied onto the crossbar. I also had a bag in which was my centrepin reel, some hooks and bread. It was a perfect June day without a cloud in the sky and very hot. My directions said that after about five miles I had to turn off into woods, keep going along a footpath for half a mile and then I would come to the lake. I found the path and, sure enough, the dappled sunlight through the trees eventually gave way to shimmering water. As I was unquestionably poaching, I hid my bicycle in some bushes and surveyed the scene. It was quite a big, oval-shaped lake of about ten acres, with an island in the middle. Thick bulrushes grew out into it and I couldn't see anywhere it was possible to fish from the bank. There was no path around it, merely trees which grew right down to the water's edge and, although the lake sparkled in the sun, it looked black and deep.

I walked through the wood carrying my tackle and soon came to a mossy glade that led down to a shallow bay. Here the bulrushes did not seem so thick and I pushed through them until, just before the water became deep, I found the huge trunk of a fallen oak. This had become jammed on the muddy bottom and made a perfect seat from which to fish. Before putting up my rod I sat and looked around me. The opposite bank was about three hundred yards away and I was lucky enough to have a light summer breeze at my back. Suddenly there was a slow swirl in the water and I watched in awe as an enormous carp swam slowly along, parallel to the shore, and about twenty yards away. Frantically, I assembled my tackle, but by now the huge fish had swum out of casting range. I quickly threw some bits of bread into the water to encourage it to return and these were blown out into the lake, but the big fish continued to swim out of range. Suddenly, one of the bits of bread was taken by another carp. This was not as large as the first, but I was not going to be too fussy about that. With shaking hands I cast out my bread crust, which landed a few feet from the feeding carp. He took another piece of bread and then came to my crust. I was trembling all over with excitement and waited for him to gobble it down. However, he swam up to it and seemed to be sniffing it. Then he swam under it, approached it from the other side and sniffed it again. He obviously thought it was safe for suddenly he opened his huge mouth and sucked the crust down with a noise like an old man supping soup.

I waited a second to allow the carp to get the bait properly into his mouth and then struck. All hell broke loose. The fish charged out into the lake leaving a wake like the *Titanic*. The old reel screamed like a banshee and I hung on and hoped for the best. Suddenly the carp turned and swam back towards me. Then he dived deep, lay on the bottom and refused to budge. No amount of side strain and pulling would move him and I was sure that he was around a tree root or something. I held on grimly and then he slowly started to come towards me. He was tiring now and, although he made one more run, I soon had him wallowing beside the tree trunk on which I had been sitting. Of course I hadn't got a landing net – they're too much trouble on a bicycle – and I had to get into the water and heave him from below onto the tree trunk. He was a beautiful common carp of about 12 pounds, certainly the biggest that I had ever caught. I took the hook out and gently slipped him back into the lake. I held him for a second and then his tail started to work and he swam away into the depths.

I sat down and relived the whole experience all over again. God, I was excited, and trembling from head to foot. I didn't want to fish, I merely wished to sit there and contemplate my luck and take in the beauty of my surroundings. The June sun was high overhead and the whole lake glittered like stars on a summer night. Suddenly, another carp wallowed just to my right and the hunting urge took over again. I re-baited and cast into the lake. This time I put on a sinking piece of bread as I reckoned the carp would have been scared from the surface by the battle.

It was then that I heard the man's voice in the distance and there was no question that he was coming closer to me. 'Jesus,' I thought, 'a gamekeeper or estate lackey. If he catches me they will be a complaint to the school and this time I'm sure I will be expelled after the Peep Hole Incident.' I crouched deeper into the bulrushes and waited. With any luck, I thought, he would pass me by on his rounds and never notice my presence. The man continued to get closer and then he stopped in the glade behind me and there was silence.

What the hell was he doing? He couldn't have noticed any footprints because the ground was too dry. I was sure that I had left no trace of my presence. There was complete silence for quite a while and then I heard rustling noises. There was the sound of heavy breathing and the occasional sigh. This was too much. Overcome by curiosity I left my rod jammed in a small branch of the tree trunk and crept slowly forward through the rushes towards the glade. As I reached the fringe a most extraordinary sight met my eyes. There, facing me, astride a man, was Miss Broadbent. Naked. She was jiggling up and down and her tits were swinging like church bells. Her eyes were shut and there was a look of extreme pleasure on her face. Underneath her the man bucked like a bronco, but I could only see the top of his head. 'Oh God that's good,' he said, and I recognised the voice – Mr Browne!

My first reaction was one of total horror that anyone as beautiful as Miss Broadbent should possibly want to copulate with the awful Browne. Then I realised that, other than the boys, there were no males under the age of fifty in the whole school and that she unquestionably had a very limited choice. Even so, I felt deeply jealous and upset. I continued to watch with glee. It was really rather exciting. Suddenly Browne bellowed: 'I'M COMING!' – and my reel began to scream.

The peel of the old centrepin could be heard in the next county. The effect on the mating couple was interesting, to say the least. They froze and then Miss Broadbent tried to get off and Mr Browne screamed in agony. She tried again but with more effort and he shrieked even louder. 'Don't bloody move,' he yelled, 'you're ripping my cock off.' I at last realised what had happened. The banshee noise of my reel had made Miss Broadbent's fanny contract and they were locked together like a pair of coupling dogs. Meanwhile my reel continued to scream erratically as the carp pulled out more line. The need to catch a fish overcame my joy at the sight of Mr Browne's misery and, even though I felt deeply sorry for Miss Broadbent, I waded carefully back to my rod, picked it up and played the fish. It was not a big one and I quickly returned it. Then I wondered what to do. I could not resist the temptation to creep through the reeds again and see what had happened. They were still in the same position and Miss Broadbent was continuing to try and eject Mr Browne but now, more gently, and obviously without success.

I decided that there was nothing I could do to help and that if they knew that I was there and recognised me I would be in deep trouble. I went back to my rod and took everything down. Then, carrying my tackle, I waded through the rushes, parallel to the bank, and headed back to my bicycle. The journey was not without incident as, at one point, the lake deepened and I had to swim across a small bay. However, I eventually reached my bike without being seen and, soaking wet, headed back to school. On the way my conscience pricked me. Clouds had built up over the sun and a cold wind was beginning to blow. Then the rain set in. I really could not leave the lovely Miss Broadbent impaled for ever on the banks of the lake in this weather. I stopped by a phone box.

'Be that Rugby school?' I said in what I thought was a broad rustic accent.

'It is,' said the receptionist.

'Oi wants to speak to 'eadmarster,' I said, determined to wreak as much revenge upon Mr Browne as possible.

'Putting you through.'

'Walter Hamilton speaking,' came the precise tones.

'Mr 'Amilton,' said I, 'Oi'm ringin' yer 'cos Oi seen one o' yer young matrons down at the Dark Pool. 'Er's in trouble wi' 'er young man. They'm be stuck together, loike.'

'Who the hell is this?' said WH.

'Never yew moind,' I said. 'Oi'm telling yew the truth. Her needs 'elp and fast.' And I put down the receiver before I became convulsed with nervous giggling.

I bicycled on and, shortly afterwards, was thrilled to see Walter Hamilton's car hurtle past heading towards the Dark Pool with the school doctor in the front seat. I pulled off the road and hid, waiting for their return journey. Half an hour later the car slowly drove past again, in the opposite direction. In the back, wrapped in a coat, was Miss Broadbent, and it was obvious from the fact she was facing me out of the rear window that she was still glued to Mr Browne. Even in her unhappy position, her face had a radiant calmness and a look of defiance upon it. Of him there was no sign and I could only surmise that he must have been stretched out flat with his feet on the dashboard. The mind boggles as to how they were helped from the lakeside glade to the car and what the headmaster must have said to them.

Neither of them was seen for a day or two and then Miss Broadbent made her appearance looking as beautiful and unconcerned as ever. Of Mr Browne nothing was ever heard again, but rumour had it that he went to Africa to teach. And there, with any luck, he was eaten.

Three days later, I was stopped by Walter Hamilton in the street.

'You didn't, by any chance, go fishing on Sunday?' he asked.

'No sir,' I replied, possibly a touch too quickly.

'I don't believe you for one moment,' he said, 'but we'll leave it there for the time being.' He paused and thought. Then he looked me hard in the eyes. 'I gather from your housemaster that you have aspirations to become an actor when you leave here,' he said. 'I have to say that I do not believe it to be the right profession for you.' And he walked away smiling to himself.

It was at this stage of my school career that I was confirmed. Everyone in the school, except the Roman Catholics or other minority religions, was made to do this. There was no choice, as there is nowadays, every pupil knew that at a certain stage in his school career (usually between fifteen and sixteen) confirmation was part of the syllabus. For weeks before this important event, the school chaplain and his assistant took special classes explaining the meaning of the ritual and its significance within the Church of England. The service of confirmation was always conducted by a bishop and was attended by all the parents and godparents of those to be confirmed. As the bishop concerned with my confirmation was the Bishop of Liverpool, the Right Reverend David Shepherd, who had played cricket for England, there was a particularly large turnout. My father, who claimed to be an agnostic, refused to attend; my mother was not allowed to attend as she was still a Scarlet Woman, and I took my grandmother to one side and told her that under no circumstances was Nanny to be sent.

I wanted to make do with my two godfathers, John Moore, the country writer whom I hugely admired and whose work, particularly *The Brensham Trilogy*, I had read and re-read many times, and Sir John Heygate, whose presence I knew would intensely annoy my father, as he was everything that my father despised. He regarded him as effete and decadent. He had been part of the generation of 'bright young things' of the 1920s and 1930s and had refused a commission during the war, preferring to be Bombardier Sir John Heygate. There was a story attributed to him, which did the rounds, which was as follows: In 1940, just after the evacuation of Dunkirk, John Heygate was having lunch in the Ritz with the homosexual poet, Brian Howard, with whom he was at Eton (Evelyn Waugh is supposed to have based his character, Anthony Blanche, in *Brideshead Revisited* on Howard). At the next-door table were two army majors who were discussing Dunkirk, from which they had recently been evacuated. They had loud, hectoring voices, which were disturbing the whole room. Eventually Aircraftman Brian Howard and Bombardier Sir John Heygate could stand it no longer, rose from their table and walked across to the majors. 'Have we been at Dunkirky-werky, darlings?' asked Howard at his most camp.

John Heygate was a writer and had been married to my

mother's sister, Gwyneth, by whom he had had two sons, George and Richard. Richard and I have been close friends from a very early age. John and Gwyneth divorced and he at that time lived with his third wife, Dora, on the family estate, Bellarena, in Northern Ireland. His main claim to fame was that he had run away with, and later married, Evelyn Waugh's first wife, who was also called Evelyn ('She-Evelyn' to their friends). He also had a certain drink problem.

On the day of my confirmation all was going well. John Moore had arrived with his wife, Lucille, and was seated. There was a hushed chattering of parents all dressed in their best finery. The confirmation was about to start but there was no sign of John Heygate. The service began and I joined the queue of those whom the bishop would bless. I shuffled forward towards David Shepherd who, with a beatific look of sheer joy, laid his hands on each boy's head and muttered an incantation. He looked as if he was about to have an orgasm. At this point the Devil supposedly leaves the confirmed child and disappears back to Hell, although why the unfortunate Angel of Darkness has to repeat this each time or how he does it has never been explained.

Suddenly, there was a disturbance and I turned round to see my godfather, who was obviously drunk, lurching up the aisle. His tie was askew and his shirt hanging out of his trousers. David Shepherd looked up mid-blessing but, experienced trouper that he was, continued with his incantation to Beelzebub. All at once my godfather stopped and pointed at the ceiling of the chapel. 'There he goes,' he shouted. 'There goes Satan, look at the bastard run, look at his tail between his legs.' He stood in the middle of the chapel, swaying visibly with a happy smile upon his face, before the headmaster kindly took his arm, led him down the aisle and escorted him out of the door.

I later discovered what had happened. John had summoned his chauffeur and his Rolls and driven from Bellarena to Rugby. The problem was that he had stopped at nearly every pub on the way and taken five days to make the journey.

When I was fourteen my grandmother sold her lovely Georgian house, the staff were all given notice, except for Nanny, and we moved to the village of Shenington, near Banbury. The reason for this was purely financial as it was ridiculous for two old ladies and a boy, who was mostly away at school, to be in such a large and impractical house. I hated the move as I loved Pyrton and missed the Ducat-Hamersleys, and Jonny in particular, enormously.

Nanny came with us as she had been with my grandmother since she joined the family, as an under-housemaid, at the age of fourteen. She had slowly been promoted until she had been appointed as my father's nanny and had then stayed on as my grandmother's housekeeper and general factotum until I was born, when she again became a nanny. She was one of the old brigade who, in their small kingdom, wielded enormous power. She never married although, like so many of her kind, she had been engaged to a soldier who was killed at the Battle of the Somme. She was an extraordinary woman who showed me great kindness and I am sure I was the son she never had. When I went away to school, firstly my prep. school and then to Rugby, it was Nanny who came to my first speech day, sent by my father, who was 'busy'. I admit, with great shame, that I ignored her and refused to acknowledge her presence. Everyone else had their parents there and I could not admit, in front of the other boys, that my nanny had come. It was an act of great cruelty, cowardice and disloyalty and I regret it to this day. Nanny, as I was told later by my very angry grandmother, caught her train back to Pyrton in floods of tears and, quite correctly, reported my deplorable behaviour. I am certain that my father also received the rough edge of my grandmother's tongue because next time there was a gathering of parents at Rugby, he came and he came alone. I was so excited that he was coming and I remember so well rushing in joy towards him as he climbed out of his car. My arms were outstretched in welcome. This was my father come, at last, to see me on his own. He held my shoulders. 'Chaps don't hug,' he said, and held out his hand to shake. After that I never told anyone when there was a speech day and, of course, my mother was forbidden to come by court order.

When we first arrived at Shenington, I had no one with whom to fish or shoot (I had now progressed from an airgun to a 12-bore shotgun). I had been told, when I asked in the village shop, that there was a lake near by called Temple Pool. It belonged to Lord Bearsted of Upton House. I looked it up on an Ordnance Survey map and found out how to walk there. It was about two miles away cross country, but I went there as soon as we arrived in our new home. I eventually found it and discovered it to be a rectangular lake, surrounded by tall trees and reed beds, except at one end where there was indeed a temple with a short lawn leading down to the water. Here I spent large amounts of the summer holidays and soon discovered there was a tumult of tench in the water, together with some roach, perch and pike. It did not cross my mind to ask anyone's permission to fish, and all the time I was there I never saw anybody.

The local squire in the village was another retired army officer by the name of Colonel Dick Bertram, a 3rd Hussar with a round Puck's face and enormous laughter lines around his eyes. He had a son called Bill with whom I became great friends. Colonel Dick and his wife Betts were very similar in character to Jack and Tara Ducat-Hamersley. They were kind and quintessentially English with all the best traits of that race. They also saw in me a rather lonely child and encouraged Bill and I to do things together. This was not difficult as we both loved the countryside, had a similar sense of humour and a certain rebelliousness. Sadly, Bill was not a fisherman despite my showing him the joys of Temple Pool. However, he was a keen shot. He was a year older than I and attended Sherborne School.

I cannot, now, understand my thinking, but I regarded all the land around Shenington as my private estate that I could walk over and shoot wherever I liked. I suppose, because I'd had the freedom to go where I liked at Pyrton, I felt that I could do the same anywhere. It did not occur to me to ask permission of anyone; I just wandered over hill and dale, field and wood carrying my shotgun in broad daylight and shooting anything I wished – in season, of course. The amazing thing was that no one ever stopped me. I regularly returned with pigeons and pheasants, rabbits and hares and was never questioned by a soul. Thus, when I became friends with Bill, I told him about this and invited him to come with me as my guest! There is something very exciting and ritualistic about shooting a game bird on the opening day of the season (hence the Glorious Twelfth for grouse), and I was determined to shoot a partridge on the first of September. During my fishing forays over Lord Bearsted's land, I had heard several coveys of partridges calling and therefore knew roughly where they would be. It is also the opening date for the duck season and I therefore planned to do both.

'My dear chap,' I said to Bill, rather pompously, one August morning, 'I would be so pleased if you could join me for a partridge day on September the first. We'll walk up the birds and then flight some duck in the evening.'

'Where?' asked Bill.

'Oh, all across Lord Bearsted's land,' I said blithely. 'I think there are quite a few coveys about so we should have some decent sport.'

'But have we got permission?' asked Bill sensibly.

'No of course not,' I said, 'don't be silly.'

'You mean we'll be poaching, will we, Mike?'

'I suppose so. I've never thought about it,' I replied. 'I shot all over there last season and had some splendid days. I don't think Bearsted minds,' I finished naively. 'But if you're worried about it I'll go alone because I've always wanted to shoot a partridge on the first day of the season.'

'Of course I'm not worried,' said Bill. 'I wouldn't dream

of being worried. It'll be terrific fun. It's just that I've never poached before.'

The day dawned warm and overcast with a moderate westerly wind. Bill and I had a good breakfast at my grandmother's house, cooked by Nanny, and at 9.30 a.m. we set off. When we reached the stubbles we walked for only about ten minutes before the first covey rose in front of us and we each had a bird down. I put them in the game bag, which I, as host, was carrying, and we continued. By lunchtime we had had fourteen partridges and a hare, which Bill, rather foolishly, had shot and which I made him carry. We never saw a soul and returned to my grandmother's for lunch where we emptied the game bag. 'You have done splendidly,' she said. I am sure she knew full well what we were up to but had the sense not to ask questions.

'Tell you what,' I said to Bill as we were finishing our meal, 'we've shot enough partridges. This afternoon we'll decoy some pigeons. I saw quite a few coming into one of the stubble fields and we can build a hide out of stooks. I don't have any decoys but we can use the ones we shoot.'

We again set off for the fields and arrived where I had seen the pigeons feeding and, as we rounded the hedge, a great flock took off. 'If we make a decent hide they'll be back in ten minutes,' I predicted. 'They've never been shot before.' I was right, and we spent a happy afternoon shooting fifteen pigeons, which went into my game bag. After that, by mutual consent, we set off for Temple Pool and, splitting up fifty yards apart among the trees that surrounded the lake, we waited for the duck.

The wind had risen as evening approached and was now strong; it was perfect for flighting. The light started to fade and at last I heard it: a sibilance of wings. The mallard were coming. Round they circled getting lower and lower while we crouched in our hiding places. Then, when they were perfectly over Bill he stood up and had a marvellous right and left. We were limited as to where we could shoot as we didn't have a dog and therefore couldn't kill a bird over the lake. Then it was my turn. I took the first duck but hurried, dropped my shoulder and missed the second. The wind was still rising but there was a lull until suddenly we both saw a plump of ducks, about twelve in number, circling. Down they dropped and passed over the pair of us so that we both shot together and each of us had one more bird. We went to pick them up.

'Stand still or I'll let the dog on you,' shouted a voice, and we both froze. A burly man with a growling mongrel and a shotgun under his arm came up to us.

'Oi'm Lord Bearsted's gamekeeper,' he said by way of introduction. 'Oi bin feedin' them duck for 'is Lordship for weeks now, and you little buggers come 'ere and 'elp your-selves. Now give me your guns.'

Reluctantly, we handed them over with the duck we had shot. The game bag with the pigeons was taken too.

'Now what's your names?' he asked. We told him. 'You're Colonel Bertram's son, ain't yer?' said the keeper and Bill nodded. 'You should be bloody ashamed o' yourselfs. Well brought-up boys like you poachin'. Now clear off. You'll hear more o' this.'

As the gamekeeper walked grimly away carrying our precious guns, the game bag, the pigeons and the duck, Bill and I both ran. I don't know why we ran, I suppose it was to let off steam, but we sprinted away across the fields in the deep twilight until our lungs were bursting and then flung ourselves down beside a hedge, not saying a word. Eventually, Bill spoke. 'We'll go to my place,' he said, 'and tell Pa. He'll sort it out.'

We arrived at Bill's home and were greeted by a stony-faced Colonel Dick. 'Right, you two,' he said, 'come into my study.' It was just like prep. school all over again. Once we were inside he made us stand while he sat behind his desk. 'I've just had a phone call from Lord Bearsted,' he said. 'I gather you've been poaching his duck.' We nodded miserably and then a smile spread over his face. 'I didn't know you two had it in you,' he continued. 'That's the sort of thing proper chaps do. Now have a drink.'

'But what about our guns?' said Bill.

'Oh don't worry about that,' said Colonel Dick. 'I'm hunting with Marcus Bearsted tomorrow and I've told him to stop grizzling and to bring them with him. It'll cost me a bottle of whisky but worth every penny. Shame you couldn't keep the duck.'

'Colonel Dick,' I said quietly, 'would you like a brace of partridge?'

(Bill Bertram went on to become the leading architect specialising in Georgian architecture in Britain. He has done much work at Highgrove for the Prince of Wales and is architectural consultant to the Duchy of Cornwall. He has written a book, *The Architect's Tale*, published by Redcliffe Press. He is still as funny as he ever was and is my great and close friend.)

Academically I found everything relatively easy at school. I loved Latin, history and English and was studying these at A-level. I enjoyed maths, tolerated geography and hated all the sciences. Perhaps I had a bad teacher, but I really don't think so. Physics and chemistry were total anathema to me but, despite studying for A-level, we were made to do one science lesson per week. I had opted for chemistry as it seemed to me the best of a very dull lot. I cannot give a good reason for this allergy to the sciences but I really didn't care what the speed of light was or whether sulphuric acid was extremely dangerous and burnt everything it touched. My attitude was that I was never going to use these things in life, so what purpose did it serve to learn about them? However, when we were told that if certain chemicals were mixed together they would explode, my ears pricked up. I stopped reading under the desk and listened attentively. It was the first time that I had ever paid attention in a chemistry lesson. This was more like it. This could be useful. This was fun. I happily ignored the science master's naïve enjoinder that we were never to try this on our own and determined that I would do so at the earliest possible opportunity. Of course, I enlisted the help of my great friend, Harry Gather-Angreigh, he of the spyhole debacle, and we decided to carry out a little experiment of our own.

On the pretext of doing homework we persuaded our

science master to allow us to remain in the laboratories after lessons had finished and thus had the run of the place to ourselves. I have, of course, completely forgotten the formula for the substance except that it was something to do with iodine mixed with something else. In small quantities this could be dropped in crystal form onto a hard floor and if someone trod on one of the crystals it would produce a minor explosion rather like that made by a Christmas cracker. It was totally harmless but most satisfactorily made people jump. This was all very well but, Harry and I surmised, would it explode if it were made in large quantities, held together with glue, and a heavy weight dropped upon it? Would it produce a really satisfactory bang? This we had to find out.

We decided to try firstly with a small amount of the substance, say the size of a tennis ball, as we didn't want to do any real damage; well, certainly not at first until we knew how much power our home-made explosive had. The ultimate aim was to put enough into a container and sink it into the Dark Pool before detonating it. We had read somewhere that this would stun the fish and we could then see how big the carp were. It did not cross our minds that this was a somewhat unsporting thing to do. It was far too fascinating an idea for that. We only hoped that, by making a relatively small amount, we would merely knock the fish out but not kill them. This was why our first attempt was to be only tennis-ball sized.

We found all the ingredients and, putting them into a small bowl, warily stirred them around. We had no idea how volatile the mixture was and obviously didn't want to hurt ourselves. However, all went well and we soon had enough to mould together into a small ball with the added glue to give stability. When it was nicely shaped into a ball we left it in the container and placed this under a pulley, which we had hung over a door, and through that ran a length of string with a shoe attached to one end. As shoes had set off the explosions in minor amounts, we surmised they would be successful for a larger quantity. The fact that the shoe didn't have a foot in it to add weight somehow passed us by. It also, thank God, did not cross our young and foolish minds to jump on the mixture.

All was ready and, with great excitement, we released the string. The shoe fell accurately onto the ball of explosive and – nothing happened. We were both bitterly disappointed.

'What we need,' said Harry, 'is a better and heavier weight.'

'I know just the thing,' I said. 'Stay here. I'll be five minutes.' I went out of the labs, grabbed my bicycle and cycled back to our house. Then I ran up the stairs to the matron's room where she kept all her medicines and, most importantly, her scales for weighing us. These were of an old-fashioned design and had weights. Making sure that matron wasn't around I stole a 2-pound weight, which was the largest one, ran down the stairs and bicycled quickly back to the lab where Harry was waiting impatiently.

'Brilliant,' he said, 'that's perfect.' Very carefully we positioned the bowl with its explosive content by the door, tied the string to the centre of the weight and passed the other end over the pulley. Then we went to the other side where we could haul it up. As this had been my idea in the first place, I insisted, despite Harry's protestations, in holding the string and being responsible for the release. Harry, with ill grace, counted me down.

'Three, two, one, GO!' he shouted and I let go of the string. There was an appalling explosion and the sound of breaking glass. Smoke and dust billowed from under the door and Harry and I stood transfixed by what we had done. Luckily, neither of us was hurt.

'God Almighty,' I said in a trembling voice, 'we must have made too much.' We peered round the door, which by sheer luck had saved us from any harm, and looked into the lab. Through the haze of smoke and dust we could see little or no damage had been done to the laboratory itself apart from all the windows being blown out. We stared in horror. How the hell were we going to talk our way out of this? Of course, it was impossible, as was quickly proved by the arrival of one of the masters. 'Daunt, Gather-Angreigh,' he shouted, 'what the hell's going on here?' He had been walking past the labs when the explosion took place and had blood on his cheek where he had obviously been cut by a piece of flying glass. And, of course there was no real answer to that question. We were immediately taken to Walter Hamilton's house, as this was obviously too serious a crime to wait until the morning. We were left in the hall while the facts were explained to the headmaster. At last we were shown into his study. Both of us were shaking but whether this was because of the retribution to come or because of the explosion I am not sure – probably a combination of the two.

Walter Hamilton was sitting at his desk and looking extremely unamused. 'I want to know precisely one thing,' he said. 'Did you carry out this experiment in order to further your knowledge of science, and chemistry in particular, or did you do it to make a bang?'

There seemed little point in lying and, with my dreadful scientific reputation, we would not have been believed anyway. 'To make a bang, sir,' I mumbled, deciding that it was best not to mention blowing up the Dark Pool.

Walter Hamilton sat in stony silence staring at us. 'In that case you will be beaten severely by your housemaster,' he said. 'If it had been the former reason I would have expelled you. You can both thank your lucky stars that I am a classicist. Now get out.' Only then did I remember that Walter Hamilton had achieved a First at Trinity, Cambridge in Classics, and despised the sciences almost as much as I did.

At the beginning of the Christmas holidays I had been invited to stay with the Ducat-Hamersleys. It was wonderful to see them all again and especially Jonny. It was like coming home, and I suddenly realised that I now had three homes but that my mother's was the most important and special one.

Shortly after I arrived Jonny took me on one side.

'Now listen,' he said, 'I was at a dance just before Christmas and there were two sisters there and I fancied one of them enormously. She's the younger of the two, so her elder sister is ideal for you. I don't really want to take the young one out alone, so I thought we'd make up a foursome and take them out to dinner together.' He looked at me hopefully and I saw that he was terrified at the thought of taking a girl out alone and then I realised that I was too. Neither of us had any idea how to talk to the opposite sex. We were both at single-sex boarding schools and the thought of being alone for a whole evening with a girl completely scared us. However, I decided it would be pathetic not to give it a go and that I would be letting Jonny down if I didn't agree to the plan.

'Yes, ring them up and arrange it,' I said blithely, without giving any thought at all to the potential problems.

'I was hoping you'd do that,' was Jonny's response.

'Not bloody likely,' I replied. 'You've met them. They're not going to take very kindly to some total stranger ringing up, are they?'

The truth of this sank in. Then, 'Where shall we take them?' said Jonny. This was a very good question as neither of us had any ideas about restaurants, pubs or hotels in the area. 'And how do we get there?' he continued. 'We can't just meet them in The Plough' – the village pub – 'and tell them to get there on their own, can we?'

The idea of the local, although it solved the transport problem, was not a good one. It was run by a very rough family, the Woodleys, and had become even rougher when the Rockers had discovered it. It was now packed every night by leather-clad youths who annoyed everyone by hurtling through the village on excessively noisy motorbikes. Only recently, there had been a fight when the Rockers' rivals, the Mods, had visited it on their scooters. The police had been called and the village had been enjoyably horrified as flashing blue lights and sirens arrived. Nothing like it had ever happened before. 'No,' I said, 'the Plough's a really awful idea and anyway it doesn't serve food. I think we'd better ask your parents' advice.'

'That's a really good idea,' said Jonny. 'We'll do it over dinner tonight.'

That evening, as we all sat in the dining room, conversation was much slower than usual. Jonny's parents sat in their normal places at either end of the table, Jonny and I were on one side and Scrute, Jonny's ten-year-old sister, was on the other. Hugh was away staying with friends.

'Been out pike fishing today?' enquired Uncle Jack.

'No,' replied Jonny, and lapsed into silence.

'Well, what have you been doing?' asked Aunt Tara.

'Nothing much, just talking,' replied Jonny.

I kicked him hard and glared at him, which did not go unnoticed by Uncle Jack. 'What's the matter with you two?' he asked and waited expectantly. Jonny wriggled uncomfortably on his chair.

'Well, go on,' I said unhelpfully.

Jonny looked down at his untouched food and scratched his ear. Scrute stared at him in expectant anticipation.

'Mike wants to take out a couple of girls and wants me to go with him,' blurted out Jonny. 'But he doesn't know where to go and I said I'd ask you.'

'You lying bugger,' I said vehemently. 'This was entirely your idea.'

Uncle Jack and Aunt Tara started to laugh and Scrute was jumping up and down in her chair with excitement.

'You two,' she shrieked, 'taking out girls.' She rolled around howling and giggling with tears running down her cheeks.

'Right,' said Uncle Jack, when everyone had calmed down, 'Mike, I want you to tell me what is going on.'

'*We* thought,' I said loyally, and Jonny looked at me gratefully, 'that we would like to take two girls out to dinner. But,' I emphasised, 'we don't know where to go or how to get there and back.'

'I see,' said Uncle Jack, with a huge twinkle. 'And what are these girls' names?'

I looked at Jonny.

'Jane and Sarah Pringle,' he mumbled.

'Oh yes, the Pringle sisters,' said Aunt Tara, 'I know their parents well. The girls are about the same age as you two, aren't they?' Jonny, bright red in the face, nodded assent.

'I know them too,' put in Scrute. 'Every single touch and tingle Pringle.' And she went into more peals of laughter. Jonny looked as if he could kill her.

Before murder could take place Uncle Jack glanced at his wife. 'We'll have a talk about it and make a plan for you,' he said, and with that we had to be content.

After breakfast the next morning we were summoned to Uncle Jack's study. This was a wonderful room with fishing rods in a corner, a royal stag's head on the wall and the smell of mothballs from the fly-tying box. I loved it.

'Your mother and I have made a plan,' he said, looking at Jonny but addressing both of us. 'You can take the girls to The Lambert Arms. I'll drive you there and collect you. The girls can meet you there. Now,' he continued, and looked hard at both of us, 'how are you going to pay for this dinner?' This rather important point had never crossed our minds and we stared at Uncle Jack in horror. 'You haven't thought about it, have you?' he said, and we shook our heads. 'Okay,' he continued, 'when the evening arrives I'll give you twenty pounds but you can repay me with labour, probably cleaning out the large game larder. It hasn't been done for years and is a threat to health. It will take you at least a day between you to do a good job. Is that fair?' We nodded. 'Now go and ring the girls and see what they say. If they've got any sense they'll turn you down flat,' he added as an afterthought.

With a lot of humming and hawing, standing on one leg and then the other, and very red in the face, Jonny telephoned. The conversation was brief. The girls said that they would love to come, an evening was arranged and their mother would, they hoped, drive them to The Lambert Arms and pick them up again. Jonny, heaving a sigh of relief, put the phone down and grinned at me triumphantly.

At that time The Lambert Arms was probably the smartest hostelry in the area. It had childhood memories for Jonny and me. When I had been seven and Jonny five we had been inveigled into a Christmas revue, which ran for one night only, in a village hall that had been turned into a tiny theatre for the evening and which, at that time, was attached to The Lambert Arms. This was a charity performance with the money going to the local hospital. I can say, without any chance of contradiction, that it was a complete disaster. I couldn't understand why most of the grown-ups were either swaying or giggling foolishly. However, the first person to disgrace himself seriously was Jonny. He had two words to say which were, 'Ugh, women.' Terrified, he waited in the wings, clinging to his nanny's legs. When the time came for him to make his entrance he refused to go on until physically pushed by his fearsome nanny. He then displayed absolutely no talent for the boards whatsoever. He stood, centre stage, and howled loudly until rescued by an embarrassed nanny. My contribution to the evening was even worse. I stood, piddling with terror in a puddle of pee, while singing, in a piping treble and blissfully out of tune, 'Daddy Wouldn't Buy Me A Bow-Wow'.

Our table was booked for 8 p.m. On the appointed day, Jonny and I, in our school Sunday suits and ties, were dropped off there at 7.45 p.m. to await the girls' arrival at 8 p.m. 'I'm picking you up at ten,' said Uncle Jack. 'That's quite late enough. I need my sleep.'

We walked through to the bar. To this day I totally fail to understand why we were served drinks as we both, un-questionably, looked well below the legal age of eighteen. However, the kindly bartender didn't seem to notice this.

'And what would you young maasters loike?' he asked in his best imitation of a Regency innkeeper.

'Two pints of your best ale, please barman,' I demanded. 'We're dining later,' I added. I had been reading *Treasure Island* and assumed that this was the way to speak. Because we were nervous the two pints seemed to slip down very fast and we ordered two more.

At 8 p.m. sharp the girls arrived. We both stood up and

Jonny began to introduce me but couldn't remember their names and we all stood, twitching and embarrassed, until the elder girl said, 'I'm Jane and this is my sister Sarah.' Jane, the one Jonny had earmarked for me, was overweight and spotty. Her sister was a petite brunette, beautiful but with a cold eye. I could see why Jonny had taken a fancy to her. They both ordered Coca-Cola and Jonny ordered another pint.

'Do you like fishing?' he asked suddenly in an aggressive voice, inferring that if they didn't there had to be something wrong with them. The girls smiled kindly but denied any knowledge of the sport. 'How about trapping moles then?' When the sisters didn't reply he went into a long and incredibly boring dissertation on where and how to find mole runs, how to gut them when trapped and what to do with their skins. I noticed that some of his words were slightly slurred. Jane and Sarah were looking bemused and, particularly when he went into great detail of where to insert the gutting knife, slightly sick. Then we all sat in silence and stared at the floor.

We were rescued by the head waiter, who took us through to the dining room which was completely empty. We sat at our table and Jonny excused himself and wandered unsteadily away to the loo. I did my best but it was obvious that the sisters were deeply regretting their decision to come out with us. Jonny returned and knocked a chair over at the next-door table. 'Fucking thing,' he muttered, which rang round the room. The girls blanched but said nothing. The head waiter picked it up and took our orders.

'Would sir like some wine?' he enquired unctuously.

'What a good idea,' Jonny replied enthusiastically.

The wine waiter appeared with a wine list almost as large as *War and Peace* and we stared at it in horror. Neither of us knew anything whatsoever about any sort of wine. Then a brainwave struck me. I had heard Uncle Jack talking about something called claret and I knew what the bottles looked like as, with their indented bottoms, they were perfect for making into minnow traps. I rifled through *War and Peace* and then gave it to Jonny.

'I thought we'd have a bottle of claret,' I said knowledgeably, 'but I can't find any.' Jonny glanced through it quickly.

'Nor can I,' he said. 'It's disgraceful. Place like this ought to have fucking claret.' And he lifted his hand and summoned the wine waiter.

'You haven't got any claret,' he slurred. 'It's appalling.' The wine waiter paused, picked up the wine list and held it open for Jonny to see.

'We serve,' he said precisely, 'no fewer than sixty-two different sorts of claret. If Sir would kindly look at Bordeaux rouge, Sir will see the claret. But,' he added in a fatherly tone, 'I'm not sure that it's a good idea for Sir to have any.'

After that everything seemed to deteriorate to its natural nadir. Somehow we staggered through the awful evening until, thankfully Mrs Pringle appeared at 9.30 p.m., summoned, I am certain, by Jane, who had made a 'trip to the loo' and had, I suspect, telephoned her mother asking to be rescued from these dreadful boys. Uncle Jack arrived at 10 p.m. and ushered us into the car. 'Did you have a good time?' he enquired kindly.

'No,' replied Jonny in a moment of honest sobriety. 'It was horrid. I'd much rather go fishing than take girls out.'

'You'll learn,' replied Uncle Jack, but until he was eighteen Jonny stuck to his preference.

I am sure that one of the reasons that my grandmother moved to Shenington was that it was only five miles from the farm that my mother had bought at Idlicote in Warwickshire. I am certain that she realised the idiocy of the court order against my mother and wanted me to have some small part of what was left of my childhood with her. Thus, when I left Pyrton, I returned to my mother's for Christmas and the remainder of the holidays. Badger's Farm was beautiful, bleak, wild and desolate. It stood on the top of a hill with views, in every direction, over glorious countryside. Here, I was thrilled to find that my godmother Inez was staying as well. Inez Nimmo-Smith, which was the final name by which we all knew her, had been married twice prior to Bob Nimmo-Smith and had also recently left him. Her second husband had been the academic, Christopher Hill, Master of Balliol College, Oxford, whom she had married aged twenty-three. She had had a daughter by Christopher, whom they had christened, perhaps unfortunately, Fanny. He had achieved fame by being a leading member of the Communist Party.

I had always adored Inez and she had been a kind and generous godmother to me. She was one of my mother's greatest friends and a true Bohemian in that she totally ignored all convention and was just herself. To be able to follow that particular lifestyle, Inez had many things going for her: she was small and ridiculously beautiful with an elfin face and a cigarettes-and-gin voice. She also had a wicked sense of humour. She loved people and everyone loved her. I was like a Red Admiral butterfly, who bathed in her sunshine and worshipped her from afar. Above all, she had an extraordinary knowledge of poetry, and could quote great chunks of Keats and Shakespeare, Byron and Swinburne and all the Romantics.

That first evening that I was home, we sat in the dining room after dinner and I felt, for the first time, that I was accepted into this exalted company as a grown-up. With encouragement from my mother, who had a passion for poetry, Inez, pink with port and pleasure, quoted Keats's 'La Belle Dame Sans Merci' and Rupert Brooke's 'The Hill', whilst I, who also loved verse, sat entranced at her feet as the beauty of the words engulfed me and her husky voice flowed over me. At last she turned to this tear-washed youth and said, 'Remind me to tell you Walter Raleigh's poem that he wrote whilst awaiting execution in the Tower of London, "As You Came From the Holy Land".'

'Please do it now,' I said.

'No,' she replied. 'It's too special for general company. I'll do it for you when we're alone.'

'Yes,' said my mother. 'That final verse really does define love as no other poem I have ever read.' And with that I had to be content. It was like a Christmas stocking: I could see the shapes and even feel the contents but had no real idea what was truly inside. With a week to go before Christmas I asked my godmother every day to let me hear the poem but she wouldn't oblige. 'No,' she'd say, 'when the time is right I'll do it for you. But it is such a special poem that I'll not waste it on the wrong moment.'

On Christmas Eve we all went to the local pub after a simple dinner. Here we knew that there would be carols sung amidst the mince pies, holly and Christmas trees. All my mother's farm labourers were there, so that it was like being in the midst of a large family. The precious and loved words of 'Once in Royal David's City' reverberated from the pub roof in rough, country accents and I wouldn't have swapped it for the choir of King's College, Cambridge, for all the money in the world. At last the final notes were sung, the last glass finished and we all lurched into the ancient Land Rover and weaved our way down the country lanes to the village of Idlicote and the old farmhouse nestling among the outbuildings at the top of the hill. As we clambered out of the Landy there was a welcoming neigh from the stable, and the warm, comforting smell of cattle and horses, manure and straw, lingered in the still, frozen air. A full moon cast its pale light upon the countryside and, from the terrace, we could look, even at that late hour, over great tracts of Warwickshire and ancient trees standing in stark silhouette against the frozen grass.

We went into the happiness of the house and in the drawing room the huge log fire flickered its warmth across the paper chains, the hanging cards and the Christmas tree bedecked with glitter. 'Well, I'm off to bed,' said my mother, 'but why don't you two have another drink and Inez can quote Sir Walter to you.'

'What a lovely idea,' said Inez. I mumbled something and disappeared to the fridge for some nourishing wine. I came back with a bottle and two glasses. Inez had put some more logs on the fire so that it was beginning to blaze and now the whole room was lit only by the flames and the fairy sparkle of the Christmas tree. I am sure that the drawing-room fireplace was the main reason that my mother had bought Badger's Farm. It was an enormous inglenook affair that burnt huge and horribly uneconomic amounts of four-foot logs. For this reason it was lit very rarely, usually only at Christmas and for winter dinner parties. In front of it was a vast silk Iranian Qom rug and from this, lying on her side and looking incredibly beautiful, Inez stared up at me.

'Put the wine on the table and come down here.' she commanded. And so I did as I was told and lay down next to her. And then she kissed me. By this time, at seventeen, I had kissed precisely three girls and these had all been at Pony Club dances. They had epitomised an adolescent's feeble, furtive fumbling. I really had no idea how to kiss and so Inez taught me. She did it slowly and kindly, biting my lips and then licking them while holding my face between her hands. I had never known anything like this and was so completely overcome that I lurched clumsily on top of her. 'No,' she said, 'wait. Now is the time for Sir Walter. Lie back and I'll come to you.' So saying, she lay on her back with her head on my shoulder and began to quote:

As you came from the holy land
Of Walsingham,
Met you not with my true love
By the way as you came?

The beautiful words washed over me and my being was
trance-like, hypnotised by her smoky voice. The fire seemed
to flicker more brightly and the Christmas tree lights to dim.
The tears flooded down my cheeks and, for the first time in
my life, I felt that overpowering feeling of passionate love
for a woman. The poem finished with arguably the greatest
definition of love that has ever been written in the English
language:

But true love is a durable fire,
In the mind ever burning,
Never sick, never old, never dead,
From itself never turning.

I lay still, with this ethereal woman's head on my shoulder,
in complete awe. In my short life I had never been so moved.
'And now,' said Inez, 'I'm going to make love to you.'

And she did. With gentleness and understanding, kindness
and passion. I was seventeen and she was thirty-eight. No
young man could have lost his virginity in a more loving or
romantic fashion. I was supremely lucky. I am sure that she
realised that I was a virgin and that she took pride, pleasure
and joy in introducing me to the secret delights. For my
part I, of course, immediately fell completely in love with

her. As we lay naked on the priceless rug warmed by the dying embers of the fire and lit by the coloured lights of the Christmas tree, I nearly spoilt it all. 'I lo—' I started to say. But Inez was too quick for me. She put her hand over my mouth and kept it there until, a little while later, we made love again.

Many years passed, and I was in a pub in Sussex with my mother and her sister, Gwyneth, my aunt. I can't remember why but we were discussing great love poems and I said that I felt that Sir Walter Raleigh's 'As You Came From the Holy Land' was for me Top of the Pops. 'That's Inez's favourite poem,' said my mother.

'I know,' I said. Then, because I was very proud of it and because I loved my mother dearly and wanted to share my pride with her, I enquired gently. 'Did you know I lost my virginity to Inez?'

'Oh darling, don't be so stupid,' she replied. 'I arranged it.'

I returned to Rugby for my last two terms to study and take my A levels in English, history and Latin, but I also had to decide what I wanted to do afterwards: I resolved to be an actor. This was mainly because I knew that it would please my mother and greatly annoy my father. I had mentioned this previously to my housemaster and had appeared in the school play as Algernon in Oscar Wilde's *The Importance of Being Earnest*. This had been an undoubted success and I had become completely addicted to the 'smell of the greasepaint and the roar of the crowd'. I had a pretty good idea what my father would say to this ambition, but I decided at least to give it a try. At the end of the summer term I left Rugby.

FOUR

The Army

Since his attempt to tell me 'the facts of life' my father had been wary of talking to me, and Monica had hardly been seen at all. During the year before I left Rugby my father visited me and took me out to lunch. The purpose of his visit was to find out what I wanted to do with my life and, he hoped, to help me towards a sensible career.

'Do you have any plans at all?' he asked. 'After all, you'll be eighteen next year and you must have thought about it.'

I had been dreading this moment. Yes, I had been thinking about it and I knew all too well that my favoured choice of career would not at all be approved by him. However, I decided that the best thing to do would be to grasp the nettle and so I looked my father hard in the eye.

'I want to be an actor,' I blurted out.

My father's reaction was worse than I could have dreamed

possible. What I had not thought of was that this would remind him of my mother and what he felt were her worst traits. He went red in the face and instantly started shouting.

'Don't be so bloody stupid, only poofs and queers are actors, not people like us. You'll be an actor over my dead body. I suppose this is totally your mother's influence. That's why I wanted to keep you away from her, do you understand?'

No, I didn't, but I knew better than to say so.

'You bloody well have another think and if you can't do better than that I'll think of something for you!' And with that he stormed out of the hotel where we were having lunch. Sadly, a great many memories of my father are of him driving away in a temper.

I have always had one major fault in life, which is that if someone says I can't do something it invariably makes me more determined to do it, even if it is to my own detriment. I therefore hatched a plan. I didn't see my father again until after I had left Rugby, but during that time I wasn't idle. One day he suddenly rang up my mother's home and announced that he would be appearing on the morrow.

'Please be outside the farm at 10 a.m.,' he said. 'I don't want to have to come in.'

When he arrived, I opened the car door and got in. I was hardly in the front seat and had not even said 'hello' before he launched into his tirade.

'Well,' he said, 'what thoughts have you had on a career?'

'I still want to be an actor, Dad,' I replied. He again went scarlet in the face but before he could start shouting, I continued: 'In fact, I've applied to RADA for a scholarship and been awarded one.'

This was completely true. I had forged my father's signature on the entrance papers and, after two days of oral and written exams, had been given the scholarship. I therefore hoped that, if I faced him with a fait accompli, he would give in and allow me to do what I wanted. However, I had underestimated my father's hatred of my mother and therefore his misplaced wish to thwart her. In fact, my mother had had little to do with my decision, except that I infinitely preferred my mother's actor friends to my father's flying ones, however brave they might be.

'You think you're clever, don't you?' my father said and his voice had gone quiet, which was always a much more dangerous sign than the shouting.

'Well, I'm cleverer,' he went on. 'How did you get into RADA without my permission? I, as your father and guardian, would have to sign the entrance papers because you're under twenty-one.' (The age of majority in this country was not reduced to eighteen until 1970.)

'I got Mum to sign them,' I lied.

'That wouldn't work,' he said emphatically. 'You may be living with her but she doesn't have custody of you.'

Suddenly, for the first time in my life, I had had enough of my father and answered him back. 'More's the pity,' I screamed, 'because she would have been a far better mother to me than you have been a father. I'll do what I fucking well want, with or without your permission.'

'You won't, you know,' he replied quietly. 'You'll go into

the army and they might knock some sense into you.' And with that he turned the car around and drove me back to my mother's.

I gave up fighting my father. I didn't like or respect him but I had little choice in doing what he wanted. I think the main reason I gave in without much of a fight was because of Colonel Jack Ducat-Hamersley and his family, and Colonel Dick Bertram and his. If the army had produced such kind and decent people as these then it must be worthwhile, I reasoned. Looking back now, I am eternally grateful for all that these two wonderful families gave me. Without them I dread to think how I would have turned out. Also, Jonny Ducat-Hamersley and Bill Bertram became, and remained, my best friends for life.

My main act of rebellion, and one which had annoyed my father intensely, was to move out of my long-suffering grandmother's home and into my mother's, where I had been welcomed with open arms. I had bicycled there carrying a suitcase of clothes hanging from the handlebars. My fishing rods, which were my only truly valued possessions, were tied to the crossbar. That first night as I dined with my mother she said, 'When I lost custody of you I was heartbroken and your Aunt Gwyff found me weeping over a cake that I was making for your third birthday – with Ada, the cook's, help,' she added honestly. 'And Gwyffy said to me, "Don't worry, darling, he'll come back one day." And now you have.' And she gave me a huge hug.

In September 1960 I entered the Royal Military Academy Sandhurst, which is the main training college for British Army officers, equivalent to West Point in the United States.

Sandhurst and I did not really like each other. There was too much of my mother in me truly to fit into the army mould. I could, and do, understand that, when in the army you must never question an order, but what I hated was the terrifying convention. The haircut must be the same, the civilian clothes the correct, boring cut and colour; the conservative views must adhere to a code. It was all so unthinking and conventional. I wanted to scream that Buckingham Palace should be turned into council flats just to see what reaction this received and to provoke some sort of argument. However, a true soldier must never question an order, or the order of things.

One of the first things that we had to do was PT. This involved half an hour of physical jerks and some vaulting over a horse. I have always rather enjoyed gymnastics and, fortunately, being well coordinated, I found it very easy. I had been posted to Ypres Company in New College and among the new arrivals in my platoon was an overseas cadet from Ghana called Ebenezer Ossai Addai. He was a cheerful soul and was well liked by all of us. At the end of that first introduction to PT we were all standing in three ranks and the order came from the PT sergeant instructor: 'In three ranks, strip.' And we all took off our vests, shorts, shoes and socks, folded them carefully and stood stark naked before receiving the order: 'To the showers, fall OUT.' I was standing next to Ebenezer and suddenly noticed the PT sergeant staring in amazement at his cock. 'Don't you point that thing at me Mr Addai, sir,' he shouted, 'it might go off.' When we were in the showers I could not resist having a good look myself and indeed it literally hung down nearly to his knees, and had a diameter of at least two inches. Ebenezer was very proud of it and waved it happily at everyone from his shower.

One of the good things about Sandhurst was that some of us were regularly invited to cocktail parties, dances and dinner parties during the last dying days of the deb season. In 1957, the Queen officially did away with the annual presentation at Court of well-bred girls. However, Queen Charlotte's Ball and the following social events continued, and this allowed certain of us to attend these functions. Most of these parties took place in the summer but in the winter there were the hunt balls. These were usually preceded by dinner parties in various glorious manors. There was one small problem, which was that I hated riding and had, and still do have, a psychotic loathing of horses. However, I was always pleased to receive an invitation (or 'stiffy', as they were called) as it meant free drink, a beautiful house and a chance of illicit sex by corridor creeping. One of these occasions I remember vividly...

Her name was Annabel and she was the most beautiful girl in the room. At last I had persuaded her to dance with me and now we were smooching happily to the haunting notes of Acker Bilk's 'Stranger On the Shore'. It was 1961 and I was at a hunt ball. I had been invited by an unknown woman because I had managed to get myself on The List. This was a collection of names, gathered from God knows where, of young, so-called 'gentlemen' who were considered eligible. Eligible? We were about as eligible as apes. We possessed *the* dinner jacket, *the* dark suit and no money. We were far too young to marry and most of us were only interested in the girls for one thing. Yet, because we were on The List we were lucky enough to stay at some of the most beautiful houses in England, gobble lobster, quaff champagne and creep draughty corridors. Often these were hung with Constables and Canalettos, Rubenses and Rembrandts, Manets and Monets. There were libraries full of first editions and furniture fashioned by Sheraton and Chippendale. We dined off eighteenth-century dinner services adorned with family crests and drank Château Latour from Georgian glasses. Few, if any, of us appreciated how lucky we were. I regret to say that we mostly took it all for granted. It was supremely British, immensely farcical and utterly stupid.

I concentrated on my partner as we waltzed around under the chandeliers. She had velvet skin, eyes in which I could have drowned, and a wonderfully slim body which now nestled next to mine. I couldn't believe my luck as she snuggled closer. Pathetically, it had taken me ages to pluck up the courage to ask her to dance. In those days most of us had no idea how to talk to a girl. We had all been sent to single-sex public schools with only our fag for comfort. I had adored her across a smoke-filled room and it wasn't until my third glass of very good brandy that I, in trepidation, approached her and, rather formally, said, 'May I have the pleasure of this dance?'

'Junt?' she suddenly announced. I wasn't sure whether she was referring to my dancing ability in a particularly vulgar manner or merely belching discreetly. To cover up my incomprehension I pulled her closer. She wriggled away. 'Junt?' she repeated aggressively. And suddenly I understood. She was asking, 'Do you hunt?' Now the truthful answer to this should have been 'no', but I knew, if I said that, all hope of seduction would be gone. I therefore half-heartedly nodded.

'Oh good,' she said, 'so you'll be out with us tomorrow?'

'I'm afraid I can't,' I replied, feeling hugely relieved. 'Sadly I haven't brought any clothes with me.'

'Oh don't worry about that,' she said, 'my brother Rupert's about your size and he's away with his regiment.'

'And I don't have a horse,' I said, laying down my ace.

'That's okay,' she replied, smiling sweetly as she trumped me. 'You can borrow Dobbin, he's the gentlest nag we've got.'

The next morning found me mounted on Dobbin and beautifully turned out in Rupert's clothes. Now, as I mentioned, I am pathological in my hatred of horses and all that goes with them. Quite frankly, they scare me to death. As I've told, I was made to ride as a child with the beastly Biddy O'Sullivan and it says a great deal for my passion for Annabel that I was found mounted at all, even on the so-called 'dearest horse in the world'. Just the short walk from the stables had been frightening as Dobbin had slipped on

Above left: My mother, Elspeth, some years after her divorce from my father, in which she was unjustly portrayed – and treated – as a 'Scarlet Woman'.

Courtesy of and © Dr Frances Dipper

Above right: Me as a small boy, looking rather more angelic than may actually have been the case.

Below: (Niall) Michael Daunt, OBE, my father (second left), a brave and skilful pilot, but a terrible parent to me. As chief test pilot for Gloster, he is shown with the inventor of the jet engine, Sir Frank Whittle (in RAF uniform), test pilot John Crosby-Warren (far left), general manager Frank McKenna (centre) and chief designer George Carter (far right). The F9/40 behind them, serial DG205/G, was one of the prototypes for the Gloster Meteor, the first British and Allied jet fighter.

© Jet Age Museum collection; with grateful thanks to Tim Kershaw

Top: The Beagle Ball at the RMA, Sandhurst, 1962 – Officer Cadet Daunt is seated third from left. 'We were far too young to marry and most of us were only interested in the girls for one thing.'   *Courtesy of Dr Frances Dipper*

Below left: Second Lieutenant Daunt, 1st Battalion, Royal Green Jackets, on active service in Borneo. I found the Iban tribesmen delightful and welcoming, despite a gruesome collection of Japanese heads taken during the war.

Below right: On the shores of Lake Turkana, Kenya, with the 80-pound Nile perch I caught with the aid of an inflated condom. Our pilot, Dave Allen, is at right; his habit of measuring his aircraft's fuel by dipping a stick in the tank was at first rather alarming.

Left: Playing a marlin from Pat Hemphill's boat off the coast of Kenya. One of the blues I caught weighed 475 pounds, and took me over an hour and a half to boat.

Right: Posing with a striped marlin I'd caught from the Hemphills' boat *White Otter*. It was a striped marlin that L. hooked, and which led to her letting Pat have a piece of her mind.

Left: With George Adamson (right) on his reserve at Kora, about 200 miles northeast of Nairobi. Two years later the great conservationist was dead, murdered by bandits; he is buried at Kora, which is now a national park.

Above: Fishing the Rynda in the Kola Peninsula, north-western Russia, with my boyhood companion and lifelong friend Jonny Ducat-Hamersley, 'the greatest friend that anyone could ever ask for'.

Below: Me (centre, with my daughter) ratting with the Ancient and Honourable Society of Ratte Catchers, essentially a dining – for which read 'drinking' – club. 'Our uniform consisted of a Ratting tailcoat in hunting green with a high black velvet collar and cuffs, white breeches, white stockings, buckled shoes and a jabot at the throat.'

Above: 'The Master' – my friend and mentor, Hugh Falkus, one of the greatest salmon and sea-trout fishermen of his or any other age. At his death, he bequeathed his Spey-casting school to me.

Right: My godfather, Sir John Heygate, Bt, whose drunken intervention at my confirmation certainly enlivened the proceedings.

Below: With my cousin and great friend, Richard Heygate, and a very small brown trout. The son of my godfather, Richard is 'the Bart' to my 'Bounder'.

Left: With two sizeable pike taken on the fly from the River Test in Hampshire. 'They are such beautiful fish, with their bodies built for speed and their big heads full of teeth.'

Right: A 28-pound salmon from the River Rynda, north-western Russia, June 2009. The rivers of the Kola Peninsula have runs of Atlantic salmon that are the envy of fishermen the world over.

Left: A day's fly fishing for trout on the River Itchen in Hampshire: 'I am an angler, and hugely enjoy the pursuit of all species of fish.

Below: With my friend and fishing companion, Chris Tarrant. 'There is nothing pretentious or 'showbizzy' about Chris. He is simply Chris Tarrant, witty, funny, naughty, kind, generous, intelligent and tremendous fun.'

Above: Fishing the Spey with Ronnie Corbett, one of 'the very select club of those that have achieved greatness but have in no way allowed greatness to spoil them.'

Below: 'The gentle and very beautiful art of Spey casting for salmon': the Bounder performing a reverse single Spey cast on the River Tamar at Endsleigh in Devon.

Courtesy of and © William Heller

the cobbles in the yard and I had very nearly fallen off before the day had even begun. Luckily Annabel was ahead and didn't see my terror-stricken face. We arrived at the front of the manor, where the meet was taking place, and here we all stood around drinking and talking. After a stirrup cup or three I felt that perhaps this wasn't so bad after all. I remembered the instruction I had been given as a child and sat upright in the saddle with Annabel next to me looking gorgeous and adoring.

Thus, as I sat, almost happily, on Dobbin and swigged my third bullshot, I felt that perhaps this time I wouldn't be overtaken by stomach-churning fear and make a complete fool of myself. The problem was that I knew from bitter experience I could look wonderful on a horse *as long as it didn't move*. The moment it started to trot, canter or, worst of all, gallop, I would be found clinging, terrified, around its neck.

At last we moved off and trotted gently to draw the first covert and I managed to rise perfectly in the saddle as dear, kind Dobbin behaved immaculately. Suddenly there was a terrible baying of hounds and blowing of horns and the whole field set off at a horrific pace across the stubble. Dobbin instantly changed into a fiend and, despite my sawing frenziedly at his mouth, was no longer a gentle, obedient and lovable nag. He took the bit between his teeth and hurtled off as if the hounds of Hell were chasing him. Somehow, I clung on as the whole field overtook me. 'Out of the way!' screamed an enormous woman with a bum like a tank, as she charged past me. Of Annabel nothing was to be seen.

I think she had suddenly realised that I was not a Jorrocks and was thoroughly ashamed of the miserable specimen who clung pathetically to Dobbin's neck. She obviously wished to have nothing more to do with me, and I couldn't say I blamed her. In her mind, awful horsemen were likely to be dreadful lovers. They wouldn't stick the pace, stay in the saddle or perhaps even rise to the occasion. And she was probably right.

By now, I was scared stiff and humiliated, and longing for this farce to finish. I think Dobbin had had enough, too. He didn't want his day's hunting to be ruined by the incompetent fool on his back. We came to a fence and Dobbin took off. As we landed on the other side he gave a sort of sideways twist (which I swear he did on purpose) and continued his day's hunting while I lay on the ground, sore, bruised and mud-covered. At last I picked myself up and limped miserably to the nearest pub. It seemed the only sensible thing to do. I desperately needed a stiff drink before I faced the derision of the manor. I would creep in through the back door, slink past the kitchens, the butler and my hostess and scurry, I hoped unheralded, to my bedroom and change, before creeping out the same way with my luggage. In the distance, I could hear the sounds of the hunt carrying across the breathless countryside. The last vestige of morning mist hung in the stark woods and that beastly woman, she of the tank arse, was still shouting 'Out of the way!' at some other hopeless fool. And Annabel? Love, lust and she divorced at that last fence and I never saw her again.

The first term of the two-year course at Sandhurst was sheer hell. It was a relentless round of drill, kit-cleaning and lectures. The only joy was the language and humour of the drill sergeants. These men, the cream of the army's NCOs and warrant officers, were all from the Brigade of Guards and were thus veterans of the drill square. At their head was the world-famous academy sergeant major, J.C. Lord. He was, literally, a legend in his lifetime, and coined the expression: 'I call you "sir" and you call me "sir". The only difference is you mean it.' He instilled terror and enormous respect into the officer cadets and I can honestly say that I was deeply honoured to have known him.

One example of his extraordinary personality was when a boxing match was held between Sandhurst and Cambridge University. The guest of honour was King Hussein of Jordan, who had attended the RMA a few years previously. He was shown to the gym, where the contest was due to take place, by the then commandant, Major General 'Geordie' Gordon-Lennox. Waiting outside the gym to greet them was Academy Sergeant Major J.C. Lord. As the King came towards him, Lord drew himself up to his full height of six-foot three and gave the King a cracking salute. 'Good evening, sir,' he said. The King couldn't help himself. After two years as an officer cadet he returned the salute – and 'Good evening, sir,' he replied.

Another 'royal' incident took place on the parade ground. One of my brother officer cadets was Prince Michael of Kent, and when Michael Kent made a mistake it was nothing to hear the drill sergeant shout, 'Mr Prince

Michael, sir, you're a fuckin' 'orrible prince.' One of the great cries at an officer cadet who had incurred the drill sergeant's wrath was, 'If I was you sir, I'd lie down and I'd die, I'd bleedin' well die.' However, once when Michael Kent made an error the drill sergeant was heard to shout the usual, 'If I was you, sir I'd...' and then he paused and realised that he couldn't suggest that a close relation of his sovereign should expire, and so he continued, 'I'd bleedin' well habdicate, sir.'

Every Sunday there was a church parade, when we were marched to the chapel and made to sit through an hour-and-a-half of God-praising. On one particular Sunday we had been warned that Field Marshal Lord Montgomery of Alamein would be reading one of the lessons. After we had made our way to our pews, we removed our forage caps and waited for the service to begin. My next-door neighbour had forgotten this respectful act. Suddenly, I saw a drill sergeant hurrying down the aisle towards us. He stopped by our pew, leant across so that he was nose-to-nose with my neighbour and, in a stage whisper that rang around the chapel said, 'Sir, take your 'at orf in the 'ouse of God – cunt.'

The service somehow continued until the world-famous field marshal climbed the steps of the pulpit, waited for the hymn to end and then surveyed the throng of officer cadets staring up at him.

'Here beginneth the seventeenth chapter of the Book of Genesis beginning at the ninth verse,' he barked. 'And God said unto Abraham...' at which he stopped and looked up, surveying us all, '…and in my opinion he was right,' he said, before continuing with the reading.

One of my friends at Sandhurst, who later went into the Coldstream Guards, was a splendid man by the name of Jeremy White. Jeremy was funny and witty and, because he was a natural rebel, we had a great deal in common. He had been accorded the nickname 'Fucker' because of his success with so many girls. One of the duties of an officer cadet was carrying out menial tasks at the local racecourse, Tweseldown, near Fleet, where regular point-to-points took place. For one of these occasions I had been ordered to be in charge of selling tickets for the car park. This was not a particularly onerous task as all I had to do was to stand on the gate in my best No. 1 uniform and, in return for £3, put a ticket on the windscreen of every car that arrived at the gate. This somewhat ruined a Saturday when there were better things to do and so I was slightly surprised when Fucker sidled up to me beforehand and offered to help.

'But I don't need help,' I said. 'It's a terribly simple task and it can be done with only one man.'

'Don't be a fool,' replied White. 'It's an easy way to make lots of lolly and I'll show you how.'

When we arrived at Tweseldown, Fucker took me to one side. 'Now,' he whispered, 'here's what we do. You put the tickets on the windscreens and I go around the car park, remove them, give them back to you and you sell them again.' It was so obvious and so simple and we made a £100 each on the day, which in 1961 was a great deal of money. Had we been caught we would undoubtedly have been thrown out of Sandhurst, although whether it would have been for theft or for behaviour unbecoming an officer and a gentleman, I'm not at all sure.

Looking back on my time at Sandhurst, although I have to admit that I wasn't a natural soldier, I enjoyed it considerably more than I expected. I had decided to go into the Oxfordshire and Buckinghamshire Light Infantry or, as they had recently become, the 1st Battalion, the Royal Green Jackets. As I had lived most of my life in Oxfordshire and it was the regiment of Colonel Jack Ducat-Hamersley, who had shown me such kindness and taught me so much when I was a boy, it seemed the natural thing to do. This was late in 1962, and I received a letter in the post informing me that I would be joining my regiment in Penang, Malaya in February of 1963. However, in December 1962 the regiment was posted to Borneo on active service to assist in putting down the Brunei Revolt, which led to the Indonesian Confrontation.

In many ways, I was enormously lucky in my short military career, and the first piece of luck was to be posted to the Far East and the beautiful island of Penang. The second piece of good fortune was to find myself on active service almost immediately afterwards in the jungles of Borneo. I flew out to Malaya from a freezing Britain, for the winter of 1962–63 is recorded as one of the coldest ever. Penang could not have been a greater contrast: the humidity was in the nineties and the sun blazed down. As the regiment were in Borneo, there were only two officers in the mess, the families' officer, who had the unenviable job of looking after the soldiers' wives and trying to ensure their good behaviour, which was a serious nightmare, and the Motor Transport Officer, who was back briefly on leave. I had never got around to taking my driving test and I knew that MTOs had the power to monitor the test and to pass or fail the applicants. Therefore, at breakfast that first morning, I asked him if he would test me.

'How much driving have you done?' he asked.

'Well,' I replied, 'I've been driving Land Rovers on my mother's farm for ages.'

'Okay,' he said, 'drop into my office this morning and I'll issue you with a pink ticket. It's no good out here but take it to a post office when you're next in England and they'll issue you with a licence.'

I looked at him in amazement and gratitude. 'Thank you,' I said.

'No problem,' he replied, smiling. 'Oh, and by the way,' he remarked, as I was about to leave, 'that's a bottle of whisky you owe me.'

I was only in Penang for a short time, to get acclimatised, before I caught a train down to Singapore and then flew from RAF Changi to Kuching in Borneo.

I almost immediately fell in love with Borneo. It was then, and to a certain extent still is, one of the few truly wild places left on earth. The Brunei Revolt was practically over before it had begun and certainly by the time I arrived there in February 1963. I was sent to A Company, then stationed in Miri, the largest city in Sarawak and the birthplace of

Borneo's oil industry. Our job as soldiers was to visit the distant villages and to win the hearts and minds of the people. In the deep jungle these were nearly all Ibans, the traditional headhunters of Borneo. They lived in longhouses, which were literally that – long houses. These were built on stilts and entirely made of wood. They were always beside a river and consisted of a series of joined rooms, with a communal room at the front, and a thatched roof. Underneath the longhouses were the goats and chickens. It was all incredibly basic but the people were some of the happiest I have ever known.

To get to the longhouses we travelled many miles up the rivers and usually found them by accident, as there were no maps in those days. Some of those deepest in the jungle had never seen a white man before, but their rules of hospitality demanded that they show us a proper welcome. This was because, for obvious reasons, no one was allowed to marry within their own longhouse and thus, when young men were seeking a mate, they travelled by canoe up or down the river stopping at other longhouses until they found the right woman. For the most part, the people were animists by religion but some had been converted to Christianity by missionaries, although in 1963 these were rare.

The first longhouse that I ever visited was up a tributary of the Baram River. My party consisted of a corporal and eight riflemen including a radio operator. We also had a civilian translator, who spoke Iban, and a boatman. On the way upriver we saw many and varied tropical birds, monkeys and, most exciting of all an orang-utan (*orang* in Malay means 'man', and *hutan* means 'forest'; thus, man of the forest or jungle). When we arrived, everyone ran to greet us and stared wide-eyed at these strange people. I had brought sweets with me, which I immediately gave to the children. We went into the main longhouse and the old headman greeted us with courtesy. It was impossible to know his age but his hair was white and his earlobes nearly hung down to his shoulders where they had been stretched. On his arms were tattoos of upside-down chevrons; I was told by our translator that each of these represented a head that he had taken. I looked at him in awe and asked where they had come from. 'They are from the Japanese during the war,' he told me proudly, and taking my arm led me into his personal quarters within the longhouse. He pointed to the ceiling and there, hanging by their hair, were a collection of shrunken heads. I tried not to look horrified and instead congratulated him on his score. I later learnt that he was a very famous headman within the community, as the Ibans believe that if you take a head in war the owner of the head will be your slave in the afterlife. This means you are hugely popular with the women, as they also will benefit from immortal slavery if the man is their husband.

The riflemen had all been adopted by different families and were being well looked after. I felt guilty that we had so little to give these wonderful people until I realised that cigarettes were the greatest present of all and, in those days, all of us smoked. We had arrived at roughly 4 p.m. and the tropical night descended with its usual suddenness at approximately 6.45 p.m.; everywhere throughout the longhouse oil lamps were lit and food began to be prepared. I insisted that all my soldiers give their rations to the Ibans and there followed a communal meal of both our foods. Theirs was rice with fish and huge freshwater prawns from the river, which were delicious. Our compo rations were nowhere near a fair swap. They also gave us an alcoholic drink called *tuak*, which was a rice wine, tasting not unlike the Japanese sake and very potent.

After the evening meal there was dancing and it was explained that the girls of the longhouse would dance in a circle and then the young men from another longhouse would do the same. If there was a mutual fancying the lads would creep into the girls' quarters when everyone had retired and if the girl felt like it, she would be sleeping alone, but if not she would be with her mother. I enquired about becoming pregnant and was told that there was a certain jungle root that prevented pregnancy. Whether this was true or not I never found out. I did, however, have a quiet word with my riflemen and told them, to much complaint, that under threat of being charged with disobeying orders they would not under any circumstances join in. We were there to win the hearts and minds of the people and the last thing I wanted was to be faced with a disgruntled young Iban, especially, as I reminded the soldiers, because these were headhunters.

The next morning the headman insisted on showing us the Ibans' most successful and dangerous weapon – the blowpipe. This was what he had used to bag all the Japanese heads that now hung in his living room. A blowpipe is roughly six foot long and made of bamboo. The darts are also of bamboo and approximately eight inches long. They have a piece of cork on the end, which makes them fit snugly into the pipe. This is then held to the mouth and the warrior takes a deep breath and expels it sharply, causing the dart to leave the pipe at surprisingly high speed. In skilled hands it is accurate to about twenty yards – more than enough for jungle warfare. The end of the dart is sharpened to a very fine point and tipped with poison. I never found out what this poison was but I am told that it is made from the sap of the ipoh tree, sometimes mixed with snake venom. The aiming point on a man is the neck, as the point needs to get into the bloodstream to kill instantly. It is a terrifyingly effective weapon. During the war, the headman told me, he used to hide in a tree at a turn in one of the jungle tracks used by the Japanese patrols. He would wait until the patrol had rounded the corner, separating the last man from his fellows so that he could not be seen, and then, at a range of little more than five yards, blow. Death was instant. By the time the patrol realised that tail-end Charlie was missing it would be too late. They would return to look for him and all they would find was a headless body. It must have terrified the Japanese patrols witless, for they would have heard nothing.

I asked if I could have a go with the blowpipe and we set up a target of paper, with a bullseye drawn on it, on a tree. I blew as hard as I could and, to derisive remarks from my soldiers, the dart just reached the tree but well below the target. However, to my joy, none of them did any better. Then the headman took the pipe, filled his lungs with air and, in a sudden explosion of breath, the dart quivered into the centre of the target. It was a wonderful demonstration of skill and I almost felt sorry for the Japanese.

We were being picked up from the longhouse by helicopter because this would save time. However, first we had to prepare a landing zone. The best flat piece of ground had a huge tree in the centre of it and I explained that this would have to be cut down. The headman demurred, looking worried, and it was explained to me that this tree was sacred as it was the tallest tree near the longhouse and that anyone who harmed it would suffer. However, he continued, if I took the first cut the evil would fall on me and no one else and then his people would finish the job. He gave me a *parang* (machete) and, watched by the whole longhouse and my riflemen, I approached the tree. There was complete silence as I lifted the parang for the first cut. In doing so, I touched a branch above my shoulder and disturbed a hornet, which furiously settled on my neck and stung me. I clasped my hand to my neck in pain and doubled over. There was an audible hissing of communal indrawn breath and it took me the next ten minutes to persuade everyone that it was a hornet that had hurt me and not a jungle god.

Eventually, a large enough clearing was made for the helicopter to land and I called up our base on the radio and said that we were ready to be collected. I had tried to explain to the headman what a helicopter was but the nearest the translator could get was to say that it was a manmade bird. It became totally apparent that none of the longhouse had ever seen a helicopter before and I was longing to see their reaction. At last there was a distant clattering, which gradually came closer, and amid clouds of dust, obvious awe and a certain amount of fear, the helicopter landed. I ordered my riflemen on board and was just about to climb in myself when the headman asked if he could have a flight. Now this was strictly against army regulations, but I thought 'to hell with that' and asked the pilot if he would mind if we took the headman for a quick flip around the area. He, being another rebel, immediately agreed, and I signalled for the old man to climb aboard. This he did and we flew him around his area, and over the nearest neighbouring longhouse, before returning to his home. As he was climbing to the ground, he explained to us that now he would be even more famous among the Ibans. We took off again and all of us waved as to a fond family, which I know we all felt they had become.

Somewhere, in a longhouse far up the Baram River, I hope that there is a man about fifty years old at whose birth I assisted. It came about as follows: We had visited, once again, my favourite longhouse, where the headman showed me all the Japanese heads that he had taken in the war and where he demonstrated what a deadly weapon the blowpipe is.

This was the third time that my soldiers and I had been there and we had established a bond of friendship with the inhabitants. In particular I felt very close to the headman and his wife. I always laid my sleeping bag on the floor of their part of the longhouse and had begun to get to know his family. I had met his son and his eldest daughter and knew that he had two granddaughters, one of whom, he told me, was with him that evening as she was due to give birth and wanted to be with her mother.

After the last glass of the delicious tuak I retired to my sleeping bag and was in a deep slumber when, at about four o'clock in the morning, I was awoken by the headman and the translator, who said that the granddaughter had gone into labour and please would I come and assist at the birth. I have to admit that this frightened me considerably, for two reasons. Firstly, because the chief and his wife imagined that, since I was a British Army officer, I would know all about childbirth, and secondly because I knew nothing. I had been present and helped deliver countless cows, sheep and horses. I had watched the miracle of piglets coming out of the sow like a string of little sausages, immediately rise to their feet, run the couple of feet to their mother's belly and instantly latch on to a teat. But I had never been present at a human birth. However, now was not the time to admit this. I woke my very sleepy wireless operator and made him contact battalion HQ. Then I asked for the Medical Officer to be woken up. Very shortly a yawning doctor came on the line and I explained the situation.

'What the hell do I do?' I asked, somewhat panic-stricken.

'Don't worry,' he said, 'her mother will know exactly what to do and those young Iban girls usually have no problems.

144

With any luck you will only need to tie the umbilical cord in two places and then cut it in the middle.' I hated the word 'usually' and the phrase 'with any luck', but I merely asked him to keep the link open. I looked at my patient, who was lying on a palliasse with her mother squatting next to her. She seemed totally calm and was having contractions fairly close together. Her mother jabbered at the interpreter. 'She say "any moment",' he translated. Suddenly the girl gave a spasm and a cry and the next second her mother was holding a tiny baby boy. I had some 20-pound nylon in my pocket, which I used to catch catfish, and with this I tied the umbilical cord in two places. Then the interpreter handed me a wicked-looking knife over which I poured some tuak in optimistic sterilisation before cutting between the ties, and that was that. I was hugely moved and felt greatly honoured to have been asked to assist, even though I had done almost nothing. I reflected quietly on the birth and thought that a spasm and a cry had probably started it and a spasm and a cry had ended it.

'What's he going to be called?' I asked the interpreter. He turned to the girl, who was now holding her baby to an almost overflowing breast. Then he looked at me and smiled.

'She want to call him Mister Mike,' he said. 'You not mind?'

'Mind?' I said. 'Mind? I am thrilled to bits.'

So, Mister Mike, I hope that the world has treated you well and that, so far, you have had a wonderful life. I will never forget how you started it. I was a very lucky second lieutenant.

During the three tours of six months each that we did in Borneo I visited many longhouses and was always shown incredible hospitality and kindness. These were mostly Ibans, who are a part of the Dayak tribe, and a happier people I have never found anywhere in the world. I once asked a headman if there was ever any crime and he didn't understand what I was saying: 'You know,' I said, 'if someone steals from someone else, that's a crime.' He thought for a moment and then replied, 'I think I was told that it happened once in my grandfather's time, but I have never known it myself.'

'And when it occurred in your grandfather's time what happened to the thief?' I enquired.

'Oh, he would have been killed,' he replied as if I had asked a particularly stupid question.

There was one other 'Iban' incident which is worth mentioning.

We had just arrived at another unmapped longhouse and I had given the children the usual sweets as they rushed to meet us. The men and women were always more dignified and waited inside to welcome us calmly but warmly as we entered. All the women were topless and the men wore small loincloths. The chief immediately took me and my interpreter to his small section of the longhouse and offered us *chai* (tea). He was a wizened, rotund old man with the traditional earlobes weighed down and lengthened by heavy rings. Soon the women began to prepare supper in huge pots outside. There were quantities of rice, fresh fish from the river, chicken and a huge wild boar that was being roasted over a spit. As darkness fell, we all sat down on the floor of the communal room in one huge group of about eighty people and started to eat. We were also again given bamboo beakers of tuak. Then the usual dancing took place, which is truthfully a mating ritual, and in which I had forbidden the soldiers to participate, and eventually everyone retired to their various parts of the longhouse for the night.

Later, the headman, the interpreter and I retired to his rooms and had one final glass of tuak together before I laid out my sleeping bag.

We chattered of fishing and hunting for a while and then suddenly the chief looked shy, if that is possible for a man covered in warlike tattoos. I wondered what was coming. He turned to the interpreter and whispered something in his ear. The interpreter started to giggle stupidly.

'What did he say?' I demanded.

'He say, maybe you like to sleep with wife,' the interpreter blurted out, staring at the floor. I looked disbelieving and amazed, for in all the longhouses that I had visited this was the first time this had happened. 'He mean it. You very honoured. Big compliment.'

The chief called out something and a gargantuan woman waddled into the room. She stood with her head bowed but peering at me from under long, lank hair with a naughty smile on her face. I turned to the interpreter. 'Tell the chief,' I said, leaning forward and thinking very fast, 'that I am indeed highly honoured by his kind offer. His wife is very beautiful [I almost made myself sick saying it] and he could not have paid me a greater compliment, but I already have a wife far across the sea in England and our God, who is an angry and vengeful God, would punish me greatly if I were to lie with another woman.' I sat back on my haunches, rather pleased with my excuse, and hoped for the best.

The chief looked more surprised than upset and squatted for a while scratching his crotch and thinking. Then his face lit up and he again leant across to the interpreter. I waited in some trepidation. It was a long conversation but at last they finished. After a moment of thinking how to phrase it, the interpreter said, 'He heard all about your nailed God from two old, round-eye women who come here year ago. They dress in long robes and tell him all about Jesus. They want him believe in Him, too. The chief tell them he have many wives and happy worshipping spirits of jungle. He tell them go away. He think it better for you if you worship jungle gods, too. Then you could lie with wife. He say she tire you out and maybe you not big enough man for her!' And they both rolled around bellowing with laughter. Even the fat old wife was creased up with giggles. I made a feeble attempt to look dignified. Then they started whispering again. I waited, blushing like a schoolgirl.

'The chief say if you cannot have wife, your corporal must have daughter. Very good for friendship between Iban and British. Sadly, she not good enough for you. Only wife right for you,' he announced and the chief turned and called again into the sleeping quarters. A curtain was pulled back and into the room came one of the most lovely women that I have ever seen. She was about twenty years old with

148

black, shining hair that hung down almost to her waist, and her naked breasts jutted proudly. She had an ethereal beauty, an exquisite figure and long, perfectly shaped legs that seemed to go on forever. She stood smiling gently at me. I stared at her stupidly and wondered how the hell I could rescind my lie about the 'angry and vengeful God'. Of one thing I was certain: my corporal was certainly not going to get his rough and horrible hands upon her. Hell! It was virtually rape.

'I am afraid,' I said, with as much dignity as I could muster, 'that my corporal also has a wife across the water and our God would be equally furious with him.' The girl suddenly turned to her father and jabbered angrily at him. Then she looked apologetically at me and said in almost flawless English, 'He and this man,' glancing witheringly at the interpreter, 'played the same trick with the last lot of soldiers who came here too. They think it's terribly funny but I hate it. I work with the nuns further up the river and teach at the mission school.' She gave a last scornful glance at her father. 'He's a Christian, too,' she said, and flounced gracefully out of the room.

The regiment completed three tours of Borneo of six months each. In between these we returned to Penang where we spent another six months. We lived a lifestyle which has now long disappeared. There were endless rounds of cocktail parties, dinners, receptions and tennis parties (the officers' mess had its own tennis court), water-skiing (we had our own boats and I was appointed water-skiing officer), scuba diving, and we even managed to organise a wild-boar shoot. There were, of course, servants galore to look after us. Drink was incredibly cheap, beer cost more than spirits and tonic more than gin. It was the last dying embers of the empire and tremendous fun. I have no doubt that the riflemen enjoyed it, too, for the night life which was available in Georgetown, the 'capital' of Penang, was much and varied and, for the most part very good-looking.

There was a clap of sex on offer and all the taxi drivers and trishaw riders pimped for the girls. I remember one who was particularly persistent. I was with Major David Wood, the second-in-command (2I/C), a pompous and correct officer, with thinning red hair, a red face and a moustache; in fact, he was a stage version of an army officer. Why I was with him I fail to remember but I do know that he had never travelled by trishaw before because he had told me so. As we climbed out, 'You want pretty girl? Clean, very cheap?' enquired the driver solicitously. This was the standard gambit which was offered to every 'round eye' during, or at the end of, every journey. 'Very decent of you to offer,' said the 2I/C, at his most English, 'but not just at the moment, thank you.' Then he looked at me and raised his eyebrows as if to say 'these fellows really are the limit'. I kept a straight face but before we could pay him, the driver, who had obviously been thinking hard, came up with his second proposal. A huge smile of understanding came across his face and he nudged the 2I/C in the ribs and winked at him lewdly, 'Oh, you want little boy,' he said, as if he had been incredibly stupid not to have thought of it before. This was far too much for the 2I/C and his face went redder than ever: 'Certainly not,' he exploded. The driver looked thoroughly taken aback and amazed. Here was a 'round eye' who wanted neither boy nor girl. This was unheard of in his book. However, he wasn't beaten yet. He scratched one armpit, then the other and finally his head while the 2I/C searched in his pocket for change and held out his hand, trying to escape from this revolting man as soon as possible. At last the driver's expression cleared and his face took on the look of one who has found the cure for cancer. 'I know what you want,' he said, and he paused for dramatic effect. 'You want goat.'

In those far-off and wonderful days when the army spoilt its officers blissfully, all of us, however junior, had a batman assigned to him. This man, usually an old lag who had been passed over for promotion, came to 'his' officer in the early morning with a cup of tea, ran a shower or bath and, while the latter was bathing, removed the charge's shoes or boots for polishing and his uniform for pressing.

In my case I was allotted Rifleman Leacock. This man, a cockney of dubious character had been in the regiment for many years but had never managed to climb higher than the rank of lance-corporal. This was usually due to being drunk and disorderly. Most of the time he was a sober, quiet and responsible soldier but once a month he would consume, as he described it, a 'rage of beer' and would then insist on trying to hit a sergeant. It was never a corporal, lance-corporal or even an officer, but always a sergeant. Any sergeant would do; he did not have preferences, but he would return from Georgetown having drunk huge quantities of Tiger (the delicious local beer) and then make his way to the sergeants' mess. Here he would walk straight in and thump the first sergeant that he saw. He was not a large man and nearly always failed in his purpose, but he would try and, of course, this was completely against all Queen's Regulations. The sergeants, for their part, would do their best to get him to the cells for the night without a punch-up, for they were all very fond of Leacock as most of them were years younger and, as I say, sober he was a delight to be with. Besides his rebellious character, one of the other reasons that I was very fond of Leacock was his broad cockney accent and his continual use of rhyming slang. I have always loved our beautiful language, in all its variations, and this particular diversion I found truly fascinating. I quickly learnt that a 'bubble' was a Greek, a 'front-wheeler' was a Jew and an 'iron hoof' a gay man.

In those days the soldiers were paid once a week, on a Thursday. They stood in line on pay parade, queuing to come to a table where their platoon commander sat and handed out the amount of money called out by the platoon sergeant. Thus you would hear: 'Rifleman Leacock, one hundred dollars,' (in those days the Malay dollar was worth 2s 4d, or approximately 12 pence in today's currency) and you would count out the amount owed and hand it over. The soldier concerned would then check it and, if it was correct, he would salute, say, 'Thank you, sir,' turn to the right, stamp his foot and fall out. It was the same every Thursday.

After yet another sergeant-bashing, and after he had

come out of the regimental nick, I had taken Leacock to one side and given him a long lecture on not getting drunk and, most importantly NOT BASHING SERGEANTS. He wasn't married and I told him to find a nice girl and let off steam in bed with her rather than punching a sergeant. This he had agreed to. Rather pleased with this solution to Leacock's problem, I awaited results. The following Friday he appeared at 6.30 a.m. as usual to do my kit, looking well and cheerful.

'Leacock,' I said, 'you look really well. You obviously didn't get drunk or hit any sergeants. Did you take my advice?'

'Oi did, sir,' he said. 'Oi done exactly as yer told me. I went dahn the Green Parrot [for some reason there is always a Green Parrot nightclub in every town all over the world where the British Army is stationed] only 'ad one beer and then Oi had a really good butcher's arahnd the place. Suddenly Oi spotted, sittin' at the bar, all alone, a really gorgeous bit o'grumble [woman]. Lovely fripnies [tits], a magnificent Khyber [arse] and glorious mystics [legs]. Any'ow, Oi went over and chatted 'er up and we 'ad a few bops on the dance floor. She couldn't speak much English but I weren't there for the chatter and after a while I suggested we walk up the apples and pears [stairs] and 'ave a Donald [fuck]. Well, when we got into bed, Oi felt arahnd. Bleedin' feller, weren't it?'

'God, Leacock,' I said in horror. 'What on earth did you do?' He looked at me in amazement as if I were mad.

'Well, Oi paid, aint Oi?' he replied.

The riflemen were not, however, the only people to take advantage of the joys of Georgetown. One evening I met a friend from England in the E&O (Georgetown's smartest hotel) for a drink. He was there on business and, after we had had a most enjoyable dinner he retired to bed early as he had important meetings early the next morning. It seemed to me too early to return to the mess and I had heard of a very upmarket drinking den called Churchill's which served great drinks and where there were pretty hostesses. I persuaded myself that it would do no harm to visit. After all, I only wanted a quick nightcap and so, foolishly, I called a taxi and was taken to Churchill's. Here I was immediately greeted with open arms by a bevy of beauties and was persuaded to have several drinks. Then one of the bevy, with her hand on my thigh, suggested that she should take me upstairs for a massage. Well, a massage couldn't do any harm, I thought, could it? And it would be wonderful to relax totally after the strains and stresses of Borneo. With this sort of drivel running through my befuddled brain, I followed The Beauty upstairs. There I stripped to my underpants and lay on the bed. The Beauty anointed me with oil and gently massaged my shoulders and back. This, through several bottles of Tiger, I found relaxing and very erotic.

'You turn over,' she said, 'I do front.' I rolled over and she immediately stared at my boxer shorts where Charlie was rearing his lustful head. 'Oh,' she said coyly, 'you want extra-special massage,' and she grabbed Charlie in a gentle fist. This was much too much for me and I nodded vigorously. 'Only twenty dollar more,' she said, and suddenly I remembered that I only had ten dollars left after all the beer and the massage and I needed this for a taxi back to the mess. 'I can't afford it. I don't have enough money,' I said, inwardly heaving a sigh of relief that Satan had been vanquished. 'No problem,' she replied, 'you British officer. I take cheque.' And with Satan the victor laughing all over his sinful face and an uncomfortable erection I wrote one out.

Three days later I started pissing red-hot pokers. There is an indescribably silly law in the army that states that it is against Queen's Regulations, in that it is unbecoming of an officer and a gentleman, to get a dose. He can certainly go to the Medical Officer, but it is the MO's duty to report him to the commanding officer. Our old MO would never have done this. He was a man of the old school who would have called me a bloody fool and cured me quietly and privately. When the regiment first arrived in Malaya, he had addressed the whole battalion as follows: 'Some of you,' he had said, 'are going to place your private parts where I would not put my umbrella,' and then he had gone on to warn of the perils of unprotected sex. I had not joined the battalion at that point but his lecture had become regimental legend. However, I knew that his replacement, a young and ambitious man with no sense of humour, would not hesitate to go snivelling and sneaking to the commanding officer who would then be forced to take action. I therefore asked at the E&O's reception desk if they knew of an English doctor in Georgetown. The manager of the hotel, who had obviously had this problem before, smiled knowingly and wrote down a name and address.

I arrived at a fashionable area of Georgetown and rang the doorbell. A pretty Chinese girl answered the door and I was shown into a waiting room. After a while a man only slightly older than myself entered. 'Hello,' he said, 'I'm Dr Tony Greenburgh. What can I do for you.' I told him my sad tale. 'Ah yes,' he said, 'I thought it might be something like that. By the way, what was her name?'

'I believe she was called Coca-Cola Annie,' I admitted, blushing like a schoolgirl.

'Oh, she's safe enough,' he said. 'A straightforward dose of clap. Thank God you didn't have the one with one leg.'

He gave me an injection and a course of pills. 'And no alcohol for a month,' he said. 'That'll be twenty dollars. It'll cost you the same to cure it as it did to catch it,' he added, and, with a broad smile, sent me on my way.

I arrived back at drinks time and the mess corporal came to take my order. 'A large gin and tonic as usual, sir?' he enquired, 'No thank you,' I said, 'I'm training for the athletics.' And then I looked around the mess sheepishly. However, I felt much better when I saw that almost every other subaltern was training for athletics, too.

To be truthful, I loved my time in Malaya and the dream of treading the boards was slowly fading. I still didn't like the convention and conformity, but I realised that without the army I would not have had the wonderful experiences that Borneo and Malaya had given me.

Before we left Malaya we were told that our next posting would be to Berlin and I think we all realised that it would be hard to find a greater contrast.

To my amazement I had been promoted to command the Reconnaissance Platoon. This is possibly the best and most exciting job that any young officer can be given in an infantry battalion. It is really the commanding officer's private army, and my wise old colonel, Oliver Pratt, had recognised the rebel in me and given me the job. His exact words to me were, 'Be as unconventional as you like, that's what the job is all about.'

Berlin, in 1965, was at the height of the Cold War. The city was divided into four sectors, each governed by one of the four allies, the Americans, French, Russians and British. However, in 1961 the Russians had erected the Wall, thus effectively cutting off West Berlin from the East. It was guarded everywhere by Russia's minions, the Volkspolizei (or Vopos as they were colloquially known). These were the East German police, armed with Kalashnikovs, who happily shot their own people on sight if they were caught trying to escape the tyranny of the East German communist regime.

My job was to patrol our side of the Wall in Ferret scout cars and Land Rovers. The Ferret was a small armoured car with a crew of two men. Down below was the driver and up top was the gunner/commander with, usually, a machine gun. The Land Rovers were stripped down without roofs or windscreens and often had a machine gun mounted on the bonnet. In these we patrolled the various areas of the British sector of Berlin and then reported on the movements and numbers of the Vopos. We were basically a mobile intelligence unit. This, after a short time, became monotonous as little out of the ordinary ever took place. I therefore decided one night to liven things up, and carefully rehearsed my platoon in exactly what they were going to do.

In the British sector was a farm, down the centre of which ran the border between West and East. The Russians had not yet built the Wall here but had erected a barbed-wire fence instead. On the Eastern side there were farm buildings and I had noticed, on previous visits, that the Vopos used these as a rest area. All the previous visits had been during the day and I was interested to see what happened after dark. At 4 a.m. on a filthy February morning we made our approach. It was bitterly cold with heavy sleet and a gale-force wind that deadened the sound of our engines. With our lights switched off we drove slowly until we were opposite the farm buildings. Here we stopped and switched off. We were about two yards from the wire and thirty yards from the farm buildings. All was quiet. There was no sign of life from the East. We were in six vehicles: four Ferrets and two Land Rovers. Very quietly, and following my orders precisely, all of us stood on top of our machines, undid our fly buttons and got our pricks out. Then I pointed a Very pistol at the black sky and fired a phosphorus flare which lit up the night sky like daylight. This was the sign for everyone to pee at the East. The result was hugely satisfactory. There were guttural shouts from the buildings opposite and out poured ten Vopos, excitedly waving their weapons, to be confronted by twelve cocks all pissing at them. Apart from the amusement value, we actually learnt some valuable information from this. Up until then it had been assumed that there were only two Vopos on the farm but now we knew that there were at least ten.

There was, however, one occasion when I could have been in big trouble. I often felt the need to escape the claustrophobia of the officers' mess and be alone. There was nothing more refreshing for my soul than to flight the duck on the nearby sewage farm at RAF Gatow. The smell was unpleasant but the peace and tranquillity refreshed me. Like so much of Berlin in those days, the sewage farm, like the divided farm, was split by the wire of segregation between West and East. One side had freedom and the other communist oppression and tyranny.

One bitter January night I was there, doing an evening flight, and very few duck had come in. However, just as the light was nearly gone, I saw a lone mallard silhouetted against the darkening sky. In great excitement at this last chance, I hurried, mismounted the gun and, to my horror, saw the mallard lurch down, a wing tip trailing, a good distance over the wrong side of the wire.

I had been taught from an early age that no sportsman worthy of the name should ever abandon a wounded bird, but this really was beyond the discipline of upbringing. If I were to be seen by the Vopos, I would either be shot or captured. If it were the latter, I would be interrogated most unpleasantly for my meagre knowledge before being spat out and returned to the West and disgrace. I would almost certainly be cashiered. However, a combination of childhood training, devilment and stupidity drove me on to the most foolhardy thing that I have ever done in my life.

I thanked God that at least it was, by now, a very black night. I left my gun and cartridges against a tussock and crawled towards the wire. I was pretty certain, from my experience of commanding the reconnaissance platoon, that this area was neither mined nor had tripwires. I also knew that there were no searchlights. This knowledge, however, did not stop me from shaking with terror as I started quietly to lift the bottom of the wire. After I had raised it enough to crawl beneath I stopped and listened. There was no sound at all except the soft sigh of a vicious north wind and my own heart pounding. I crept under and entered East Germany. I had marked the direction of the duck carefully and now decided that speed was of the essence. I stood up and ran fast towards where I thought it was. Suddenly it helped me by flapping near by. I grabbed it quickly, wrung its neck, and ran back towards the hole I had made. I couldn't find it. Somehow, in my haste, I had lost direction. I forced myself not to panic and lay flat, feeling first to right and then to left. Then I found the gap and, drenched in the sweat of fear, wriggled through. In the far distance I saw a flare and a shot was fired. I had been very lucky. The Vopos had been too distracted by some poor devil trying to defect to bother about a fool retrieving a duck.

In the summer of 1966, I was ordered to be guard commander of Spandau Prison for twenty-four hours, which at that time held just three prisoners. They were Baldur von Schirach and Albert Speer, who were each serving twenty years, and Rudolph Hess, who had been ordered to be imprisoned for life.

In many ways, I have to admit I greatly looked forward to the duty. I had read all about the prison and, in particular, the background to Hess's confinement, and realised that I would be living history. In May 1941 Hess had made an unauthorised and unwise flight to Scotland, flying himself in a Messerschmitt 110, in order to negotiate peace with the British government (that should not, he stipulated, include Winston Churchill). He had parachuted out of the aircraft, which went on to crash land in a Scottish field, and been marched off to the police at pitchfork point by a Scottish farmer; he had been in captivity ever since.

The prison was built in 1876 to hold 500 prisoners as a military detention centre. It was within the British sector of Berlin but was guarded by the four allies on a rota system. When I was in Berlin there remained only the three prisoners but when von Schirach and Speer were released on 30 September 1966, only Hess, who was then seventy-two years old and completely mad, continued to serve his lonely penance. There was thus the farce that this huge ugly, forbidding, austere, nineteenth-century monstrosity now held captive only one senile old man. To guard him was a fourteen-foot wall, an electric fence, a platoon of armed soldiers and eighteen civilian warders. This ridiculous situation remained until the death of Hess in Spandau in 1987. The three Western allies regularly suggested to the

Russians that he should be released but the Soviets were obdurate and insisted that he should die in Spandau. The reason for this was that guarding Spandau gave them access to West Berlin and permitted them to march troops into the British sector.

I arrived with my riflemen at the prison promptly at 8.45 a.m. to carry out the changing of the guard at 9 a.m. I forget much of the ceremony and it is unimportant, but I vividly remember, as I supervised the assigning of my soldiers to their various watchtowers, looking at the horror that was Spandau. On three sides were tall, drab walls with slits for windows ('That little tent of blue which prisoners call the sky,' as Oscar Wilde described it) and on the fourth side was a fourteen-foot wall with an electrified fence on top. The wall was interspersed with the watchtowers, in each of which was an armed man. After I had finished there was little more for me to do until lunch, but I knew that all the three inhabitants exercised at 11 a.m. I read the potted history of each and the guard commander's orders. ('Should a prisoner attempt to escape you will open fire immediately.' God help us!) Just before the hour, I went out into the central square. At the precise time a door in the great walls opened and out came the prisoners. Von Schirach and Speer immediately set off at a brisk walk, talking animatedly to each other and, as they passed me, nodded a compliment. Hess was entirely different. He shambled round on a lonely path of his own making, his head bent forward, staring at the ground. He mumbled continually to himself and occasionally raised his voice in apparent anger like a meths drinker under the arches at Waterloo. It was an unhappy sight.

At lunchtime I made my way to the officers' mess. There was an extraordinary contradiction between the bleak austerity of the rest of the prison and the mess. Here all was comfort and style with cold waiters serving cool drinks. All the four wartime Allies were represented here and opposite me, guzzling his wine, was a fat Russian colonel. Out of boredom and wickedness, although I knew the answer, I could not resist asking him why Hess could not be released. He ignored me. When I repeated the question more loudly his face suffused with anger and he spat out the reply I expected.

I visited my soldiers in the afternoon and again in the early evening. All was well. No prisoners had escaped! I retired to bed early and read my book, reflecting on the misery I had seen. I slept fitfully and was awoken by the alarm, which I had set for 3 a.m. I put on full service dress uniform and went round the riflemen again. 'Number one tower present and correct, SIR,' shouted the first soldier and presented arms. I saluted back and continued my dawn stroll. Suddenly, I stopped in my tracks and listened. It couldn't possibly be. But it was. In the middle of this grimness a nightingale was singing near by, and from where its lovely song came, drifting on the warm still air, was the comforting smell of nicotiana and roses. In the centre of the exercise square was a tiny garden with a small tree which Albert Speer had lovingly tended for twenty years and now, in the midst of man's cruelty and madness, nature had proven that it would always be there – like the poppies of Flanders.

After the death of Hess in 1987, and to ensure that the prison did not become a neo-Nazi shrine, Spandau was shut down and demolished. Being guard commander of the prison was an experience I shall never forget, and which I was very privileged to have carried out.

Whilst I was learning my trade as reconnaissance platoon commander I was briefly attached to the Queen's Own Hussars, one of the 'smartest' regiments in the army. As a cavalry regiment they had long ago dispensed with their horses and were now equipped with tanks and armoured cars. Since my reconnaissance platoon patrolled the Wall in Ferret scout cars I needed to learn about these and the QOH were the ideal people to teach me. They were a very friendly lot and welcomed me into their mess with enormous courtesy. Most Saturday evenings there was a roulette session run by the then commanding officer, Harry Dalzell-Payne, who later went on to be General Officer Commanding the 3rd Armoured Division. These sessions were highly popular among the officers' messes of the other regiments stationed in Berlin and, I have no doubt, highly profitable for the QOH.

Among the officers that I met there was Michael Parker. Michael is a highly talented, artistic person and one day he cornered me in the mess and put a suggestion to me.

'You had a scholarship to RADA,' he said. 'As a change from military duties I want to produce a play. I am *not* thinking of some small amateur dramatics but a show that will run for a week before an audience of at least 3,000 per night.'

I looked at him in amazement.

'And where would we produce this incredible show?' I asked, noting to myself the pronoun that already showed my commitment.

'I thought we'd use the Kuppelsaal,' he announced airily, 'and that we'd do Shakespeare's *Richard III*.'

I stared at him. This was a huge undertaking, even if the authorities allowed us to do it. The Kuppelsaal was part of the German 1936 Summer Olympic Games structure and had been used during the war as a briefing room by Hitler.

'Oh,' continued Michael, 'and I've written to Laurence Olivier, who produced and directed the film version besides playing Richard, and asked if we can hire their costumes. I'm going to play Richard and you can be Buckingham. Thus my costume will hold the name Laurence Olivier and yours will be Ralph Richardson.'

'Have you had a reply yet?' I asked.

'Yes,' said Michael smugly, and he pulled an envelope from a pocket in his service dress. The letter inside was from Laurence Olivier personally and, besides loaning Michael the costumes for FREE, he also wished us luck. I stared at it in amazement. This was a letter from God. No actor in the world was more famous, and to receive the great man's blessing was beyond belief. All my old love of the acting profession overtook me. I started to shake, and found I had a huge lump in my throat. I looked at Michael.

'Of course I'll do it,' I said. 'I can't wait to start.'

Taking me with him, Michael made an appointment to see the assistant commandant of the British sector, Brigadier

Allan Taylor. The brigadier turned out to be a keen theatre buff and immediately agreed to help in any way possible. He did, however, stipulate that his daughter, Jacky, should be given a part. This was the military equivalent of a casting couch and we had little option but to comply. Luckily, Jacky was both beautiful and talented and was immediately cast as the Lady Anne.

'What we're going to do to cover our arses,' said the kindly brigadier, 'is to say that this is part of the English-Deutsch Gesellschaft [or let's be nice to the Huns],' which was, at that time, top of the politically correct pile. 'That way I can also get you lots of money – and you're going to need it,' he continued practically. 'I'll write a letter to the sector paymaster telling him to give you a decent allowance.'

He was as good as his word and Michael soon had a telephone call from the paymaster asking him to come and see him. Again taking me with him for support, Michael made all haste and went to his office. He was a small half-colonel, with a moustache and glasses, who said that he would be more than happy to back the enterprise. Actually, he hadn't much option as he had virtually been ordered to cooperate by the brigadier.

'However,' he said, 'I would love a small part in the production.' Here was the military casting couch again. Michael prevaricated and said that he would love to give him an audition.

'Of course,' said the paymaster, 'the amount of money I allow you is entirely within my discretion. So would it be possible to do without an audition?' Michael stared at him and realised that he was completely over a barrel.

'Let me think what would suit you,' he said tactfully, and we backed out before there was any further attempt at blackmail.

'How about giving him Edward IV?' I suggested. 'It's a small part but sounds large and I'll bet the old fool doesn't know the play.'

'Great idea,' Michael replied, 'but that's the last bit of blackmail we're having.'

The paymaster, in rehearsals, was every bit as awful as we had feared. He could easily have had his name put forward for an Oscar for Worst Ever Actor Award. His looks did not help, as not by the strongest effort of imagination could his face, etched with centuries of plebeian blood, ever be considered royal. Michael had edited his lines to be as short as possible, but even these were delivered with an eccentricity peculiar to himself. However, he saved his greatest achievement of dreadfulness for his one major speech. After he has been told that Clarence is dead, King Edward asks a series of rhetorical questions beginning with the word 'who':

> Who sued to me for him? Who, in my wrath
> Kneeled at my feet, and bade me be advised?
> Who spoke of brotherhood? Who spoke of love?
> Who told me, in the field by Tewkesbury,
> When Oxford had me down, he rescued me,
> And said 'Dear brother, live, and be a king?'

The problem was the word 'who', which our paymaster colonel delivered with a long and desolate wail – 'whoooo' – so that he sounded like a blocked owl. At rehearsals there were queues of people waiting in the wings for him to play 'the Constipated Owl Scene', as it had been christened, in order to see for themselves quite how bad he was. No amount of gentle coaching from Michael could cure him. He was a small man, with a small man's obstinacy, and determined to play his part as he saw it. He was only just persuaded to remove his spectacles and his watch after Michael pointed out to him that it was unlikely the Plantagenets wore such things.

Other than this minor problem we were remarkably trouble-free and the dress rehearsal approached fast. For this we had an audience of soldiers from both the Queen's Own Hussars and the Green Jackets, who had been ordered to attend and who couldn't wait to see their officers making fools of themselves. The reasoning behind this was that should there be any obscene barracking, it was better that it was limited to a 'soldiery only' night. All the ushers were subalterns from both regiments and we even had usherettes from Queen Alexandra's Royal Army Nursing Corps.

All went well until Act Two, Scene One, the Constipated Owl Scene, as King Edward, in a long flowing cloak, waited in the wings to make his entrance. At this point there was a small problem. Some subalterns had surreptitiously nailed his cloak to the floor and the audience were amazed to hear, off stage, the sound of swearing and tearing cloth. Eventually King Edward made his entrance to find his fellow actors,

Rivers, Buckingham, Dorset, Hastings, Grey and Queen Elizabeth, clutching themselves, weeping and rolling on the floor with laughter.

Despite this, however, the play ran for a week to packed houses every night. To Brigadier Taylor's relief, it proved a huge success and even made headlines (and excellent reviews) in the British newspapers.

[Note: Michael Parker went on to run a series of major events in Britain including the Queen's Diamond Jubilee and the Millennium Military Tattoo. Known affectionately as 'the Queen's Showman', he is now Major Sir Michael Parker, KCVO, CBE. He has also written an autobiography: *It's All Going Terribly Wrong. The Accidental Showman*, published in 2012.]

Berlin has been renowned for many years as the nightclub centre of Europe. It is famous for its decadence and one evening, after rehearsals for *Richard III*, four of us, including the brigadier's beautiful daughter, Jacky, decided to see what the city had to offer. We ordered a taxi, told the driver that we wanted the naughtiest bar or nightclub in Berlin and left it to him.

The taxi drove down a backstreet near the Kurfürstendamm and stopped outside a nondescript door with a spyhole. The driver got out and pressed the bell. A voice asked who it was, our driver explained and the door opened. Suddenly we were in a different world. Through dim, discreet lighting I could see a large, comfortably furnished room with a bar down one side. There were tables spread across the floor and a stage at one end. It was crowded with obviously opulent, well-dressed men and women. We were shown to a table and a waiter took our orders for drinks.

After a short while, the curtains of the stage drew back and a master of ceremonies announced a striptease called 'Beauty and the Beast'. This consisted of a rather ugly girl slowly taking off her clothes and being helped by a man in a gorilla's costume. 'Which is Beauty and which is the Beast?' Jacky asked in a stage whisper which rang around the room. The waiter came over. 'Zer must be no tokking durink ze acts,' he ordered. It was pretty unexciting stuff and it was obvious, from the lack of applause, that the audience thought so, too. The curtains closed and we all had another glass of beer and waited.

Eventually the MC pushed his way between the curtains and, I suspect for our sakes, addressed the audience in rather broken English. 'Und now,' he started, 've commen to ze highlight off our evenink. Zis iss ze moment ven Hans und Hildegarde vill do ze act of lov for you ont ze stage. Zis iss a most emotional moment for zem so I vould ask, pliz' – and he stopped and looked at us hard – 'for complete silence.' He bowed, walked off and the curtains went back. The stage was in complete darkness and then suddenly the floods blazed on to show the rather ugly girl, who was either Beauty or The Beast, kneeling, stark naked, sideways on a bed. Then, onto the stage, came a man, also stark naked and sporting an enormous erection ('Bet it's the Beast,' whispered Jacky). He turned and proudly faced the audience, with his mammoth monster rearing straight at us. It was at this point that Jacky pointed at it and screamed with laughter. The mammoth monster drooped and shrivelled. It quickly became a mini mouse and the audience started to boo. 'Time we left,' I said, 'before we start World War Three.' And, giggling hysterically, we made a fast exit into the street.

Looking back on my time in the army I have to admit to enjoying a great deal of it. However, after serving five years' commissioned service I felt it was time to move on. So, when my two years in Berlin were finished, I handed in my papers and resigned my commission.

FIVE

London

When I first left the army a feeling of immense freedom came over me. For too long I had bottled up my natural free spirit. I had dressed like everyone else, I had worn no outrageous shirts or ties. I had not voiced any unconventional views in the mess and I had kept my hair at the expected length. Now I badly needed to let it down – literally. I therefore gleefully followed the fashion of the time and grew it to my shoulders in true hippy fashion. I didn't particularly like it like this – it felt uncomfortable and got in the way – but it was an outward expression of freedom.

One weekend I was staying with some friends in Sussex and on the Sunday we all went to the local pub for a pint of beer before Sunday lunch. In those days almost every pub in Britain, and certainly in the countryside, had a resident retired army officer. Tweeded and moustached, regimental or minor public-school tie ostentatiously to the fore, they sat alone on the same bar stool every day and sipped their pink gins. They were virtually all either ageing majors or decrepit colonels and insisted on their rank when being introduced to anyone. In their lonely corner they snarled at the twentieth century while the rest of the world went on about them. People had long given up speaking to them because they had either been bored to an early grave by the exaggerated war memories, or they had been growled at through the tobacco-stained whiskers. There were rarely ever Mrs Colonels or Mrs Majors as these had either long ago exhaled a grateful last breath or had disappeared as early as possible with the local Italian waiter. Such a man I immediately spotted as we went into the pub.

He was in a corner of the bar and there was a small space around him as if there were an electric fence keeping him apart from the rest of the pub. However, as this was the only empty part I made a beeline for it so that I could buy my host and hostess a drink. I stood and waited to be served and was immediately aware that the Major was rudely staring at me with a look of profound horror on his face. I decided that attack was the best form of defence.

'Have we met before?' I asked politely, and, receiving no reply, held out my hand. 'Hello,' I said, 'I'm Mike Daunt.' I could feel that everyone around was watching this exchange with glee, particularly my host and hostess. The Major ignored my proffered hand and then to the joy of the surrounding throng, 'Her-her-her-hermaphrodite,' he stuttered and spluttered.

To live in London in the Swinging Sixties and Sexy Seventies was incredibly exciting. It was a hugely creative time, and a renaissance of so much: fashion, music, theatre, writing and food, to name but a few. More than anything else, however, it brought a sexual revolution. Because of the newly launched Pill, which was received by a grateful world, women could at last take control of their bodies and make love with the virtually certain knowledge that they were not going to become pregnant. Naturally, both sexes revelled in this knowledge and took immediate advantage of it.

Mainly for this reason, nearly all of us, male and female alike, were more promiscuous than at any other time in history. Nowadays, young people are far better behaved than their parents ever were. But this is not for any moral reason. Sadly for them, it is because there are far more nasty diseases around than in the sixties and seventies. It is fair to say that, in those gloriously free times, almost all of us rogered each other unrestrainedly, with joy and enthusiasm, whenever and wherever we could. This may explain why we behaved, as I shall describe later, in the way we did in the Rossetti Gardens flat. There was nothing unusual about this; in fact it would have been strange had we *not* done so. Almost everywhere, and certainly in the south of England, there were regular threesomes (of both combinations), orgies and swaps. To be a single man or girl at that time was to hold a passport to sexual adventures of every kind. It was tremendous fun and, I truly believe, all of us who were lucky enough to participate in those gloriously free years loved every moment of it.

What was happening in the rest of Britain mainly passed

the army by. Although The Beatles roared out of barrack rooms and The Stones from subalterns' bedrooms, the rest of the creativity of the decade was largely ignored. To be in London and free after the confines and conventions of the army was, for me, joy beyond belief, and I felt that a great weight had been lifted from my shoulders. What I was going to do now to earn a living, I had no idea but, with the optimism of youth, I was certain that everything would work itself out. However, at least I had somewhere to live. Initially, I had been invited by my cousin and great friend, Richard Heygate, to share a flat with him in Rossetti Gardens Mansions, just off Flood Street in Chelsea. Richard had bought a sitting tenancy with his mother, Gwyneth, of this extremely comfortable four-bedroom flat. However, Gwyneth was never going to be there as she had an antiques business to run in Bradford-on-Avon and Richard and I therefore had it to ourselves. It had, however, four bedrooms and we decided to find two flatmates to defray the costs.

We put a small advertisement in *The Times* and waited to see what happened. It ran as follows: 'Wanted. 2 beautiful girls to share Chelsea flat with 2 beautiful bachelors, OWN BEDROOM and ideal for philandering'. It was, we decided, short, pithy, to the point and would attract a certain type of girl with a sense of humour with whom we could have some laughs. The night before the advertisement appeared, Richard and I went to The Surprise pub, which was just across the road in Christchurch Street. We were lucky to have The Surprise as our local as it was one of the very last Chelsea pubs not to have been 'improved'. It was rough with bare floorboards, had a dartboard and served excellent beer.

'Now,' said Richard, 'I want to make some ground rules for the flat. If we get any replies to that advertisement tomorrow we'll interview the girls, choose the prettiest and most amusing and there we are, BUT,' he continued, 'we will not bonk them under any circumstances because that will only lead to trouble.'

'Of course,' I replied. 'I couldn't agree more. I'm sure that, whoever they turn out to be, we'll all become *just* good friends.' And I think both of us actually believed our own rubbish.

The next day the phone didn't stop ringing. We ended up with twenty-eight girls that we had to see. We became very blasé and only made notes of those that sounded serious fun. Several of them came as pairs and these we interviewed that evening. At 6 p.m. sharp the first couple arrived. One was blond, and the other brunette. Both wore miniskirts and had legs up to their armpits. 'Oh God!' I thought, 'if we choose these two we'll never be able to stick to our rules.' However, there was something not quite right about them. There was a certain toughness, a feeling that they were holding something back, and although they had upper-class accents, these were affected and didn't ring true. Suddenly I realised what was going on. I looked hard at them.

'You're on the game, aren't you?' I said. They looked at each other and giggled.

'Okay,' said the prettiest one, 'here's the deal. We'll pay triple the rent and you can each have a freebie once a week.' Richard and I started to laugh.

'Sorry girls,' we said. 'It's a wonderful offer but we honestly don't want to run a brothel. But many thanks and good luck to you.' And with that we all parted on the best of terms.

It was a long night and by 10.30 p.m. we had had enough. We were totally spoilt for choice. Nearly all the girls were beautiful and fun, and we both felt that we could be great mates with any of them. We decided to finish the rest on the morrow and then make our choice. Richard went to work at 8 a.m. and I, who was living on my savings and hadn't yet decided what to do, was just making a cup of coffee when the doorbell rang. I answered it and there were two more girls.

'Have you let the rooms yet?' they said. 'We only got back from the south of France late last night and read your advertisement on the plane. Sorry to just drop in but it seemed our best chance. Oh, by the way, I'm Susie and this is Hazel.'

'Come in,' I said. 'I've just made some coffee, would you like some?'

They came in and we all sat in the kitchen with our cups of coffee. Susie was somewhat overweight but so full of laughter that I immediately liked her enormously. Hazel was tiny and beautiful and obviously awash with naughtiness. By the end of half an hour I knew these were the girls for us. I left them in the kitchen and went into the drawing room so that I could phone Richard in private. I told him what had happened and what I felt and he said that he would put off everyone else for another evening and that he would trust my choice. However, he would meet them at 6 p.m. when he returned from work and if he liked them they could move in as soon as they liked. I told the girls this and they went away very pleased.

Richard and the girls arrived at the flat at almost exactly the same time and we all decided to adjourn to The Surprise for much-needed refreshment. It soon became obvious that Richard and Susie really liked each other. She was his sort of person: intelligent and unconventional. She also had a boyfriend, which seemed a very good thing.

'There's only one problem,' she said. 'He's married.' I think that by now both Richard and I were well pleased with our choice and we didn't care what her boyfriend's situation was.

'Don't worry,' said Richard. 'It's nothing to do with us.'

'He can only escape occasionally,' continued Susie, 'so he won't be staying very often.'

'And what's your situation,' I said, turning to Hazel, who was very much my cup of tea, as she brought out all the ridiculous male protectiveness in me. The girls looked at each other and started laughing. 'Mine's married, too,' she said.

After these admissions the evening seemed to flow as fast as the drink until at closing time the four of us, visibly swaying, made our way back to the flat.

'Where have you got to get to?' asked Richard.

'Fulham,' said the girls.

'Of course, you could always stay,' I said, completely forgetting our agreement not to bonk the flatmates. Richard looked hard at me and the girls looked at each other.

'GOOD IDEA,' everyone cried in chorus.

It was a fine arrangement and everything could not have worked out better. Susie's and Hazel's lovers occasionally stayed the night, but otherwise, when anyone felt the need, either the girls wandered into our bedrooms or we crept into theirs. Everyone was happy with this wonderfully lax arrangement; I was Hazel's bit of casual and Richard was Susie's.

One summer's evening we had all been to The Surprise yet again and, as was usual when we were slightly pissed, had ended up in each other's rooms. 'For God's sake,' I heard Susie telling Richard, 'wake me up early, The Lover's due back from Hong Kong tomorrow on the early flight and it gets into Heathrow at 6.30 a.m., so he might come straight round here for a quickie on his way to the office.' Richard assured her that he would kick her out with the dawn.

I'm afraid that what I did next was irresistible. I simply couldn't help myself. I set my alarm for 7 a.m. and at 7.15 Hazel and I crept out of bed, let ourselves out of the flat and rang the doorbell long and hard. The result was deeply satisfying. There was a shriek from Richard's room, where he and Susie were having a dawn chorus, then the door crashed open and Susie flew out and ran, gloriously naked, down the passage, nearly taking Richard's cock with her, while Hazel and I rolled on the hall mat weeping with laughter, fast joined by Susie and Richard, who also saw the joke. Then we heard the lift coming and, just in time, rushed to our separate rooms, where we had to pretend that we had just woken up as The Lover rang the doorbell. That evening

Susie thanked me profusely for ensuring that she was in her own room.

My main problem at this time was that I still had no work and was fast running out of my meagre savings. I simply could not decide what I wanted to do. The following Friday I went fishing on the Kennet at Kintbury, in Berkshire, and stayed at The Dundas Arms for the night. I came in for dinner and was informed by the owner, Pip Piper, that everything was on the menu except for salmon or any other type of fish, as the fishmonger had forgotten to deliver. 'That bloody man,' said Pip, 'that's the last time I'll deal with him. The problem is that he's the only fishmonger for miles around and virtually has a monopoly.'

'Do you sell a lot of fish each week?' I asked.

'Yes, we do,' replied Pip. 'Especially in the summer.'

'I've just started my own fish and game dealing company in London,' I said. Well I had. Two seconds ago. 'I'll deliver here once a week and twice a week if it's worth it.'

'Right,' said Pip, 'here's an order but I want it on Tuesday.'

'No problem,' said I, not having the faintest idea how to fulfil it. But I was determined to find out.

Thus started a business that I ran for the next twenty years. However, as it involved rising with the dawn to be in Billingsgate, I needed a flat of my own, as I woke up everyone else in Rossetti. My aunt Gwyneth was also returning to London and, not unnaturally, needed her flat. Also, Hazel's lover had left his wife and she wanted to move in with him. And so ended a joyously happy four months. I looked around for a suitable flat and eventually settled on one of the singlebedroomed ones in Nell Gwynn House on Sloane Avenue. This was an ideal bachelor pad with one large bed-sitting room, a tiny kitchen and a bathroom, and was easy to keep clean and tidy. It was in the area of London that I had come to regard as 'my patch'. It also had a very good local pub, The Admiral Codrington in Mossop Street, just around the corner.

After finding a flat, I decided that I wanted to set up a new bank account in the area in which I lived. I therefore went to see the manager of the Midland Bank, Thurloe Square branch. I was incredibly lucky in my choice because the manager, John Evans, became a friend and looked after me like a father. Sadly, I was only with him for six years before he retired, but during that time we formed a close bond.

In 1968 the relationship between a bank manager and his clients was very different from the sanitised situation of today. Regrettably, nowadays, the computer has totally taken over everything and all possible situations are covered by rules. Thus if you have an X credit rating you are allowed to borrow up to Y amount of money. There is no flexibility in this and little, if any, humanity. When I first started my little fish-and-game business I paid myself a set amount per month, which John, my bank manager, knew all about. However, occasionally I needed help from the bank. John was a keen, if not very skilled, fly fisherman and quite often we had a conversation on the telephone which went roughly as follows:

Me: 'John, could I possibly be allowed an extra fifty-pound overdraft this month, please?'

John Evans: 'Now, I know, Michael, that you have access

to some very good fishing on the Kennet near Kintbury. Would it not be a fair swap to take me for three days' fishing in return for my financial help?'

Me: 'One day, and I'll throw in the correct flies as well.'

John Evans: 'You're a mean bugger but okay, I'll arrange it.'

And everyone was happy. Not in a million years would anything like that happen today.

One day when I returned to my flat there was a message to ring John at the bank.

'Michael, I wonder if you'd mind coming in and seeing me?' he said.

'Of course,' I replied, 'Anything wrong?'

'No, nothing at all. I just think I may be able to help you with some advice.' And we made the appointment. I duly appeared at Thurloe Square at the appointed time and was shown into John's office. After the usual pleasantries he addressed the matter in hand.

'Michael,' he started, 'you're paying yourself a reasonable wage and the business is doing well but at the end of each month you're usually on your uppers with very little money to spare and then you come to me and we do a little bartering.'

I nodded in agreement.

'Now,' he continued, 'I'm not unhappy with this arrangement but I feel you could do better and save yourself a lot of money. I notice from your cheques that many of them are made out to restaurants and the odd nightclub. What you're doing, I presume, is taking girls out in the hope of getting them into bed.'

I was somewhat taken aback by this, and wondered where it was leading, but I nodded in agreement.

'Now,' continued John, 'occasionally, I'm sure, you don't succeed in your dirty purpose and therefore you've wasted all that money on nothing.' He paused and ran his hand through his thinning hair. 'Let me tell you,' he continued, 'that Mrs Evans and myself have been happily married for over thirty years. However, every man likes a little variety and I know a splendid girl in Soho called Maisie who, for only five pounds will do a very good turn. You spend your five pounds with her and you're *guaranteed* to get your leg over, whereas if you take some bit of tottie out to dinner, which will cost you eight to ten pounds, you only *might* get her into bed. So I'm going to give you Maisie's number and you can start saving money.'

It is a sad fact that this is unimaginable nowadays. I thanked John and tried to point out that I rather liked the uncertainty of the chase, but I don't think he understood.

I soon established a daily routine. I would get up at 4.30 a.m. and drive to Billingsgate Market. Here I would fill my newly acquired Ford van with fish. Following that, I would prepare the orders in a fishmonger's near Duke Street, St James's, which was owned by Ewan Hilary, an Old Etonian friend of mine, and then I would spend the morning delivering. At lunchtime I went to various drinking establishments, one of which was just around the corner in Jermyn Street. It was called Jules Bar.

This splendid establishment, sadly no more because of the value of the property, used to have a wonderful lunchtime trade and there was always a hilarious crowd drinking there. One of the regulars was a somewhat overweight woman by the name of Clarissa Dickson Wright, who later went on to achieve huge fame as one half of the cooking team for the television series *Two Fat Ladies*. Clarissa and I became good drinking friends; she could consume vast quantities of gin and tonic and made me laugh a great deal. She had a wonderful brain and, providing that she was remotely sober, was one of the wittiest and funniest people I have ever known. She was, at that time, however, an unemployed barrister as her drinking habits had embarrassed her chambers and she had been asked to leave. One lunchtime she came into Jules Bar looking particularly pleased with herself.

'What have you done?' I asked.

'On my way here,' she replied, 'I was waiting for a bus when a large black man [her words] tried to mug me and take my handbag.'

I was horrified. 'What did you do?' I asked.

'Hit him very hard and laid him out,' she replied proudly.

After everyone had stopped laughing, I enquired, 'Did you call the police?'

'Certainly not,' said Clarissa. 'What a waste of time that would have been with endless questions and the snail-like taking of notes. No, I left him on the pavement and caught my bus here.'

I thanked God it wasn't me, as I had no doubt that an angry Clarissa could undoubtedly pack a very mean right hook. I suspected that her assailant was deeply regretting his actions.

On another occasion Clarissa had come into the bar with a very small, bespectacled man whom she could virtually carry under her arm. As usual we all chattered away and the company was full of mirth and laughter, to which Clarissa's little companion contributed nothing. He merely stood next to her, sipping his half pint of bitter and looking bored. After a while, he made his way to the loo for a pee. My curiosity overcame me.

'Who on earth is that?' I enquired. For the first time ever I saw Clarissa embarrassed. She looked down at the floor and blushed like a schoolgirl. Then her natural, ebullient character reasserted itself. She looked me straight in the eye: 'I know he's dull,' she said, 'but he possesses a huge cock.'

After a somewhat liquid lunch I used to retire to my flat for a good sleep before getting up around 7 p.m. ready for the evening's entertainment. This usually entailed a visit to The Admiral Codrington, which was run, in those days, by a wonderful East End cockney character called Mel Barnett. He had a very beautiful wife named Susan. One day Sue wasn't there and I enquired as to where she was.

'She's touring America wiv 'er sister,' said Mel. 'She rang me last night to say that she was in Dallas where JFK was assassinated. 'Ang arahnd a bit, says Oi.'

One of the people I met there was a very pretty American girl called Jo Anne. She didn't seem to be with anyone in particular but was just part of the crowd. She told me she was an antiques dealer and had a shop in Ebury Street. She was fun, interesting and intelligent, and one evening I asked her out to dinner.

'Oh Mike,' she said, 'that's real kind of you and you're great to be with and we get on real well but I have to tell you that I'm the other way inclined. I live with my girlfriend just round the corner in First Street. She works in the evening for the BBC, which is why I come in here occasionally until she gets home.'

'No problem,' I said, thinking 'bugger, bugger, *bugger!*'

Two nights later I was again in The Cod and there was Jo Anne, but this time with a tall, good-looking girl whom she introduced to me as Hilary. This was her famous girlfriend, whom I was fascinated to meet, as I had never knowingly met a pair of lesbians before. I think that I foolishly imagined that they would have moustaches and was idiotically surprised to find that, of course, they were the same as everyone else. I thoroughly enjoyed their company and we all bought each other lots of drinks. Just before closing time Hilary turned to Jo Anne and me. 'Let's have dinner together,' she said. 'We can go to Nineteen Mossop Street.' This was a splendid little bistro-style restaurant literally next door to the pub. 'In that case we need to go now,' I said, 'because we'll never get a table once the pub closes.'

As we left The Cod laughing together, nothing was further from my mind than a bit of wickedness. I had been told the position by Jo Anne and she and Hilary seemed a very happy pair. After an excellent dinner I was invited back to their flat on First Street for coffee, just a minute's walk away from the restaurant.

I still thought that nothing more would come of the evening. I would just have a cup of coffee, maybe a drink, and then walk back to Nell Gwynn House. However, it was soon made very clear, especially by Hilary, that much more was expected from me. As soon as I sat down, she snuggled up to me on the sofa and put an arm round Jo Anne on the other side of her. 'Come on,' she said, 'bugger the coffee, let's all go to bed.'

I could not believe my luck, and thought that God was definitely in his heaven and all was very right with the world. It is every fellow's fantasy to be in bed with two beautiful girls who also fancy each other. Any man who denies this is either a liar or grossly undersexed. It is Nirvana; it is paradise on earth; it is perfect bliss. It took us all only seconds to be undressed and in bed and I happily jumped on Hilary, who seemed the keener of the two. When that was over – and I regret to say that I was so excited that my performance epitomised the expression 'It won't take long, did it?' – the two girls made love together and the sight of this ensured that Himself was soon rearing to go again. However, remembering my manners, I looked at Jo Anne and raised an optimistic eyebrow. It seemed the polite thing to do. Jo Anne shook her head.

'Mike,' she said, 'the only reason you're here is because Hilary said that I ought to try a feller some time. But having seen you with her, no way.'

So I leapt on Hilary again.

And that should really be the end of the story. However, there is a rather sad postscript. A few nights later I was again in The Cod and saw Jo Anne sitting at the bar.

'Have a drink,' I said. 'How's Hilary?' And she burst into tears.

'She's left me for a feller,' she wailed.

Besides The Admiral Codrington I also used to drink in The Nag's Head in Kinnerton Street, Knightsbridge and The Australian in Milner Street, Chelsea. In the evening there could be found in either, and sometimes both, of these pubs, an amusing crowd of lads of about the same age as myself. These were mainly law students, but there was a smattering of other professions as well. The two pubs were very different. The Australian was large with two bars which faced each other and which both spilled out into the street. There was no public or saloon bar; they were both of the same class and usually packed out. This was because it was very much a family-run pub. Ted Saunders, the landlord, and both his children, Barry and Rita, were behind the bar, and Ted's wife, Anne, was in the kitchen. The Saunders family were friendly and laughing and seemed to enjoy the, often, abysmal behaviour of their clientele. They put up with the drunken singing and broken glasses (provided they were paid for), and tolerated the bounced cheques. When Ted's daughter, Rita, a large, comely girl with the warmest of hearts, gave birth to a son, Ted introduced the baby to us all by saying, 'Now you lot had better be nice to him, you might want to cash a bouncer with him in years to come.'

The Nag's Head in Kinnerton Street was a very different establishment. The landlord was a large, overweight cockney called Len Cole who had a lit cigarette permanently hanging from the corner of his mouth. He had neither charm nor humour; I never saw him smile. There was no Mrs Cole and thus the pub was seldom cleaned and never dusted. For reasons I totally fail to understand, he tolerated us. And, in fairness, we tolerated him. We never complained about the dirt or the smell from the lavatories (in truth, did we even notice it?) and we regarded the place as our club, for there were few other customers. Sometimes our behaviour became too exuberant and Len would threaten to throw us out. He never did.

The pub was divided into two bars. There was a ground-floor room, which was tiny, where Len had his domain. Here, he stood behind the minute bar, where there was barely room for him to move his vast frame and handed out the drinks. There was no food as such, but squashed into a corner of his bar there was always a ham. This he used to carve with meticulous care but always with the inevitable cigarette hanging from his lower lip, from which occasionally the ash used to drop onto the plate. How no one was ever poisoned by this ham is amazing; it was never put into a fridge and merely remained on a shelf under the optics from one day to the next until it was finished and replaced by another.

There was also a downstairs bar, in the basement. This bar was the main reason we drank in The Nag's Head. It was run in the evenings by another law student, who went by the aristocratic name of Jeremy de Calthrop. Jeremy was immensely generous to his friends and, when we were down on our luck or had run out of money, he handed out pints for which he 'forgot' to charge. Why this was never noticed by Len I have no idea. However, I suspect that, provided he had enough to pay his bills and exist, he took no interest in the pub's finances at all.

By drinking in these two pubs I was lucky enough to become friends with a bunch of law students who had formed themselves into a club called The Ancient and Honourable Society of Ratte Catchers. This was essentially a dining club and was loosely based on an eighteenth-century association of Regency bucks of the same name, who hunted the taverns with a pack of hounds and thus had the perfect excuse to go on a pub crawl. I was given the great honour of being invited to become a member. There was a slight drawback in that members had to wear Ratte-Catching uniform for the dinners that were held once a month. This uniform consisted of a Ratting tailcoat in hunting green with a high black velvet collar and cuffs, white breeches, white stockings, buckled shoes and a jabot at the throat. I was told where to have this made and duly went to the tailor in Savile Row, but was terrified of the cost. 'Don't be silly,' explained Cephas Goldsworthy, the leader of the Rattes, 'he'll send you an account, and anyway, no gentleman ever pays his tailor.' Cephas later went on to become a very distinguished criminal defence QC.

The idea behind the Ratte Catchers was one of comradeship and mutual assistance in trouble. For instance, I was once hauled up in front of the magistrates for some minor driving offence and was represented in court by another member whom I shall call Bill Kinsman, who was, by then, a qualified barrister. We had no defence against the charge but to try to keep the fine to the very minimum Bill pleaded extreme poverty for me. The conversation between the chief magistrate and myself then went as follows.

Magistrate: 'Mr Daunt, if you are as poor as you claim to be, how come that you can afford a private barrister?'

Me: 'Mr Kinsman is a friend of mine, sir.'

Magistrate: 'Do you mean that he is defending you free of charge?'

Me: 'No sir, for a case of rather good wine.'

Magistrate: 'What wine and what year?'

Me: 'Château Lynch-Bages 1966, sir.'

Magistrate: 'Oh lucky, lucky man.'

Essentially, however, the Rattes was a dining and drinking club and our great claim to fame was that we had never been allowed to eat at the same establishment twice. A classic of this was the night that we dined at Rules in Maiden Lane, which is London's oldest restaurant, having been established by Thomas Rule in 1798. The problem with all of our dinners was that we met beforehand in the house or flat of one of our members, where vast amounts of Ratting Punch was drunk. This immensely alcoholic concoction meant that we always arrived at the chosen restaurant in an interesting condition. For this particular dinner we had all met in Ebury Mews and, as it was a beautiful summer's evening, had been standing outside in all our Regency glory quaffing large quantities of punch. We had also, wisely, hired a minibus and driver for the night. Just as we were all climbing into this vehicle, a passing American tourist and his very beautiful woman asked who and what we were. One of our members, a young film director called Bill Orde, grabbed the pretty girl and hustled her onto the bus, which, entering into the spirit of things, quickly drove away. As Bill was a good-looking man and the girl was given a pint of punch, she was thrilled to bits to join the party, especially when she was told that she was being taken out to dinner. Singing joyously, we drove to Rules.

I do have to admit that the management, seeing the state we were in, was not overjoyed to welcome us to their extremely respectable establishment. Sensibly, we were shown to a private room and, hardly had we been seated for five minutes, when a yard of policemen, led by a chief superintendent, pulled up in two squad cars. Now for the police to arrive *before* dinner was unusual even for us, and we all fell silent as they trooped into the room. In the rear we suddenly noticed the American from whom we had removed the girl. 'That's her,' he shouted. 'This lot kidnapped her. Arrest them all.' This was obviously going to produce a problem for the police as the 'kidnapped' girl was passionately kissing Bill Orde at the time, and didn't want to be rescued. 'Oh piss off Hiram,' she said. 'I'm enjoying myself.' The police and Hiram beat an embarrassed retreat, the latter bleating, 'Oh Margie, how could you behave like this?'

However, I suspect at the restaurant's request, the chief superintendent remained behind 'to keep an eye on things and ensure decent behaviour'. He was immediately invited to join us for dinner and, protesting feebly, had a glass thrust into his welcoming hand. At the end, the Ratting version of the German national anthem was sung:

Ours is not a happy family,
No one ever laughs or smiles.
Mine's a dismal occupation,
Crushing ice for grandpa's piles.
But we must not be downhearted,
We must not be put about.
Baby's been and gone and farted,
Blown his arsehole inside out.

The management asked us to leave as we were disturbing other customers. We refused and sang another song. 'Leave or we will call the police,' they foolishly threatened, and then remembered that the chief superintendent had never left. That gentleman was asleep on the table with his head on his folded arms. Eventually, we clambered into our minibus with the exception of Bill Orde who, in the true tradition of the 1970s, took Margie back to his flat.

Cephas Goldsworthy was the leader of the Rattes and a man of huge charm and great wit. He was built like Falstaff with long, flowing, dark locks, a tiny waist, huge belly, great presence and a wonderful brain. I always enormously enjoyed his company as he was a brilliant raconteur. Many times I have heard him tell the same tale, but it has never ceased to leave me weeping with laughter. His timing was that of the greatest actors, which I am sure enormously contributed to his taking silk. One evening, over several pints in The Australian, I asked him if I could come and see him perform.

'Of course you can, dear boy,' he said. 'How about

tomorrow in the afternoon when you've finished work? It's an interesting case. I've been defending a well-known burglar who has pleaded not guilty to nicking a great many valuable jewels from a raid in St John's Wood. This is the second trial. You see, when I was making my final address to the jury in the first trial, I had nearly finished when the judge called time for lunch. Now, when the jury all have their heads down it's a very bad sign and usually means that they think the accused is guilty, and when I had been making my final address they had all stared at the floor.'

He continued: 'After lunch, and just before we went into court, I had a word with my client as I was not at all happy about the likely outcome. "How do you think it's going?" I asked him. "No problems, guv," he replied. "That foreman of the jury's a noice guy. O sent 'im a point in the pub at lunchtoime." "You did what?" I asked, horrified. "Oi sent 'im a point, din'Oi, 'e's a good bloke." Well, of course I had to tell the judge, who asked the foreman of the jury what had happened. He vehemently denied receiving any drink from the accused, so the judge sent for the manager of the pub and the barmaid, both of whom said that they had never seen the burglar, let alone served him. But justice had to be seen to be done, and the judge, quite correctly, dismissed the jury and ordered a retrial. This morning you will see the last of the judge's summing-up of the new trial before the jury retire. Meet me in The Viaduct Tavern, which is near the Old Bailey, at 12.30, and I'll fill you in, but we should get a verdict in the afternoon.'

I was there promptly and, when Cephas appeared, I asked

him how it was going. 'Well,' he said, 'I've found a tiny point of law which may help.'

'What did the jury do when you were making your final address?' I enquired.

'Looked me in the eye,' replied Cephas with a smile, 'so I'm hopeful.'

After lunch I went into the public gallery and we all sat and waited. Eventually they returned.

'What is your verdict?' demanded the clerk of the court.

'Not guilty, my Lord,' said the foreman.

I joined Cephas outside the Old Bailey and was just congratulating him when his client, the burglar, came up to him.

'Oi just wanted ter fank yer, guv,' he said. 'Yer did a brilliant job.'

'Thank you,' replied Cephas. 'But before we part, I just want to know something. Did you really send the foreman of the first jury a drink in the pub at lunchtime?'

'Nah, 'course Oi didn't,' replied the burglar, 'but Oi didn't like the look o' that lot.'

On another occasion, Cephas kindly invited me to come with him to an inquest. In this he had a watching brief for the deceased, a man who had been shot by the police during an armed raid on a bank. His job was to protect the interests of the family. 'There won't be a lot of action,' he said, 'but if you've never been to an inquest before, particularly involving a police shooting, I think you'll find it interesting.'

I duly appeared at the appointed hour and made my way to the public gallery with family members and some press.

We all stood when the coroner appeared in front of us and mounted a raised platform and, when the formalities were over, waited for the first witness to be called. This was the policeman who had carried out the shooting. He was a man of about twenty-five wearing an ill-fitting, shiny blue suit. He had acne and his eyes were far too close together. I understood entirely why Cephas had said to me several times that it was often difficult to differentiate between the villains and the cops, other than that the villains were usually better dressed and more fun. The policeman went into the witness box and addressed the court in the formal sing-song voice so beloved of the police when giving evidence:

'I am a member of the Authorised Firearms Squad of the Metropolitan Police. On the seventh of November I was called to Barclays Bank in Penge High Street and upon entering I saw the deceased holding a sawn-off shotgun to the cashier's 'ead. With my Heckler and Koch MP5SF at the ready, I therefore knelt behind a pillar and addressed the deceased. I said to 'im, "Lay down your weapon or I will have to use the minimum force required to restrain you." I repeated this warning three times. 'E then turned round and pointed 'is gun at me. I carefully aimed at 'is legs but regrettably missed and 'it 'im in the 'ead.'

During this time, the coroner took lengthy notes and, when he had finished, the second witness was called. This was an old lady of diminutive size, wearing a grey linen dress and black stockings. On her nose was a pair of pink-framed spectacles. She reminded me of my nanny. Her evidence went as follows:

'My name is Lily Foord and I'm an actress. That's with two Os not the common F O R D but F O O R D,' and she spelt it out, almost shouting. By now everyone in the court, from the most cynical hack to the grieving parents, was listening intently to her. The old lady, who was obviously revelling in the attention, looked around the room before continuing:

'On the seventh of November, or was it the sixth? No it was the seventh because I was cashing a cheque to buy a present for my nephew. It was his twenty-fourth birthday on the eighth. No, I'm sorry, I'm wrong – it was his twenty-third. I know because his name is Charlie and his sister is called Marge and C comes before M in the alphabet, doesn't it?' She paused and looked at the coroner for guidance who nodded with a pained expression on his face.

'Anyway,' she continued, 'where was I? Oh yes, I was telling you about Charlie and Marge. You see Charlie is younger than Marge because C comes before M. So it must have been the seventh because Charlie's birthday's on the eighth.' She stopped and smiled charmingly and with pride at the coroner.

'Please try and stick to your evidence,' said that man, somewhat brusquely.

'Oh but I am, sir,' she replied. 'But I wanted to make sure I had the correct date. I mean it would be awful if I said it was the seventh of November and really all this happened on the sixth. What would happen to me if I made a mistake like that, sir?' she enquired. 'You'd probably do me for penury, wouldn't you, sir?' She looked like the original innocent old lady who was everyone's granny, but I was sure that she was enjoying herself at the coroner's expense. By now that unfortunate man was deeply regretting interrupting the witness.

'What do you mean "penury"? Why should your being poor have anything to do with this? And why would you imagine that I would, er, um, "do" you for it?' he enquired testily.

'You know, sir, when someone tells a porky pie in court they're done for penury.'

'You mean "perjury",' snapped the coroner. 'Now, please, Mrs Foord, stick to your evidence.'

'It's Miss, sir,' she said.

'It's miss what?' said the coroner, who was being stupid.

'It's Miss Foord,' said Lily. 'Miss Lillian Ethel Foord. Not Mrs Foord, because I've never been married. I've had plenty of lovers but I've never tied the knot. Mind you there was one who—'

'Yes, yes, Miss Foord,' shouted the coroner sternly, by now terrified of losing control of his court, where considerable sniggering and suppressed giggling was taking place. 'I know you are an actress, but please remember that this is not a theatre and do not treat it as such.'

'I know that, sir,' she replied sweetly, 'because then I would be up there where you are and you would be down here where I am.'

After the laughter had ceased, Lily continued with her evidence.

'As I was saying,' she went on, pausing and looking hard at the unfortunate coroner. The words 'before I was rudely interrupted' hung in the air but remained unspoken. 'On the seventh of November I was in Barclays Bank in Penge High Street cashing my cheque for five pounds, which I felt was quite enough for Charlie's present as he never came to see me in my last play,' she added, staring at the coroner and daring him to interrupt her again. However, the man had, wisely, learnt his lesson and kept his head down. 'Suddenly,' she said, 'just as I was signing my cheque, a horrible, tall, black man ran into the bank holding a sawn-off shotgun which he pointed at the cashier's head and demanded money.'

She paused dramatically and looked round the room, and the coroner foolishly interrupted her again. 'How do you know it was a sawn-off shotgun?' he demanded, trying to get his own back. 'Have you ever seen one?'

Lily stared at him with contempt and amazement. 'Dozens,' she replied. 'The props department of every theatre in the land is full of them. Anyway,' she continued, as if the coroner was a minor irritation, 'the poor cashier started to empty his tills with the black man still pointing the gun at him whereupon this nice policeman ran into the bank, knelt behind a pillar, said, 'Goodnight Sooty' and shot him in the head.'

There was, of course, complete uproar in court, with Lily centre stage and loving every minute of it.

Another member of the Ratte Catchers was Anthony Jennens, known to one and all as 'Jennens'. When I first met him in The Australian he was attempting to become a barrister, having left Sandhurst under a cloud. Jennens was six-feet four-inches tall, a man with a commanding presence, and not just because of his height. He was also highly intelligent and very amusing. His life was best summed up by another Ratte Catcher, Jeremy Wingate-Saul, the son of a High Court judge, who said, 'Jennens's problem is that if there is a simple, easy and honest way of getting a hundred pounds and a difficult, complicated and totally dishonest method of acquiring the same sum, Jennens will always choose the latter.' And in those days I am afraid that this was true.

He also had a certain drink problem. We all drank too much in those halcyon times, but Jennens was excessive. Breakfast for him consisted of a pint of vodka and orange juice, mixed, as he put it, half-and-half with plenty of vodka. This was poured down his throat with a shaky hand, usually in one gulp. Because of his affliction he soon gave up the law and then lived from hand to mouth from various dubious enterprises, which earned him little except a very bad reputation. But he was a Ratte Catcher and the Rattes looked after their own, and he was amusing and interesting when not too drunk to speak.

It was at this point that we all decided Jennens needed help with his drink problem and he was persuaded to go into a clinic to dry out. What none of us realised in those innocent days was that an alcoholic needs to reach the lowest of the low and be begging for help before there is any chance of successfully curing him. Jennens at that point had not reached the necessary nadir of his life and was only agreeing to go into a clinic to keep his friends happy. Thus, to give himself courage, he one day drank even more than usual before booking himself into The Priory. This was then, and still is, one of the foremost clinics for treating addictions in the world. It is also hugely expensive.

However, Jennens had completely the wrong attitude towards The Priory and so spent a relatively enjoyable month there. During this time he was a disturbing influence upon the other inmates, often encouraging some of them to accompany him and escape unnoticed to the nearest pub. He 'consoled', too, several of the neurotic but beautiful women who were also being 'dried out'. Thus, he did not, in any way, help the rest of the inhabitants to rid themselves of their addictions. This regrettable behaviour eventually came to the notice of the senior staff of The Priory and he was asked to leave. With a cry of 'I've been thrown out of better places than this. Send my account to my home address,' Jennens summoned a cab and disappeared into the night, neither regretting nor regretted.

Another month passed, and Jennens was just enjoying his usual bottled 'breakfast' when the postman delivered the account from The Priory. This was for the staggering sum of more than £5,000, and as Jennens did not possess, in those days, even £5, he ignored it. One month later another unwelcome brown envelope fell onto his doormat, and again Jennens took no notice. The third bill appeared, but this time it was accompanied by a terse letter to the effect that if the account was not settled immediately, The Priory would put the matter into the hands of their solicitors. At this point, Jennens decided that action needed to be taken. He therefore 'borrowed' some of his father's writing paper, which was headed: 'From P.K. Jennens, Chairman The Bath Club' (which he was) and composed the following letter:

> Sir,
>
> I am in receipt of your account for my son, Anthony Jennens, who entered your establishment four months ago in the hope of being cured of alcoholic and suicidal tendencies.
>
> It is with deep regret and sadness that I have to inform you that my son, tragically committed suicide two weeks after leaving your premises. I wish to hear no more of this matter.

And no more was ever heard.

However, in the late 1970s, Jennens did, apparently, fall on his feet, as the very foolish owners of a large house in Hill Street, just off Berkeley Square, made him caretaker, and here he resided in great style, free of charge. The house had many and large bedrooms, a huge drawing room and a well-appointed kitchen. There was even a lift. Jennens was a generous soul and there was always a bed for the night for a Ratte Catcher, or any other friends, the rent for which was a bottle of vodka. To this day I have never understood how Jennens managed this arrangement or who the foolish owners of this enormously valuable property were. When asked, Jennens would be vague in his reply and murmur quietly about a company waiting for the price to be right in order to sell. One of the many outstanding features of the house was the marble mantelpieces, which so enhanced the main rooms. These were over two hundred years old and carved exquisitely by order of the architect Robert Adam. They were of great complexity and beauty and were, arguably, the most important and valuable of the house's many assets.

Sadly, there was, of course, a lead lining to this particular cloud, and eventually and inevitably it brought the cloud crashing down. I cannot now remember what trouble Jennens was in. What I do know is that the police were after him and had not yet discovered that he was living in Hill Street. He had therefore decided that it was time for him to 'do a runner'. Sadly, however, he was faced with one huge problem: he had no money with which to run. One evening, just as I was leaving for the pub, I was telephoned by Jeremy Wingate-Saul to say that Jennens had hopped it to America. 'Where has he got the money from?' I asked. 'Ah,' said Jeremy, 'it's an interesting tale. I am sure that you remember all those beautiful mantelpieces in the house in Hill Street. Well, he had them professionally taken out and they have gone, I suspect abroad.'

'Wow!' I replied. 'Where is he now and do the police know?'

'He's gone to California,' replied Jeremy, 'and I don't know about the police.'

'Well, good luck to him,' I said.

After that, little was heard of Jennens for a year and then one day we were all drinking in The Australian and someone asked if there had been any news of him.

'I believe he's selling pictures in an art gallery,' said Jeremy, who always seemed to know everything about Jennens.

'Yes,' commented Cephas, 'but does the man who owns the art gallery know that he is selling them?'

Eventually, Jennens returned to his native land and the mantelpiece episode seemed to have been forgotten. It was also a different Jennens; this one really, genuinely, wanted help with his drinking. He had, at last, descended to his nadir. Quietly, he disappeared for three months and dried out completely. Since that day, and it is now many years ago, he has not touched a drop of alcohol. However, his generosity is never failing and there are always large measures, from his well-stocked cellar, given to the many friends who are always welcomed at his home.

Tragically, through smoking dozens of Gauloise cigarettes and stuffing various substances up his nose, Jennens suffered from emphysema and eventually had to have a lung transplant. He was, in those long ago days, extremely racially prejudiced and so it gave his friends enormous joy to tell him that the donor of the lung was black and that Jennens would be spitting up his or her phlegm for the first few days. However, the operation was an enormous success and he is now, at seventy, one of the oldest surviving lung-transplant recipients.

I am sure that, whatever God there may be, has, firstly, an enormous sense of humour (otherwise he would not have invented the pleasurable but deeply undignified and ridiculous act of procreation), and secondly, that He has a very soft spot for amusing sinners and rewards them for making him laugh. He certainly did this with Jennens, to whom he gave a very wealthy maiden aunt who, just as he became 'dry' (Jennens, that is, not God), died and left all her worldly goods, and they were many and very valuable, to her nephew, one Anthony Jennens. He has never had to earn a living since that day but spends his time doing Good Works by helping those addicted either to gambling or to alcohol.

PS: In the New Year Honours List of 2015, Jennens was appointed OBE for services to charity. To have come on the long and arduous journey from the pits of alcoholism to the heights of such a medal is an extraordinary achievement and a great example of what can be achieved despite being an addict of any sort. It is something for which anyone should be rightly proud.

PPS: Sadly, as this book was going to press, my old friend Anthony Jennens, OBE, died. His epitaph should read: 'You really can fool all of the people all of the time if you try hard enough.' I shall miss him a great deal.

One of the people with whom I always kept in touch, wherever I was in the world, was my godmother and remover of my virginity, Inez Nimmo-Smith. We had had little opportunity ever to repeat our love-making, and anyway I was, of course, far too young for her to consider as a serious *amour*. However, I had fallen deeply in puppy love with her and although she had slowly, kindly and gently weaned me away, I had remained a close friend. I had written to her from the wilds of Malaya and Borneo and she had always replied. Her letters were a collection of robust and unconventional observations on life combined with suggestions of books for me to read and poetry that I might enjoy. It was through her that I discovered the works of Evelyn Waugh, whom she knew personally, and his book *Brideshead Revisited* still shines for me as the greatest English novel of the twentieth century. My uncle, Sir John Heygate, the father of Richard, with whom I had briefly shared the flat in Rossetti Gardens Mansions, had run away with Evelyn Waugh's first wife, 'She-Evelyn', and it had been Inez who had introduced them.

Her collection of friends was extraordinary, and her dinner parties, in her tiny basement flat in Belgravia, were famous. I was often lucky enough to be invited to these. The table could easily consist of royalty or dustmen, provided they were interesting, original, amusing and had an interest in the arts. Her acquaintances were many, eclectic and from all walks of life and everyone always felt honoured to be invited. The food was very basic, usually spaghetti Bolognese, and the wines the cheapest plonk, for Inez had very little money. She augmented her tiny income by gardening and was famous for pulling up the flowers and watering the weeds. Nobody cared. Such was her personality that everyone loved her and employed her for the happiness of her company. When my telephone rang and the well-known voice of gin and cigarettes said, 'Hello my darling, it's me,' I was always excited and couldn't wait to find out why she had rung.

One day, at midday, just as I had returned to my flat, the phone rang and it was Inez. 'Darling,' she said, without preamble, 'I want you to come to dinner tonight. I know its short notice but I've got two people coming who I am desperate for you to meet. Whatever you're doing, drop it, grab a bottle and come to me. It's the only night these two can make for ages; they are very special and you will love meeting them.'

'Who are they?' I asked.

'You'll see when you get here,' said Inez. And with that I had to be content. She was, of course, absolutely correct in assuming that I would attend. If I had been invited to dine with the Queen that night I would have wriggled out of it because Inez's dinner parties were always special, and if she said that this was a seriously unusual couple then I wasn't going to miss it for anything in the world.

Carrying my bottle of Rioja I made my way to Bourne Street, which is just off Ebury Street, and arrived punctually at 7.30 p.m. I rang the doorbell and Inez answered it and gave me my usual huge hug and kiss. 'They've just arrived,' she whispered and, taking my hand, led me into her tiny drawing room; there, smiling hesitantly, were Richard Burton and Elizabeth Taylor.

I have to admit to goggling, for these two were then at the height of their world fame, both for their work and their private lives. However, I am sure that Richard (or 'Rich' as I quickly came to know him), in particular, was obviously used to this idiotic reaction and quickly and kindly went out of his way to put me at ease. Luckily, we both immediately liked each other and shared a mutual passion for poetry and bad behaviour. Liz Taylor was an entirely different kettle of fish, however. She was obviously used to men instantly taking an enormous fancy to her and making her the centre of attention.

I managed to get both these necessities wrong because I had never fancied her on film and felt even less attraction in the flesh. Hers, to me, were not the fine, exquisite looks of a true beauty. She had, I admit, amazing eyes, but that was all. I am afraid that I virtually ignored her as Rich and I told each other wild stories, and I knew enough poetry to prompt him into quoting. We got on to the subject of Dylan Thomas.

'You know he was a friend of your mother's?' enquired Inez.

'I know,' I replied. 'She told me that he wrote a parody of *A Shropshire Lad* for her.'

'I want to hear it,' said Rich immediately. 'Can you do it?'

I composed myself and then quoted:

The cow lets fall at evening
A liquid shower of shit.
And Terence you are under
And never mind a bit
Who once so hated it.

And when the lusty reapers all
On wedlock turn their backs
And lift their tools to Ludlow
Comparing Tom's with Jack's
And piss against the stacks.

You, lad, are lying lower
Than wind or water's fall
Though cock and bull be calling

You do not hear the call.
You are beneath it all.

'And that's unknown Dylan Thomas?' said Rich.

'Allegedly,' I replied.

'How wonderful.'

'Now it's your turn,' I said. 'One of my very favourite poems is one of Dylan Thomas's which starts something like: 'Do not go softly into the night.'

Rich smiled, and I am certain that he knew exactly what I was doing. 'You mean, "Do not go gentle into that good night",' he said, and looked around the table for silence before quoting the whole wonderful poem. His voice is, to me, still the most beautiful that I have ever heard and long before the end both Inez and I had tears streaming down our cheeks. When the final glorious words were spoken there was a breathless and awed silence into which Liz Taylor, who had been far from the centre of attention for the whole evening, said, 'Well that's cheered everyone up, hasn't it?' and gave a silly little giggle.

It was a wonderful evening, despite Liz Taylor's obvious jealousy of Rich, and when I left I felt totally drained emotionally but alight with pleasure from the poetry. Rich asked for my phone number. 'Let's keep in touch,' he said. 'We'll have a badly behaved lunch and make each other laugh.'

Six weeks later Rich rang. 'Hello, it's me,' he said. 'Let's meet for lunch.'

'I know it's you,' I replied. 'Where shall we go?'

He named a fashionable restaurant near Sloane Square

and I said I'd be there. 'Oh, and bring your ferrets,' he said. 'I'm longing to meet them.' Over dinner with Inez I had told him how I kept a pair of ferrets, a hob and a jill, in my flat and what great fun they were. I was not surprised that he had rung at the last moment as his schedule was ridiculously busy, and I dropped everything to meet him. Then my phone started ringing and I realised I was going to be late. I grabbed Fanny and Fred from their cage and took them to the car. I put them into the back seat and leapt in the front. I always allowed them the freedom of the car and they nearly always jumped onto my shoulders, nibbled my ear, and stared fascinated out of the windscreen.

Because I was late, and because I was looking forward to seeing Rich again, I parked the car, most illegally, as near to the restaurant as I could. Then I grabbed Fanny and Fred and dashed inside. Rich was at his usual table and was indeed thrilled to meet the ferrets, which he petted for quite some time, to the horror of the restaurant owner and quite a few customers. Eventually Rich had obviously had enough and I decided that I was thirsty anyway.

'Order me a drink, please,' I said, 'and I'll take them back to the car.' I took the ferrets from him and dumped them in the car again before hurrying back to the restaurant, eager for a drink and Rich's company.

We had a glorious lunch full of poetry, wine and laughter, and eventually lurched outside. Rich grabbed a taxi and I went to my car; except that it wasn't where I had parked it. 'Oh hell,' I thought. 'I bet it's been towed away. My poor ferrets. I'll have to get it back as quickly as possible.' I returned to the restaurant and rang the police. Eventually, I was put through to a Very Senior Policeman. 'Your car, sir,' he said, 'has been driven away by one of my officers as it was illegally parked. However, you will find it five hundred yards down the road from where you left it. My unfortunate officer was driving it away when he was attacked by wild animals which bit him on the ear so that he nearly crashed it.'

I tried to suppress my laughter but a series of snuffles went down the line. 'It is no laughing matter, sir,' said the VSP. 'Just collect your car and kindly remove the wild animals before you park on a double yellow line in future.' That evening I rang Rich, who could not stop laughing.

Life, however, was not all laughter, drinking and women. I also needed to earn a living, although that too proved to be tremendous fun. That very first order from The Dundas Arms in Kintbury, which I had somehow fulfilled, had mushroomed into a very good little money-spinner in the form of my business, which I had named The Salmon Pool. It was hard work as I generally had to be in one of the markets, either Billingsgate or Smithfield, at 5 a.m., but I loved the buzz that was Billingsgate. The bustle and hustle, the cockney voices with their rhyming slang, the slime on the floor and the smell that permeated everything had a colourfulness which was life at its cheerful best, and I revelled in it.

Of course, to begin with, I was badly ripped off. But everyone has to learn their trade and this was part of the learning process. For instance, sometimes I sold fish to the market as well as buying it. I drove up to Scarborough and negotiated with six lobster fishermen to take all that they caught and would then drive it down to London and sell it. This I did once a week. To begin with I couldn't understand why the weight of lobsters that I bought in Scarborough was always considerably more than that which I sold in Billingsgate. When this had happened to me twice I commented on it to the buyer. 'You must 'ave weighed it wrong, Mike,' he said as he counted out the readies.

Next time, I very carefully watched his scales as the lobsters were weighed and still it was a good 40 pounds less. 'They must be ripping me off in Scarborough,' I decided, and the next week I watched very carefully as the catch was weighed. The lobsters were caught in pots off the coast and then held in one big holding cage just offshore until they were put into plastic trays for the journey south. This time I insisted that everything was weighed twice. The readings were the same each time: 673 pounds of lobster. I packed them into the van and immediately drove down to Billingsgate, sleeping in the van on the way and arriving just as the market opened. I carried the lobsters in their trays to my buyer and watched with corvid eyes as they were weighed: 621 pounds. I was horrified. Again I had lost 50 pounds in weight of lobsters. I still made a profit, after I had deducted my petrol, but nowhere near such a decent one as I should have done. The buyer paid me and saw my stricken face. He was a thoroughly decent man and suddenly took pity on me. 'Mike,' he said, 'this is going ter cost yer a bottle o' whisky, but I fink I knows where yer goin' wrong. When yer in Scarborough,' he continued, after I had agreed to the whisky, 'Wot 'appens when yer buys the lobsters?'

'Well,' I replied, 'they are brought in from their holding cage. We weigh them, put them into the trays, which we then load into the van. I pay the fishermen what I owe them and drive down to London as fast as possible.'

'Oi fort that was wot yer was doin',' said my buyer. 'Wot yer needs ter do is ter get the lobsters out of the 'olding cage and inter the trays *and leave them there for at least two hours before you weighs them.*' He looked at me hard. 'They needs ter drain,' he said. 'Yer buyin' fuckin' water, ain't yer?' I couldn't believe I could be so stupid. It was so obvious and yet, through my crassness, I had managed to lose a fair amount of money. The next time I made a lobster run I did exactly as my buyer had suggested. 'Ah woondered 'ow long it'd take thee to twig,' laughed the fishermen's leader.

My main customers were in the directors' dining rooms in both the City and the West End, and on these I concentrated all my efforts. Restaurants, hotels and pubs understandably cut the price to the lowest possible and there was a great deal of competition for their trade. The in-house dining rooms were nearly always run by 'fritefully' decent young 'gals' with blue eye shadow and Alice bands. Price really meant very little to them provided that the quality of the fish was of the best. Very soon I had a great many of these as my customers and decided that I needed to employ someone because I couldn't manage the work alone. All I wanted was a van driver. However, having thought about it hard, I decided only to employ a good-looking public-schoolboy who would chat up and charm all the cooks, who were almost entirely from the same background. This strategy worked brilliantly. My new employee, Willy Cooper by name, not only delivered all the fish and game but also, in the afternoon, went round a great many other directors' dining rooms, charming all the girls and getting more business. He also took out the pretty ones and appeared most mornings, at 8 a.m., slightly hungover and well bonked!

I also employed a secretary to cope with the telephone, the orders and the books of the ever-expanding trade. I myself prepared the fish and did the, now well-drained, lobster runs. Having started in my flat, I very soon needed premises and, as I wrote earlier, these I found with a friend who already had a fishmonger's just off Jermyn Street. We were not in competition as he was not interested in directors' dining rooms and I was not interested in hotels, pubs and restaurants.

One girl, found by Willy, placed an order almost daily. She was called Melissa and worked for a firm of solicitors. She seemed only to want high-value fish such as Dover sole, turbot and lobster. One day I answered the phone in the office myself. A very sexy voice cooed at me. 'Hello, it's Melissa,' she said. 'I've heard all about you from Willy. I'd love to meet you. Why don't you do the delivery tomorrow yourself?' I am a great believer in good service so I immediately agreed, particularly as the voice had seemed to promise delights beyond lobsters.

'What's she like?' I asked Willy.

'Er, a little large,' he said, 'but I flirt outrageously with her and that's why all these orders flow in.' The next day I delivered 10 pounds of turbot fillet and four lobsters. Willy's description was an understatement, to say the least. The poor girl weighed at least twenty stone, but she was pleasant and had this amazing voice. I felt that it had been well worth my while doing the delivery as the large, expensive orders continued to flow in.

And then suddenly they stopped. After four days, without a murmur from Melissa, I decided to ring up and find out if we had done anything awful. 'Hello,' I said, 'may I speak to Melissa in the kitchen please.'

'Who's speaking?' asked the receptionist.

'It's Mike Daunt from The Salmon Pool,' I replied.

'Ah yes, Mr Daunt, our senior partner, Mr Faversham, would like to talk to you. I'll put you through.'

Eventually a male voice came on the line: 'Mr Daunt, Charles Faversham here. I wonder if you could come and see me? Yes tomorrow at two p.m. would be fine.'

I dressed in a jacket and tie and, somewhat apprehensively, turned up at the appointed hour. I waited in reception until Mr Faversham came through. He was a distinguished-looking man in his early fifties and greeted me with courtesy.

'Your company has been supplying fish to us for the past year,' he said.

'That's correct,' I replied. 'I do hope that it has been up to the required standard.'

'It has always been superb,' replied Charles Faversham, 'but I wonder if you would mind coming with me for a moment?' Mystified, I followed him through to the kitchen where a new girl had obviously taken over Melissa's place. It was a large kitchen and along one wall were three big chest freezers. Mr Faversham opened them. They were all full to overflowing with Dover sole, lobsters, crabs, turbot and almost every other imaginable fish. 'There are only four partners in the firm and I'm afraid we'll be living off fish for at least the next year,' he said with a rueful smile. 'Most regrettably, Melissa was obsessed with your delivery man and couldn't stop ordering from you because she wanted to see him every day. It's not your fault, but do explain to your chap that he should, perhaps, be a little less flirtatious, particularly with frustrated, overweight ladies.'

Every morning, once I had bought the fish in the market, I needed to prepare them and I had learnt well how to fillet and skin. However, one morning the knife slipped and I opened up the palm of my left hand, with which I had been holding a Dover sole, with a deep two-inch cut. It didn't hurt a great deal but bled profusely. I tied it up with a spare rag and, having told someone else to finish my work, I drove to the outpatients of St Stephen's Hospital in Chelsea. Annoyingly, as it was eight o'clock in the morning, all the wounded drunks from the night before lounged in the waiting room and it was packed. 'I'm afraid it's a good two hours' wait,' said the receptionist, a woman of middle age with a moustache, a pair of Edna Everage glasses and a brusque manner. I took a seat, snoozed and waited patiently.

Suddenly, I was awakened by a man tripping over my

foot. He swayed towards the reception desk and stood there blinking owlishly. The receptionist stared at him in disapproval. 'Well, what's the matter?' she demanded. The drunk leant forward until his face was nearly touching hers. She visibly retreated and the smell of stale drink wafted across the already alcohol-permeated room. He whispered something and lurched back. 'I couldn't hear a word – speak up, man,' she said. The drunk again pushed his head forward, the receptionist retreated and again he only murmured quietly. 'I can't hear a word,' said the woman. 'Speak up!' The man took a pace backwards and stared at her. Then in a broad Irish brogue he announced, 'Some focker's kicked me in de bollocks.'

Even with this little bit of joy, I seemed to be waiting for hours. Suddenly I'd had enough. I remembered hearing that hospitals didn't like blood. It was messy and upset the other patients. I therefore carefully, and unseen by anyone, unwrapped the rag from around my hand. The wound had stopped bleeding, but I soon remedied that by pulling the lips of the cut wide apart. It didn't hurt much but the results were exactly what I wanted and blood squirted everywhere. Nurses immediately came running and I was removed to a private cubicle where almost instantly a doctor appeared, stitched up the cut, gave me a tetanus injection and sent me on my way.

One evening at a dinner party I met a man called David McLaren. He was amusing, fun and had an unconventional, rebellious and creative mind. We got on like a house on fire and to this day he is a close friend of mine. At that initial meeting we sniffed around each other like a couple of Labradors, decided we liked each other's smell, and relaxed. In the course of our talk I told him I was a fishmonger, which amused him, and he told me that he headed Collett Dickenson Pearce, which I knew to be Britain's most glamorous and influential advertising agency, generally regarded as one of the finest in the world during the 1970s and 1980s. It had among its clientele such huge names as Harveys Bristol Cream, Bird's Eye, Parker Pens, Fiat, Ford, Acrilan, Pretty Polly, Ronson and Benson & Hedges. Some of its slogans, such as 'Happiness is a cigar called Hamlet' and 'Land Rover: The Best 4x4 By Far', became bywords of British culture. I immediately realised that David must be quite some man to be the boss of such a legendary company.

'Why don't you come round and see me in the office,' said David as we were all departing into the night. 'I'll introduce you to the brilliant Sam Redhead who looks after all our dining rooms. If we were open to the public, Sam would have been awarded several Michelin stars by now, so good is her food.'

I rang David the next day and made an appointment to go and see him. I duly arrived in Euston Road at the huge building that was the CDP offices and caught a lift to the thirteenth floor, where his secretary was waiting for me. David greeted me like an old friend, led me back to the lift and we descended to the ninth floor, which was entirely given over to a huge kitchen and three dining rooms. I was expecting another blue-eye-shadowed-Alice-banded young girl, but what I was introduced to was a very beautiful, statuesque woman in her mid-thirties who radiated style and personality. David left us together and Sam and I chatted. I showed her our list of products and at the end she said, 'Okay, I'm going to give you a trial for a month and we'll see how it goes.'

During that month I did every delivery myself and they were huge. Each day I carried up vast quantities of every conceivable fish and shellfish to Sam's domain. I also got to know Sam very well. I tried to make my deliveries either at about 9 a.m. before preparations for lunch had really started, or in the afternoon when lunch was finished and Sam was relaxing. She was a lady of great wit and character and we became such good friends that she came to my dinner parties and I went to hers. It was she who had collected L. from Mombasa airport when she flew out to join me in Kenya, and at whose house L. and I met up. When the month was finished and nobody mentioned the trial period, I presumed that we had passed, but I still continued to do all the deliveries myself.

One day, as I was sitting having a cigarette with Sam in the afternoon, she said, 'Next week it's the fiftieth birthday of the managing director of Fiat (UK) and he's coming for lunch here. I want to do something special. How about peacock? I'll need two. I want them sitting on the table facing each other with their wonderful long tail feathers wafting down each way.'

I am a great believer in saying 'yes' to anything, as there is always a way of getting what you want with a little initiative and thus I, of course, agreed. That evening I rang The Trout at Wolvercote near Oxford, which I knew had peacocks running around in the garden. Obviously, no one would sell me one if I said that I wanted to eat it and I therefore had my story ready. 'It's my mother's eightieth birthday next week,' I lied to the landlady, 'and I want to give her a really special present. She lives in our old ancestral home with a huge garden. She had peacocks there when she first married my father but I'm afraid they have all died now and I would love to give her a new pair for a present.'

There was silence on the line and then the landlady said, 'Well, we have got a young pair which were hatched last spring but I'm afraid they're both peacocks. We've no young peahens.'

'That couldn't be better,' I said. 'She won't want to breed from them. My mother will be so thrilled to see them display.'

'All right,' said the landlady. 'They're called Chico and Charley' – and here her voice suddenly hardened as she named an outrageous price, and then softened again as she said, 'But they will be happy, won't they?' I quickly agreed as I knew Sam would be thrilled with them. I arranged to collect them at the beginning of the following week, two days before 'The Lunch'.

When I arrived at The Trout at 10 a.m., before it opened for business, I found the landlady waiting for me. 'I've kept them in their shed,' she said.' Have you brought a cage for them to travel in?'

'Don't worry about that,' I said. 'They can run free in the back of the estate car. We haven't far to go.' We went to the shed and Chico and Charley were perfectly happy to be picked up and carried to the car. The landlady had tears in her eyes as she said goodbye, but they soon dried when she saw the wad of £20 notes I counted into her eager hands. I am sure that, at the price I paid, she'd have sold her sister. Then I drove round the corner from the pub, clambered into the back and, feeling a total shit, wrung the birds' necks. I then took them to London, plucked and dressed them, keeping some of the tail feathers for Sam, and delivered them to CDP the next morning. Sam was thrilled, as was the managing director of Fiat.

CDP were famous for their hospitality, and the wonder of the wines combined with the fabulous food was legendary. One of the senior management, who was renowned as a gourmand, was John Ritchie, the deputy chairman. I got to know John well as he was mad about fishing - as, of course, was I. One day Sam said to me, 'Try and do a delivery at lunchtime tomorrow. It's John's fiftieth birthday and the directors have laid on a special lunch for him. We've got some brilliant beef. It's his favourite.' Of course, I said that I'd be there.

Earlier, I had noticed a crane outside the building and saw that some work was being carried out high on the ninth floor where the dining rooms were, but had thought little of it. John was particularly fond of rare roast beef and what had been done for his birthday was this: the company had bought the prize bull at Smithfield. This had been put into a crate and driven to the CDP offices. Here, the wall to one of the dining rooms had been dismantled, the bull's crate lifted by the crane to the dining room and the animal persuaded into it with hay and apples, his favourite food. He was a docile creature so that when John was ushered into the dining room for his birthday lunch, which he had been told was rare roast beef, he found the bull contentedly chewing the hay and apples. The wall had been bricked up again so that it was impossible for John to see how it had arrived. The whole process then had to be carried out again and the bull lowered and re-sold. The cost was astronomical but the company considered it worth it, for the story had been leaked to the press and the free advertising was extensive.

After John's lunch, which I was lucky enough to attend, I was invited for a final drink in David's office. Over a large glass of very good brandy I said, 'What has become of your lovely doorman?' Ever since I had been serving CDP a happy, smiling doorman had greeted me. He was a tall black man, by the unlikely name of Ernest, who welcomed one and all with the same cheerful, broad grin. Over the years I had become rather fond of him and recently had felt sad to see a new doorman in his place.

'Ah,' said David, looking pensive, 'thereby hangs an interesting tale.' He refilled our glasses and continued: 'About a couple of months ago I was just leaving the building and stopped to have a quick chat with Ernest. "Have a cigar, sah," he said and offered me an enormous Monte Cristo. Now those things aren't cheap but I thought no more of it until three weeks later when I again stopped for a gossip. "Oh, sah," said Ernest "you must see ma new car." He led me out of the building and there, parked near by, was a brand-new BMW. I knew what I paid Ernest and, unless a rich aunt had died and left him all, he couldn't possibly have afforded it. Now, I am very fond of Ernest but I also have a responsibility to the company and, if something naughty had been taking place, I needed to know. I am afraid that I hired a private detective with instructions to find out where Ernest was getting his money.

'For three weeks I heard nothing, and then the private dick asked to see me. When he came into my office the full story emerged. By 8 p.m., at the latest, this building is empty. Ernest was responsible for locking it up and unlocking it in the morning. However, when we had all gone home to our families, Ernest came into his own and made his fortune *by letting our offices to ladies of the night.*'

I stared at David and started to laugh. I looked at the expensive leather sofa and the Persian carpet in David's office in an entirely different light.

'I know,' said David, 'it makes you think, and the imagination runs riot, doesn't it? When I summoned Ernest and confronted him with the evidence – and there were photographs of nearly every office in the building being put to nefarious use – he could not have been more open. "Oh sah," he said, with his usual wide smile, "Ah knew Ah'd be caught eventually but Ah's made a fortune, more money than Ah's ever seen in ma life. Ah'll just have to find another job like this one. Thank you, sah, for all the fun. It's been a wonderful company to work for." And with a broad wink he walked out. You can't help liking the old rogue. The new one's nowhere near such fun.'

I ran The Salmon Pool for just over twenty wonderful, funny, laughing years but at the end I was doing that which I'd sworn I'd never do. Because it had become so successful, I was permanently at a desk and never had the time to do the amusing jobs. I still looked after CDP as much as possible but that was the only one. And so I decided to sell the company and do something else.

SIX

Falkus
Fishing

'The Chelsea Home for Destitute Prostitutes,' I said, answering the phone in my flat. I had just returned from yet another drunken lunch since selling my company and was in a flippant and idiotic mood.

'Is that Little Daunty?' said a distinguished voice at the other end. I almost stood to attention for I knew the voice to be that of Hugh Falkus, film-maker, presenter and writer of the most acclaimed books on salmon and sea-trout fishing of the twentieth century.

'I can't call you Daunty,' continued Hugh, 'as I always called your father that.' He and my father had flown fighters together before the war and had been friends.

'Now,' Hugh went on, 'you've done very well, but what are you going to do now?'

'I haven't any idea yet,' I replied. 'Go travelling and fishing for a year and think about it.'

'Very bad idea,' said Hugh. 'You'll drink far too much and almost certainly get the clap.'

There was a pause as he let the hook sink in right over the barb.

'Come and work with me,' he continued. 'We'll have a lot of fun together.'

And we did. We taught the gentle and very beautiful art of Spey casting for salmon.

Because of other commitments I could only work with Hugh on a part-time basis, but even that was tremendous fun and it's fair to say that he had more influence on my adult life than any other person. He was arrogant, intolerant, rude, kind and wildly funny. I loved him dearly as a father and I know he thought of me as a son.

The very first time I taught with Hugh, what should have been an easy morning went horribly wrong. There were two clients. A general from the Grenadier Guards and a young man of about twenty-five who had been given a lesson with Hugh as a Christmas present by his father. 'I'll teach the general first,' said Hugh, 'and you can have him after lunch.' This seemed reasonable; I knew that Hugh and the general had been corresponding about which rod to buy as the old soldier wanted a new one. Hugh had told him to buy one of the fifteen-foot Bruce and Walker Hexagraphs, which Hugh had endorsed with his name.

We were teaching on the lake owned by Bill Arnold, a friend of Hugh's who lived about two miles from his cottage near Ravenglass in Cumbria. I could easily see Hugh on the other side of the lake and it was obvious by his body language that all was not well. However, I continued with my pupil and we all joined together at lunchtime. Hugh turned to the general. 'You'll be with Daunty this afternoon,' he said.

'I'd much rather stay with you,' replied the general, who obviously regarded me as very much second best. 'Yer see, I think the problem is with this rod yer recommended. Doesn't suit me at all, yer know.'

'I'm sure that's true,' replied Hugh, 'you're much better suited to a hand line.'

'There's no need to be rude, Falkus,' said the soldier.

But Hugh, by now, had had enough. He had come to the end of his very short fuse. He was puce in the face and his chin was sticking out aggressively. I knew the expression well and waited with gleeful expectation for the explosion. 'General,' he shouted, 'just fuck off! I don't want your money or your company.' And the general fucked off, muttering angrily to himself. 'Typical bloody senior officer,' said Hugh. 'Wouldn't do as he was told and wouldn't listen.'

Hugh was never an easy man. His mind was too demanding for the niceties of life and he did not suffer fools. Nor did he tolerate pretension. If these two facets of humanity were combined in someone, the unfortunate person concerned would be put down, often harshly.

Whilst fishing a river without Hugh I had met a very amusing Lord of the Land. As is often the case in fishing lodges, after dinner we had been discussing women in general and our wives in particular. The Lord of the Land had kept quiet during this idiotic chatter until there was a small silence, when he interjected in a sad and doleful voice: 'Do you know,' he remarked wistfully, 'I have never seen my wife naked.' As they had four children my imagination ran riot. However, he was a very kind and funny man and extended an invitation to me to fish his piece of Tweed 'if you are ever in the area'. He was also a great fan of Hugh's.

Later that year, in October, Hugh and I were fishing on the Junction Pool of the Tweed and the Teviot in Kelso, arguably the most famous salmon beat in Scotland. During a drink in the bar on the first evening I suggested that we had the Lord of the Land and his wife to dinner with us in the Ednam House Hotel in Kelso, where we were staying. Apart from anything else I badly wanted to see what this blushing mother was like. I had told Hugh the story of her unwillingness to strip and he too was dying to meet her. Before the evening arrived, I briefed Hugh.

'I'm going to seat you next to Lady Margaret at dinner,' I said, 'and, for God's sake chat her up and be nice to her. She and her husband own one of the best beats on Tweed and we'll be invited to fish if all goes well.'

'Don't you worry, Daunty,' replied Hugh. 'I'm very good at that sort of thing.'

We sat down to dinner and it soon became apparent why the Lady Margaret had never displayed herself to her husband. She was an overweight and overbearing battleaxe, stupid and boring. She was also very pretentious.

'Do you know,' she said, turning to Hugh, 'Ay do a lot of Good Works. Ay visit all those poor [she pronounced it 'poo-er'] girls who have gorn orf the rails and ended up in prison. Many of them are, of course [and here she whispered the word as if it was very daring] *prostitutes*.'

Because I knew him so well, I could see that Hugh couldn't stand her and was about to say something awful. I kicked him hard under the table. 'Why are you kicking me, Daunty?' he enquired loudly. Then he turned back to the non-stripper. 'Please tell me something, Lady Margaret,' he said, 'didn't you ever have a fuck before you married?' The Lord of the Land caught my eye and winked hugely. Surprisingly, we never were invited to fish the Famous Beat.

To his close circle of great friends Hugh was enormously kind. 'In this life,' he used to say to me, 'kindness is all.' And he lived by his own maxim. On the same trip to the Junction Pool that had featured the unfortunate Lord of the Land, I was the recipient of some of this kindness. We had been fishing all day and had had some success, with eight fish between us, including two 20-pounders (we were sharing a rod), and had returned to the Ednam House Hotel to celebrate. As we were drinking our first whisky the telephone behind the bar rang and the barman answered it. He turned to me. 'It's for you, Mr Daunt,' he said. 'Take it in the booth in reception.' My mood of jubilation had changed. I had been dreading this phone call. I knew that it would be from my wife, and the marriage was going through a very bad patch. I picked up the receiver. 'Hello,' I said. A stream of abuse hurtled down the wires. 'Darling,' I said, in my most conciliatory tones, 'if you tell me quietly what the matter is, I'll try and sort it out.' There was another series of screeches from the phone and then a click as the receiver was slammed down. I walked back miserably to the bar. Hugh immediately saw from my face that something was very wrong.

'What's the matter, Daunty?' he said.

'That was my wife,' I replied. 'I don't know why these bloody women bother to ring up if all they are going to do is scream down the phone.'

'Oh, I understand it very well,' said Hugh. 'You see, every time you go fishing they always think that you've got another woman with you.' There was a long pause and then a wicked smile spread over his face. 'Well, of course, they're usually right.'

Looking back over the years, I still cannot believe that I was so blessed as to have laughed and drunk, fished and shot and had such a close friendship with such an extraordinary and unusual human being. Possibly Hugh's greatest asset was his originality of thought. He questioned everything. When his book, *Sea Trout Fishing*, was first published it revolutionised the sport. Nothing like it had ever been written before. The same is true of its sister book, *Salmon Fishing*, although to a lesser extent.

A classic demonstration of the Falkus gift for innovation had taken place even before he had written *Sea Trout Fishing*. It was all to do with the history of the salmon fly. (For those readers who are not interested in fishing, please skip forward a couple of pages where there might be more sex.)

Jock Scott and Green Highlander, Mar Lodge and Silver Grey: these are all classic salmon flies which evoke nostalgia for those of us of a certain age. When I first started fly-tying, at the age of eight, I spent hours marrying up the fibres of the various feathers to make the wings for these flies, for in that faraway time, these were the traditional built-wing flies we were told were necessary to hook a salmon. Nowadays, nearly all the birds from which the feathers came to make these flies are on the worldwide list of-protected species, or it is illegal to import them. In those days nobody used hair-wing flies, which, of course, are simple and cheap to tie. We all fished with these elaborate, expensive concoctions which, I have no doubt, are not as effective as our modern lures anyway. Aesthetically, there is no comparison. The difference is as great as that between a Regency buck and a chimney sweep. They are exquisite creations, have such beautiful names and yet their history is one of snobbery, power, dishonesty and calumny.

The story really starts in about 1820 with a man called John Colquhoun who lived by Loch Lomond and was an aristocrat whose elder broher was Sir James Colquhoun of Luss, fourth baronet and the head of the Clan. Colquhoun fished all over Scotland. He only used one fly but in different sizes. This was made from the feathers of the glede, or red kite as it is now known. He exhorted his followers to shoot this bird and obtain as many feathers from it as possible because it was becoming exceedingly rare and before it became extinct! A more thinking man, and one who had great influence on salmon fishing, was William Scrope of Kelso, the leading fly-tier of his day. His classic book on the sport of salmon fishing, *Days and Nights of Salmon Fishing on Tweed*, was published in 1843. He used only six flies, among which were ones with such esoteric names as 'Meg with a Muckle in her Mouth' and 'Meg in her Braws'. These were tied on large hooks and made with chicken, buzzard and bittern feathers. They were fished with a sunk line and were great killers, possibly because, in that gentle age, there were so many salmon in the rivers. Scrope had a flourishing business at that time and nearly all the aristocracy who fished in Scotland bought their flies from him.

In 1867, a man called Francis Francis became fishing editor of the British countryside magazine *The Field*. Francis was not the surname with which he was born. He arrived in the world as Francis Morgan but he had an uncle surnamed Francis, an exceedingly rich man, who said that if Morgan changed his name he would leave him everything in his will. Naturally, he couldn't carry out his uncle's wishes quickly enough. In the late nineteenth century and well into the twentieth *The Field* was the only publication that could claim to be the voice of the countryside and, in that much more rural age, was overwhelmingly dominant. It was published weekly and the fishing editor was an extremely powerful man. Francis used his position to influence completely the world of salmon flies and their tying. He informed his foolish readers that the salmon had grown wise to, and was tired of, the old-fashioned flies as tied by Scrope and would be unlikely to take them. What they would fall for, Francis told the world, were the new flies he personally recommended. In his tome, *A Book on Angling*, he wrote, 'The fish have undergone a complete change in their taste [on Tweed] since I was there; for when I was there they preferred a sober-coloured fly but of late years they prefer showy ones.' These flies needed numerous rare and exotic feathers with which to tie them. The Jock Scott, for instance, in its full classical glory, requires no fewer than twenty-eight different materials with which to tie it and these do not include the hook or the tying silk.

Francis had found, while visiting Ireland, that the feathers of such birds as blue chatterer, blue macaw, Indian crow, toucan, and jungle cock, to name but a few, were being imported into the West coast ports, and that Rogan's of Ballyshannon, which was founded in 1830, made the best flies available. Soon, to supply the new demand, three different Irish families had set up shop in Ballyshannon. Because of his enormous influence over the sportsmen of that age, everyone believed what Francis said and poor Scrope was fast driven out of business. In an ill-disguised swipe at Scrope, Francis wrote, 'There are many persons who hold that half a dozen flies are enough to kill salmon on any river in the kingdom and who despise the use of such an extended list of flies. To such irreverent scoffers and heretical unbelievers I have nothing to say. Let them indulge in their repertoire of a bit of old turkey carpet and a live barn door rooster.'

Francis imported these Irish tied flies into Britain and they were sold through the now defunct London Salmon Fishers Club. The most expensive of these cost the ridiculous sum of 10 shillings (50 pence), which nowadays would be the equivalent of roughly £30 per fly. He also wrote that each river demanded a different fly, and set up fly-tiers in various parts of Scotland to cater for this artificial and unnecessary market. For instance, Francis wrote that on the Rivers Nith and Annan the salmon would best succumb to flies made with brown turkey! Despite the astronomical prices of these lures and the complexity of their design, the gullible and ever-optimistic salmon fishing fraternity could not buy enough. Francis did not act in this, almost criminal, deceit for financial gain, as he did not need money; he had plenty of private income from his change-of-name inheritance. His actions undoubtedly increased the circulation of *The Field*, which would have enhanced the one thing with which Francis was besotted: power. He revelled in the adoration of the aristocratic fishermen and their innocent belief in his apparent knowledge. He was invited to all the best rivers and country-house parties. He dined with dukes and lunched with earls. He was the darling of country society and he revelled in every ill-deserved moment of it. He died a contented and fulfilled man and almost certainly went to his grave believing his own nonsense.

Francis's influence continued for the next fifty years, which does not say a great deal for the originality of thought of the salmon fishermen of that era, but rather a great deal about their conservative behaviour. Yet this age was the heyday of salmon fishing on all the British and Norwegian rivers, and enormous catches and monster fish were recorded, particularly in the 1920s. The exquisite built-wing flies continued into the 1950s, when Hugh Falkus saw the idiocy of using these costly confections, which were also ensuring the rapid decline of some of the world's rarest birds. He began to use hair-wing salmon flies and to write about them. He quickly found that these flies were equally as effective, if not more so, than their gaudy cousins, were far cheaper to make and considerably less destructive to wildlife.

It really all came about by mistake. Hugh had gone for a day's fishing on the Dee. When he arrived on the riverbank in the morning he discovered to his annoyance that he had left his fly boxes behind. The river was in perfect ply after a spring spate and he was not going to waste time driving to fishing-tackle shops to buy new flies. In his lapel he had an old eel hook and he had his black Labrador, Prince, for company. He cut some hair from Prince's neck as a wing, but what could he use as tying silk? At that moment he spotted a pretty girl walking along the riverbank. Hugh was always charming and he was also very good looking. Women adored him. He explained his needs and the girl laughingly disappeared into the bushes. Two minutes later she reappeared with some nylon thread from her knickers. The Dee Special was born, and that was the end of eighty years of idiocy.

It is easy to write disparagingly of Francis, and yet how many of us would not have succumbed to these same temptations? He was a man of the Victorian middle classes and to have been revered and fêted by the British aristocracy of that time must have been wonderful for him. What *is* extraordinary is that his influence lasted for as long as it did. However, with the enormous amount of salmon that in those halcyon days swam in British waters, it would have been easy to believe that paradise was immortal and that there was no need for change. If some modern guru wrote that the hairs from around the pubic area of a cat were guaranteed to take a salmon and sold them for a vast price, I wonder how many of our modern fishing fraternity would fall for it? He could even call the fly 'The Pussy Killer', for it would certainly affect the well-being of the cat population, which in turn, might, perhaps, not be such a bad thing.

Much later, Hugh also applied his innovative mind to Spey casting and reinvented this beautiful cast and art form. This is what he and I taught together for nearly five years before Hugh became too ill to teach.

After the final seven-day course held at the Boat Hotel, Boat of Garten, we needed to take some rods and reels back to Mortimer's fishing-tackle shop at Grantown-on-Spey. After we had returned all the equipment we had borrowed, we set off back to the hotel to pack. I was driving and, as we drove across the bridge over the Spey, Hugh asked me to stop and I drew up at the side of the road. We got out of the car and Hugh leant on the parapet in the centre of the bridge and looked upstream, then he crossed the road and stared downstream. I was next to him and suddenly he started to quote from T.S. Eliot's 'The Love Song of J. Alfred Prufrock':

I grow old… I grow old…
I shall wear the bottoms of my trousers rolled.

Shall I part my hair behind? Do I dare to eat a peach?
I shall wear white flannel trousers, and walk upon the beach.
I have heard the mermaids singing, each to each.

I do not think that they will sing for me.

I was standing to one side of him so that I saw him in profile, with his long, white hair streaming in the wind and a look of infinite sadness upon his rugged face, and I realised that he was saying goodbye to the river he loved so well. I admit openly that the tears streamed down my cheeks because I knew then, with certainty, that he was dying. I knew, not from what I saw, but what I felt from the wings of the Angel of Death fluttering grimly over him. When he had finished, he turned to me and realised at once how upset I was. With typical abruptness he said, 'Oh, for God's sake, Daunty, stop grizzling and let's go and have a drink.'

Shortly after this Hugh was diagnosed with cancer of the colon and was forced to have a colostomy. When he arrived at his local hospital for the operation he had all the normal tests and then was questioned by a junior doctor about his habits.

'How much do you drink per day?' he enquired.

'Not a lot,' replied Hugh. 'Only about one bottle of whisky.'

'That's far too much,' said the tyro medic, foolishly.

Hugh looked at him hard. 'Go and get the results of the tests on my liver,' he ordered, 'and bring them here.'

To the chagrin of the poor, inexperienced young man they were perfect.

Hugh faced the misery of the operation with his usual bravery. I visited him in hospital regularly and after it was over I asked him how he felt. 'They've taken a thing out of me the size of a hedgehog,' he replied descriptively.

Hugh recovered from the operation and we continued

teaching. However, an incident took place, which, sadly for medicine, was never taken forward. Hugh had arranged for the local district nurse to visit him at Bill Arnold's home, Knott End in Cumbria which, as I wrote earlier, was about two miles from Hugh's cottage. Here we did all the Spey-casting teaching on the lake. The nurse duly arrived and Hugh and she went off to the fishing hut where she was to show him how to change his colostomy bag. She was a comely woman in her mid-forties and very obviously in awe of the Great Man. When they had finished they joined the rest of us on Bill's veranda and Hugh persuaded the nurse to have a glass of whisky. After three of Hugh's measures the nurse at last rose to her feet and tottered towards her car. As she left Hugh slapped her on the bottom. 'I'll tell you something, my dear,' he said, 'if I was fit and well and ten years younger, you wouldn't have got out of here with your knickers intact.' The nurse loved it. But after she had gone his face changed. He had that thinking expression, which I knew always preceded an original idea. 'You know, Daunty,' he said, 'there's a better way of doing it. That bloody bag, I mean. And I know what it is. I must tell the right people.'

Three months later he died. However, just before that happened, we were talking in his study. 'I've left you my name,' he told me. 'Keep it going.' Although he was an atheist, he was determined to be immortal.

Because of business commitments I returned home to the south. On the night of his death I was at a hilarious dinner party with friends and, suddenly, amidst the laughter and the storytelling, I felt Hugh go through the room. I turned to my next-door neighbour, Cressida Sykes, a wonderful fisherwoman, a close friend and big fan of Hugh's: 'He's just died,' I said. He had fulfilled the wish that he had told me only a few weeks previously: 'Keats wrote it,' he had said, '"to cease upon the midnight with no pain." I so hope that I do that, Daunty.' The time was ten to twelve.

Hugh's funeral was entirely typical of the man. He had left very detailed instructions. It was to be held in the open, in a field next to the Esk, the river that Hugh had made famous in his film *Salmo the Leaper*. There was to be a trailer-load of champagne on ice, which the assembled guests were to finish to the last drop. There were about sixty of us gathered in the field to say farewell and I am certain that there were at least a hundred and twenty bottles of champagne spread out in the trailer. It was, of course, raining, a gentle, soft April shower that penetrated the clothing, but we were all country folk so it made little difference. I had been asked to read the beginning of the introduction to *Sea Trout Fishing*, Hugh's best-known book, and this I did. Then we all moved to the banks of the river, where Bill Arnold, Hugh's neighbour and great friend, was to lay Hugh's ashes. Kathleen, Hugh's wife, had chosen the spot carefully. It was where Hugh's old Labrador, Prince, was buried. 'He loved that dog,' said Kathy. 'He won't have a row with him. He'll be at peace there.' The casket of ashes was placed in the deeply dug hole by Bill and the earth thrown on top of it. Then Bill lifted the heavy stone with Hugh's inscription and was about to lay it over the grave when a strange thing happened.

Carried on the April wind, as lovely and haunting as

fairies singing, came the voices of wild geese. Everyone stared up as the skein of six greylag circled the grave, calling their mournful epitaph. Then, as if saluting a fellow flier and wanderer, they circled again before flying away into the chill April sky. It was a fitting valediction.

Long before Hugh had died I had started teaching in the south. True to Hugh's wishes I had called the enterprise 'The Hugh Falkus School of Spey Casting', later shortened to 'Falkus Fishing'. I taught on a lake near Andover. This lake was essentially a day-ticket trout fishery, but I built two platforms at one end and from here I taught Spey casting. From the beginning, I was fully booked. This was due to a combination of Hugh's name and the location, which was right in the middle of chalk-stream country.

There was one very small blot on the landscape, an organisation called APGAI. This acronym stands for The Association of Professional Game Angling Instructors and, at that time, at its head was a somewhat pompous man who was extremely aware of himself. He was an Old Etonian and insisted on wearing his old school tie even in the depths of the wilderness; he was the antithesis of Hugh and me. One day, after the school had been going for some weeks, I received a phone call from this man who informed me that Hugh and I should, if we wanted to teach and, cheekily, 'charge the sort of prices that you chaps charge', be members of APGAI. I replied that if Hugh was willing to become a member, then I would too. 'Why don't you ring him up,' I said. 'Here's his number.' I immediately rang Hugh and told him the story.

'By God,' said Hugh, 'if that little bugger rings me up telling me what to do he's not going to get a flea in his ear, he's going to get a hornet.'

Joyously, I waited to see what would happen. An hour later Hugh rang me. 'I've told him exactly what to do with himself,' he said. 'It was short, pithy, to the point and biologically impossible. We'll hear no more from him.' But, surprisingly, we did. A few days later I received a letter. In this the APGAI man went out of his way to denigrate Hugh and state that he was totally out of date in his methods. I cannot imagine what he thought he would achieve by this piece of foolishness, but I certainly wasn't having any of it and replied as follows:

Dear Sir,
I am in receipt of your letter and only wish to say one thing: Hugh Falkus's methods will be practised and his name remembered and revered long after yours has, thankfully, been forgotten.
Yours faithfully,

After that neither Hugh nor I heard any more. Hugh insisted on taking out an advertisement in *Trout and Salmon* magazine, which stated: 'Learn to Spey cast with Hugh Falkus, proudly **not** a member of APGAI.'

There was also a most satisfactory postscript. I was telephoned by a client who had recently returned from fishing the River Spey where APGAI had joined the party for one day. During the morning, he was walking down the bank and stood for a while watching my client fishing. The client was a well-known name in British industry and APGAI obviously wanted to get to know him. Whilst APGAI watched, my client faultlessly performed one of Hugh's innovative and unusual Spey casts, which I had taught him.

'Where on earth did you learn that?' enquired APGAI.

'I don't think you want to know,' replied my client with a huge smile and, with a heavy frown, APGAI quickly went on his way.

It wasn't too long before I had built up a substantial client list, and I was asked by the sporting agents, Roxtons, to take a party of fishermen to Russia. Roxtons had also made a video of the amazing fishing and for this I had done the voice-over. In those days Russia had only just begun to allow Westerners to fish its rivers, but it was well-known among the cognoscenti that the Kola Peninsula in the country's far north was a salmon fisherman's paradise, and had rivers where the salmon run was larger than anything that had been seen in Europe since the Industrial Revolution.

In June 1996, with my party, which consisted mostly of close friends, we flew to Helsinki, where we spent the night, before catching a very early flight to Murmansk the next morning. The International Airport of Murmansk was, in those days, a time warp. The men's lavatory, in particular, should have been in a museum. At the entrance was a woman in a kiosk who charged 20 kopecks (approximately ⅕ of 1p) to enter. Of course, none of us had any roubles as everyone in Russia dealt in US dollars and we had carefully taken only this currency with us. Thus, when we needed a pee, after drinking in the airport bar and paying in dollars, the happy harridan in her kiosk was more than pleased to be given a dollar to let us enter the loo. Inside was a strong smell of disinfectant and a running, open drain into which we peed. If a shit were required this was more of a problem, especially for the elderly, as the loos were of the squatter variety and had no doors. They were particularly unpleasant, as around the hole into the long drop was a great deal of evidence of where people had missed.

After spending several hours in the airport bar we were eventually called to board our helicopter to fly to the river. Yet again, we went through security with our bags and fishing rods. This took a long time as every official, from passport control to security, took his job very seriously and spent several long minutes looking at our passports and then at the security screens. When it came to my turn, and while waiting for the official to check my baggage on the TV monitor, I leant forward and peered surreptitiously so that I could see the screen. *There was nothing on it.* What the official was looking at was completely blank, as the monitor obviously wasn't working. However, he needed to pretend to do his job and therefore went through an act all day to justify his existence. It would have been very cruel to point this out and I therefore kept quiet.

Eventually, we all piled into a very old Russian helicopter and flew to our base on the Upper Varzuga. This was an entirely tented camp, which was actually very comfortable, and had a central mess tent where we ate, drank and told stories. The moment we had climbed out of the helicopters we had put our rods up and gone fishing. I remained with the camp manager because I wanted to be taken round all the beats so that I would know them. I did, however, take a rod with me so that I could have the occasional cast. We travelled everywhere by jet boat, roaring up the river, over fast runs, small rapids, and somehow avoiding the multitude of rocks. It was incredibly beautiful and a salmon fisherman's dream. When we had seen most of the beats we stopped and I made a cast into the tail of a pool. My fly was instantly grabbed by a salmon. I later found out that the Varzuga River was so prolific that it was almost too easy. That first week in Russia with six rods, three of whom were very experienced, we caught 192 salmon. I had never known anything like it anywhere on earth, and, for an experienced fisherman it was too simple, but it was an ideal place in which to teach.

The Varzuga is in the southern Kola Peninsula and here the rivers are fecund with salmon. They are not large, however, averaging 6 to 7 pounds. I knew that the northern rivers of the Kola had fewer fish but that there was every chance of catching a 30- or even 40-pound trophy. The winter after the first Varzuga expedition, in 1997, I heard that an Englishman called Peter Power had bought a huge land holding in the northern Kola which included some of its most famous rivers. This was confirmed when I received a telephone call from Peter inviting me to fish these rivers the following season. However, the chosen week clashed with the one that I was doing with Roxtons with a party of eight on the Upper Varzuga. Totally unfazed, Peter suggested that I spend three days teaching on the Varzuga and that he would then send a helicopter down to collect me and fly me up to his rivers in the north. Thus I had my own private helicopter to fly me across the whole of the Kola, which was a wonderful experience.

Arriving at the Kharlovka base camp I was met by Peter. We immediately recognised each other from our days at Rugby, where we had both been at school, although Peter had been three years senior to me. So who is Peter Power, a man who, despite achieving many newsworthy deeds in his life, has always shirked publicity? He is an extraordinary human being. Well over six feet tall with a full head of long, flowing grey hair, he emanates the confidence and charisma of the natural leader. He is highly intelligent with an unconventional mind that asks the question 'Why?' to almost everything. In that respect he is very similar to Hugh Falkus. The two never met, although I suspect that, if they had, they would have hated each other, as both would have vied to be the centre of attention. Nothing that Peter has ever done has been by the book, and I have no doubt that there are many conventional souls who have been horrified at both his lifestyle and his success.

By the age of thirty-four he was already a multi-millionaire with his own global organisation. He is a man with a very addictive nature and in those heady days his addiction was making money. In 1992, at the age of fifty-two, he sold his company and this, for him, was a disaster. Suddenly he had little to do, and without his work as his 'fix' his boundless energy had no rocks upon which to beat itself. 'I was a lost soul,' he told me. 'Drink became my passion and

I suddenly stopped seeing sunsets, birds or flowers.' Three years later he entered a clinic and eventually emerged into the world again, entire and sober. Since then he has not touched alcohol.

However, his addictive nature demanded a 'fix' and he had quickly to decide what this was to be so that he did not relapse into boredom and alcoholism. His answer was to buy a forty-nine-year lease on two million acres of Arctic tundra in the northern part of Russia's Kola Peninsula. This huge holding included the rivers Rynda, Kharlovka and Eastern Litza, together with the little-known but equally prolific Zolotaya. Peter was determined that these rivers should be the best on earth. They had the potential, but when he bought them, they were under-capitalised and badly poached. Through extraordinary attention to detail and an addict's single-mindedness he quickly succeeded. The rivers are, to this day, a flourishing, prolific flow. The rod catch has trebled and the standard of comfort and service is second to none. The world's rich and famous flocked to fish them, but soon found that money alone could not buy a place here. Everyone, whoever they were, had to write to Peter Power personally to secure an invitation, and if they did not contribute to the common weal, or behave to his liking, they were banned from ever returning.

To go back to my first visit to the northern Kola, I soon found that I was among the elite of the game-fishing world, which included both instructors and journalists, everyone excited to try these new rivers. The northern Kola rivers are far more challenging than the southern Varzuga, Kitza or

Pana. They are big, fast and rocky, and not for beginners. Granite cliffs loom over the black flowing water and the tundra is springy underfoot. Eagles soar in the heights and ptarmigan flee before you. The landscape has a barren beauty and is very similar to Sutherland in Scotland, apart from the fact there is no peat underfoot because only two feet down there is permafrost. The trees, larch and silver birch, are small and look young but, in reality, are stunted and over a hundred years old. The summer is short and the ice-clamped rivers only break free of their frosty prison in June and are solid again by November.

That was the first of many visits and I took myriad parties there to fish. Parties of twelve rods fished the rivers, but Peter would only allow me to take six people as he wanted to fill the remaining places himself. The first party I took there consisted entirely of friends, amongst whom was a man called Daniel Busk. Daniel farms 1,000 acres of Hampshire and owns two beats on the River Test. He is the archetypal English eccentric: very funny, intelligent, kind, and occasionally blissfully outrageous.

On the first night it was obvious that the two parties were never going to mix well. Peter's clients tended to the pompous and pretentious; Daniel loves to shock and is very good at it. After dinner all of us were relaxing away from the dining table in order to allow the staff to clear the detritus. We had large brandies in our hands but had sadly split into two groups, with my people telling stories and laughing uproariously while the others looked on with somewhat pained expressions. This, Daniel decided, was his moment; he stood up, looked around until he had everyone's full attention, and then gloriously remarked, 'Well, I'm off to bed now for a seriously good wank.'

For many seasons, I took parties to fish Peter's rivers and it was always tremendous fun. On nearly every visit Peter was kind enough to allow me to bring one of my sons and my second boy, Will, repaid him by catching a fish of 42 pounds, thus completely putting his poor father in the shade because, despite fishing some of the greatest salmon rivers on earth for many years, I have never caught a fish of more than 29½ pounds.

Almost certainly I shall never visit those amazing Russian rivers again because in 2012 Peter Power sold his two million acres. I want to remember that wonderful place, and all the fun and the fish, as it was when he owned it.

One of the great joys of teaching Spey casting is the people that I teach. Some have become close friends and most are fun and keen to learn. Something I did not expect, however, was that sometimes I would be treated as an agony aunt. Husbands and wives tell me things that they would tell no one else. Infidelities are commonplace for both men and women.

I was once teaching a racing trainer and his wife. People quickly tire from using different and rarely used muscles, and they learn more quickly if you take plenty of breaks. I was relaxing for a moment after teaching the wife, who was a large 'earth mother' type in her fifties. We were chatting away when suddenly she turned to me and, with a slightly embarrassed smile on her face, said, 'I'm having a most splendid affair,' as if referring to a good gallop across the downs. 'He's one of my stable lads and twenty years younger than I am. I know there's no future to it but it's such fun and it makes me feel young and beautiful again. I don't know why I'm telling you this. But it's wonderful to tell someone. It lessens my feeling of guilt. The problem is I'm terrified that my husband will find out.' She looked hard at the next-door platform, fifty yards away, as if he might be able to hear. 'You see, I do love him and I'm very happily married to him, but this perks me up and keeps me cheerful.' I mumbled a non-committal answer and continued with the teaching.

Later I went across to the husband and, during a rest between casts, he asked how his wife was getting on. I told him she was doing really well and then enquired how long they had been married. 'Just over twenty-five years,' he replied. 'And it's a good marriage. We're very lucky. We get on well and rarely have a disagreement.' He was silent for a moment then said, 'The trouble is I'm sure she's having an affair with one of our stable lads.'

'Oh God,' I said. 'I'm so sorry. What are you going to do?'

'Ignore it,' he said. 'It makes her happy and I'm not going to destroy a good marriage for something as unimportant as that. It won't last and I don't see the point in a confrontation. But,' he continued, and his face hardened, 'when it's over I shall find a reason to sack the lad.' There goes a wise man, I thought to myself.

Several months later I bumped into them at a dinner party

and they were obviously happy together. At one point the husband and I were alone. 'All okay?' I asked. He looked at me and smiled. 'All okay,' he replied. And I knew from the contented grin that it truly was.

Stories don't always have happy endings, however, and what happened, on a glorious sun-beaten day in May, was utterly heartbreaking.

I rarely teach trout casting but I had been asked by a man to give his wife, as a birthday present, a day on a chalk stream during the mayfly. We duly met up at the hut of a famous beat on the Test. I had never met either of them before but, apparently, I had been recommended by a fisherman friend of the husband who knew that his wife was keen to learn to fish. We shook hands and the man almost immediately excused himself and left, having arranged for me to give his wife a lift home at the end of the day as they lived near by.

She was in her fifties, with auburn hair and the high cheek-bones of the truly beautiful woman. She had the figure of a girl of twenty and there was a sparkle in her eye and laughter in her face. As I usually do, I asked her why she wanted to learn to fish.

'Because it's always seemed to me to be such a gentle and contemplative pastime,' she replied. 'Because, for the most part, you are on your own and because you are hunting beautiful creatures in beautiful surroundings. I can put them back if I don't want to eat them and, sadly, I can't do that when I'm shooting.' I taught her to cast and she was a 'natural', as so many women are. I explained to her the mystical, magical life cycle of the mayfly. How it only lives for one day and has no mouth because it does not need to feed and how its mating dance is one of the great beauties of nature.

'I'm sure we'll see that happen today,' I said.

'Oh, I so hope so,' she replied.

Then the mayfly started to hatch and the trout to rise. For the first one, we held the rod together and I showed her the timing of the strike. As she played her fish I could see that she was shaking with excitement. I landed it for her. It wasn't a monster but it was her first trout and she knelt among the kingcups and stared at it. 'God, it's so beautiful,' she said. 'Let's put it back.' I gently complied.

We had a marvellous day together and loved each other's company. Towards evening, as we stood in the warm, fading May sunshine, watching the ethereal, enchanted dance of the countless mayflies, she turned to me and thanked me. 'I so wanted to do this before I died,' she said, and I felt my heart go cold because I knew that this was some awful truth. 'No one else knows this except my specialist,' she continued. 'He told me three weeks ago, and I want you to promise me that you'll keep my secret, but I've only got three months to live. I'm not going to tell my husband or my children until the very last minute, so that we can all enjoy what little time we have together completely.'

I knew that she was telling the absolute truth and put my arms around her and hugged her while she wept against my shoulder. I didn't know what to say, so I said nothing and there was comfort for both of us in silence. 'Now,' she said, eventually, wiping her eyes, 'let's catch one more fish and then you must take me home.' In the deepening gloaming the rings of a final trout spread across the mirrored river. Inevitably, she caught it.

I took her to her house and gently kissed her on the cheek in the car before she went back to her husband, and I hoped so much that he realised what a brave and wonderful woman he had. I kept my promise and, six weeks later, I heard that she had died.

Sometimes I am asked to go to someone's private stretch of river that they own and either they want me to teach their children or a friend. One day, twenty years ago, I was on my way to the River Dun near Romsey and was driving through the village of Dunbridge when I spotted what looked like a really lovely pub. It was called The Mill Arms and I determined to enjoy a pint there after I had finished my day's teaching.

I kept my promise to myself and, in the evening, on the way home, I dropped in for a much-needed drink. The pub was as lovely inside as it had looked from the outside and I was relaxing on a bar stool when a man sat next to me.

'Been fishing?' he enquired, and I introduced myself and explained about teaching. 'I know exactly who you are,' he said. 'I've read about you in *The Telegraph*' – there had been a big article in the 'Weekend' section. 'You're the Spey-casting man and run the Hugh Falkus School. I'll give you a ring and bring a friend. I love fishing myself and I long to learn to Spey cast. By the way, my name's Sean O'Brien.'

Two weeks later, Sean rang me and made a date to come for a day's lesson in Spey casting and he brought with him

Chris Tarrant; the three of us have remained good friends ever since. Both have been to Russia with me and enjoyed it so much that they made another date to fish there, but at prime time. During this trip, when fishing at dawn in the Tent Pool on the Eastern Litza, Chris landed the biggest salmon so far caught on The Three Rivers. It weighed 47½ pounds and a wood carving of it hangs on the wall of Chris's house.

Chris is an enormously famous presenter and his hugely popular show *Who Wants to Be a Millionaire* had the greatest audience rating of any game show ever. It has been adapted all over the world and Chris's name and face are internationally famous. However, and this is why he is such a good mate of mine, there is nothing pretentious or 'showbizzy' about Chris. He is simply Chris Tarrant, witty, funny, naughty, kind, generous, intelligent and tremendous fun. He and I went through acrimonious divorces at almost exactly the same time. That summer we were fishing the River Itchen together and during a break I remarked, 'You know, Chris, if you and I had had our bollocks removed at birth we would both be considerably better off.'

'Yes,' replied Chris. 'In my case five million per bollock.'

One evening I took a girlfriend to watch Chris recording *Who Wants to Be a Millionaire*, and afterwards in the bar he asked me if I would like to do a show with him on fly fishing for pike in Chew Valley Lake in Somerset. I told him that I couldn't think of anything I would enjoy more but that I knew nothing whatsoever about it. 'Nor do I,' said Chris, 'but there's a guide, John Horsey, who knows everything and he'll tell us what to do.'

We arrived at Chew and Chris gave me a little lecture. 'Now Daunty,' he said, 'this is a family show so we don't want any of your foul language when we're on camera.' I was horrified and slightly hurt that he should even ask. 'No, of course not, Chris,' I replied. 'I wouldn't dream of it.'

John Horsey drove the boat out into the lake. It was pretty crowded with the three of us and a cameraman, but somehow we managed not to hook each other. When we arrived at John's chosen spot he showed us the flies to use and how to fish them. I cast out and followed John's instructions. Suddenly the line went tight.

'I've got a fucking pike,' I screamed. 'Bugger my old boots, look at the fucking fish run. Fucking marvellous.'

'Thanks Daunty,' said Chris. 'That's at least another hour in the cutting room.'

Chris Tarrant and Sean O'Brien are of a very rare breed. They are both true fishermen. They are just as content, and just as good at, fishing for salmon and trout as they are for pike, barbel or any other fish. The only really annoying thing about Tarrant is that, having caught his huge, nearly 50-pound salmon, he tells all his friends and anyone else who will listen, 'Of course I've never caught a thirty-pound salmon.'

'There's been a telephone call,' said my wife, in great excitement. 'Of course, I recognised his voice immediately and you are to ring him back as soon as you can.'

'Who?' I said patiently.

'Oh sorry,' she replied, 'Ronnie Corbett.'

I have to admit to being excited too, as I am a great fan of Ronnie, who really is one of Britain's greatest entertainers. I rang him back and the Great Man himself answered the phone. He explained that he had bought two days' salmon fishing on the River Spey at Craigellachie in a charity auction at his local golf club. 'It's something I've always wanted to do,' said Ron, 'but I know nothing about it and everyone tells me you're the man to teach me.'

We made a date and duly met at the lake where I was teaching. I liked him from the first moment. Like Chris Tarrant, Ron is just himself; there's no pretension or acting and he is naturally very funny with a huge sense of humour. Spey casting is very similar to golf; the action is all timing and technique and Ron is a keen golfer, so he took to it like a bird to flight. In fact, in my opening demonstration I say, 'Spey casting is like making love to a good woman; it is done with timing, technique, kindness, thought, gentleness and care' and I make the line waft across the water. 'It is *never* done with strength,' I continue, slamming the cast down with an enormous splash. 'That's like doing it with an old hooker and you should be ashamed of yourself afterwards.' It gets people's attention and makes them laugh, which is what teaching is all about. It is also very good advice.

After I had told Ron this he thought for a moment and then asked, 'What happens when you make love to a bad woman?'

'Same thing,' I replied, 'but rather more fun.'

Ron and I had a great couple of days together and at the end of it, he suggested that I come with him when he fished at Craigellachie. 'I might just about be able to cast,' he said, 'but I know nothing about how to fish a fly. I would love it if you could come to Scotland with me, stand next to me in the river and tell me what to do.' I jumped at the chance as we had had such fun over the two days that I had been teaching him that I had nearly suffered a heart attack from laughing so much. I told Ron that I would supply all the necessary equipment so that he didn't have to buy it, but that he must get himself a pair of chest waders. 'Tell me what I need,' said Ron, but I did better than that and took him to the Rod Box in Kings Worthy, Winchester, to get him kitted out.

Ron is a very big man in character but, at four foot eleven inches, he is a very small man in stature. I had an awful vision of the chest waders coming over his head. However, all was well and we found a pair that fitted, and I insisted that he bought a life jacket as well. I was not going to be responsible for the drowning of one of Britain's most loved performers if he should be swept away by the strong Spey current.

Ron brought his wife, Anne, with him and we all met at Heathrow to catch the flight to Edinburgh, where Ron had hired a car. Anne Hart, as she used to be, was a successful actress in her own right but gave it all up to marry Ron and has been a tower of strength and support in his life. It is one of showbiz's happiest marriages, and one that has lasted for fifty years. She is a warm, kind woman and, in looks not dissimilar to Betty Boothroyd, and I liked her immediately.

On the drive from Edinburgh to the Spey, Ronnie and

Anne wanted to stop and shop in the House of Bruar, just off the A9 where, inevitably, he was recognised and mobbed by autograph hunters.

'Don't you get tired of it?' I asked. 'Wherever you go being bothered like that?'

'No,' replied Ron, 'because those are my public and they are the people who made me the success I am. I owe them a huge debt.'

'And you work jolly hard,' added Anne proudly.

We stayed at the Craigellachie Hotel and fished the Craigellachie beat of the Spey, but however hard I tried, and whatever method I used, I could not get Ron a salmon. The fish simply weren't there despite the conditions being perfect. It is a tragic fact that the salmon fishing on the River Spey, which used to be the undoubted queen of all Scotland's many salmon rivers, is a pathetic shadow of its former self. A great deal of the responsibility for this tragedy lies in the uncaring hands of the river's landlords. If they followed the example set by the owners of the River Tweed and cared for their river in the same loving way it would not be in the miserable mess it now is.

Despite the dearth of salmon it was a marvellous two days, full of laughter and kindness. I count myself enormously lucky to have spent such prime time with Ronnie and Anne Corbett, a truly lovely couple.

Every sport has its all-time superstar and in Rugby Union this is undoubtedly Gareth Edwards. In a poll conducted by Will Carling, the former England captain, Gareth came out as the best Rugby Union player there has ever been. One of the joys of writing for *The Field* is that I am sometimes asked to write about unusual and varied field sports. Thus, when I was commissioned to cover the unique and wild Slebech shoot in Pembrokeshire, owned by Sir Edward Dashwood, I was thrilled, particularly when I found that Gareth was one of the guns.

Slebech (pronounced 'Slebidge') is arguably the best woodcock shoot in Britain. Ed has cut out the tops of the Sitka spruce to make them bushier and thus give shelter to the woodcock. These are perfect conditions for the bird. He has allowed wet grasslands to revert to rough pasture, which is ideal for snipe. He has excavated extensive ponds, which are quiet, sheltered and well fed to attract teal. It is a fine example of what a shoot should be and of tremendous benefit to local wildlife, allowing a great variety of plants and insects to flourish, including the rare marsh fritillary.

During a break between drives, I managed to talk to Gareth and he told me how much more he preferred this type of wild shooting to the ritual slaughter of half-tame pheasants. 'It's like being in a maul within five yards of your opponent's line,' he enthused in his lilting Welsh accent. 'You never know which way the bird is going to go. You have to anticipate every possibility and then be very fast. I much prefer it to the predictable driven shoot for pheasants. It's the difference between fishing for sewin in a wild Welsh river and catching rainbows in a stillwater.' I remember thinking at the time what a wonderful analogy that was.

Gareth had given me his telephone number and email

address and so, when I was researching an article on the coracles of the River Towy, I rang him and asked if I could meet him on the way down. Typically, because he is naturally a kind and hospitable person, he invited me to his home for a cup of tea, despite the fact that he had only just flown in from commentating on a match between Italy and Wales in Rome. 'I've only been back about ten minutes,' he said. 'As the plane was about to take off BA discovered that the numbers of passengers and luggage didn't tally. The aircraft was packed with Welsh supporters and the Welsh team so that when the stewardess foolishly announced: "Is there a passenger on board called Jones?" virtually half the occupants of the aircraft put up their hands.' We had been chatting in the kitchen when Gareth said, 'Come through to the living room, there's something there that will interest you.' We went through to a huge room, with a full-sized snooker table, and Gareth pointed to a glass case on the wall. It contained an enormous pike. I stared at it in awe. 'Is that your record fish, Gareth?' I asked because I had read about him catching a monster of 45 pounds 6 ounces from Llandegfedd Reservoir in South Wales in 1989.

'No,' replied Gareth, 'that's a thirty-pounder. The record fish is in the photograph above it.'

I stared at the photograph. 'That is truly vast,' I said. 'It must be near the British record.'

'For a short time,' Gareth replied, 'it *was* the record but was beaten from the same reservoir only two years later.' I asked him to tell me about it.

'As chairman of the fishing committee I had organised a

charity day for anglers of renown to fish for the big pike that we all knew were in there. By lunchtime very little had been caught. I went out after lunch, sharing a boat with the then Welsh pike record holder. Twenty yards away from me, in the next-door boat, was that doyen of pike fishermen, Fred Buller. I had rarely fished for pike before and had been lent all the tackle. I was using a number five Mepps spinner and, at virtually my first cast, this fish took. When we had it in the boat and had weighed and photographed it, we put it back. It was typical of Fred Buller's generosity of spirit that he said he was so thrilled to have been present when a record was caught. I was incredibly lucky to catch it.'

I felt that it was I who was lucky to have met and chatted with such a legend as Gareth, and reflected on the fact that he, like Chris Tarrant and Ronnie Corbett, was in the very select club of those that have achieved greatness but have in no way allowed greatness to spoil them.

Sir Max Hastings is a wonderful writer and a hugely successful journalist. Thus, when he rang me to say that he wanted to spend a day being taught by me so that he could do a piece for *The Field*, I was seriously thrilled. However, things turned out to be not as easy as they might have been, and I had to work exceptionally hard for my free publicity.

We met at the lake and I gave him my usual demonstration and chat about Spey casting being like making love to a good woman. Halfway through I knew this was going to be a difficult day. Not a smile crossed the great journalist's face. Not by so much as a glimmer did he acknowledge any of my attempts at humour. I suddenly knew what it felt like to be a comedian when the audience does not respond to your jokes and, as you deliver the punchline, it falls flat and you are left with silence. It is a horrid and frightening feeling. I demonstrated the roll cast, upon which all Spey casting is based. There is a point where, after the line has been drawn back in a curve and the rod is at its highest, it is imperative to wait. If you do not wait at that point the cast cannot and will not work. In fact, many people who have been taught by me tell me that wherever they are in the world, and whichever river they are fishing, they can hear me, at the back of their mind, shouting 'WAIT'.

And Max Hastings would not wait. I demonstrated, I shouted, I explained the reasons for the 'WAIT', but still he held the rod in a vice-like grip and cracked the line like a whip. To this day I cannot work out whether his stubborn resistance to anything that I told him was arrogance or wilfulness. Or perhaps he wanted to see how I would react to his behaviour for journalistic reasons? Whatever the cause of his incompetence we were getting nowhere and by midday I was in despair, while there remained on his face a blank, cold look, as if he despised me, which he probably did.

Suddenly, I didn't care about the article he was going to write. What I did care about was the fact that he would now go fishing, show off his abysmally awful Spey cast and then say that he had been taught by me. I therefore thought very carefully about what I was going to say before I said it, and realised that if he walked out I didn't give a damn.

After the next dreadful attempt at a roll cast when, yet

again, he had not waited and the line had cracked like a pistol shot (and it was my line too that was being destroyed, too) I said, 'Max, could you lay the rod down a moment, please? I want a quick word.'

He peered down at me from his six foot four inches.

'Yes? What is it?' he barked.

'Tell me,' I enquired gently, 'have you had a lot of problems with women all your life?'

'What the bloody hell are you talking about?'

'Come a bit quick, do we?' I said, and waited for the explosion, which amazingly never came. The first smile of the day spread slowly over his face. Not saying a word, he picked up the rod, drew back the line, *waited* and executed a near perfect roll cast. After that, the remainder of the day was fine, and he eventually even wrote a complimentary article about me.

The managing director of Collett Dickenson Pearce, the advertising agency that I had looked after when I ran The Salmon Pool, was, as I have said, a lovely man named John Ritchie, who was a keen trout fisherman. One day he invited me round to his house for a drink and then asked if I would take his twelve-year-old son fishing and teach him how to catch a trout. This was easily arranged and two days later I picked the lad up and we drove down to the River Kennet at Kintbury.

I showed him how to cast and then we walked around the beat. There was very little rising and, by lunchtime, we had caught the only trout that had been feeding. I had run out of cigarettes and so, leaving the boy by a bridge with his cheese sandwiches, I went to the local shop to buy a packet. When I returned he proudly showed me three lovely trout that he had caught. I hadn't been away for more than ten minutes and there was still nothing showing. I was therefore fascinated to see what he had caught them on.

'They all took the fly you gave me,' he said, not looking me in the eye. Now, at one time, many years ago, I was twelve myself, so I knew all about the best way to catch trout illegally because I had done plenty of it myself.

'Well done,' I said non-committally and, opening the mouth of one of them, I peered down its throat. There, just as I had suspected, was a small sliver of cheese taken from his sandwiches.

'You caught these on cheese, didn't you?' I asked. The boy looked down at the ground and mumbled. 'I'm not angry,' I said. 'I would have done exactly the same thing when I was your age, but that's enough. If we catch any more, we put them back.' The boy nodded and from then on we were friends, and he did very well in the evening with the fly when the trout eventually rose. His name was Guy and he went on to marry Madonna and made a series of highly successful films such as *Lock, Stock and Two Smoking Barrels*.

In fact, I had committed a rather worse sin. As boys, I and my great chum, Jonny Ducat-Hamersley, had gone to tea with a friend of Jonny's father who had kindly taken us to a stream he had dammed up and in which he had reared some rainbow trout to an enormous size, and which he fed every evening. They were his pets and had names. The largest was called Fred. It really was too much for two fishing-mad boys and, when we knew he was away in London, we bicycled over, hid our bikes under some bushes at the beginning of the drive to his house and, with a short, stubby pike rod, made our way surreptitiously to his dam. The trout, which were used to being fed, surged towards us eagerly, led by Fred. Jonny, who had won the toss to fish, dropped a worm in front of his nose and five minutes later a very indignant Fred was on the bank. I was therefore in no position to criticise young Ritchie.

The river keeper on one of the most famous and prolific beats of the River Test is a man called Phil Walford. He looks after the Compton Manor stretch. Compton is particularly renowned because, at one time, it was owned by Tommy Sopwith, a friend of my father's and the designer of the World War I single-seater Sopwith Camel, among many other famous aircraft. One day Phil rang me. 'Next time you're passing here,' he said, 'could you drop in, please?' I wondered what was up but a week later, on my way to Stockbridge, I called in at Compton. I found Phil in the fishing hut and, after he had kindly made me a cup of coffee, he told me what he wanted.

'One of my rods here,' he said, 'is world famous. He's been incredibly kind to me and invited me shooting on several occasions. I want to try and repay him a little. He's mad about fishing and I know he would love to learn to Spey cast. Could you give him a few hours' tuition, please. He'll be here next Thursday. If you could arrive at about ten o'clock that would be wonderful.'

'Who is he?' I asked, fascinated.

'I'm not telling you,' said Phil. 'You'll find out when you come.' Phil has been very kind to me in the past. He has allowed my children to fish in the hallowed Hatch Pool, which is heaving with enormous trout up to 20 pounds in weight. No one is allowed to fish it but, out of season, Phil allowed my youngest son and daughter to have a go there. They caught several trout up to 10 pounds, which gave both of them, and particularly my son, an appetite for the sport.

The following Thursday I arrived at the hut. 'I'll just go and get him,' said Phil. 'He's expecting you but is fishing until you arrive.' I sat and waited, wondering who on earth it could possibly be. There were footsteps, the door opened and in walked Eric Clapton. I was thrilled to meet him, as I am an enormous fan of his. My oldest son is a professional guitarist and I knew that he would be incredibly jealous that I would be teaching this legend of the music world.

We spent the next three hours together before Eric wanted to return to his fishing, but I taught him as much as I could in the time available. He was an apt pupil and when we took a rest it gave me a chance to ask questions.

'I'm a huge Rolling Stones fan, and Mick Jagger in particular,' I said. 'I must say, I would love to meet him.'

'Well, if you do,' said Eric, 'don't take any woman that you care about anywhere near him.'

'Why not?' I said, although I thought I knew the answer.

'He's sex mad, that bloke. He's a male nymphomaniac. He can't keep his hands off anything at all. I was at a party with my wife and we bumped into Jagger. I went to the loo and he immediately tried to jump on her. I mean, he'd only met her ten minutes beforehand. Bloody sex mad, he is.' I laughed, but the subject had obviously greatly annoyed Eric, so I changed it.

'"Tears in Heaven", the song you wrote for your son,' I said, 'was composing it a catharsis?'

'Yes it was,' Eric replied, 'and I know that many other people in a similar situation have gained great comfort from it.'

We went back to the hut and Eric introduced me to his fishing companion, Ivor Powell. Then Eric went off to fish, but before he left he said, 'Here's my email address, it's right up your street. Keep in touch.' He then told me an email of such filth that I cannot include it, even in this book.

I stayed chatting to his friend.

'Have you known Eric long?' I asked.

'All my life,' replied Ivor. 'We grew up together as boys, fishing for roach in the canal and shooting sparrows with catapults, and we've remained mates ever since. He's been a wonderful friend to me. Through all his success and fame he's always treated me the same. I'm just an ordinary working man and I couldn't possibly afford to fish here or go on the shoots with him, but every year I keep him company. He never makes it obvious; he just asks me along and quietly pays. He's a true friend, he is.'

I said goodbye to Phil and went on my way, reflecting on the complicated, hugely talented character that I had taught, who seemed to hide his kindness and loyalty under a front of moody surliness. I wondered why.

Epilogue

Out of us all
That make rhymes,
Will you choose
Sometimes –
As the winds use
A crack in the wall
Or a drain,
Their joy or their pain
To whistle through –
Choose me,
You English words?

I know you:
You are light as dreams,
Tough as oak,
Precious as gold,
As poppies and corn,
Or an old cloak ...

from 'Words' by Edward Thomas

That's it now; I've told my tale and loved the telling. We have such a rich and beautiful language and I am so lucky to love it so. That love was mainly given to me by my English master at prep. school, John Farrar, but my mother had a passion for words, too. I must tell one last tale of my mother. My brother Roger and I had taken her to The Ypres Castle pub in Rye for a drink. She was then in her eighty-first year but still sprightly, still witty and, gloriously, still naughty. We were at our table and Mum was drinking whisky with great enjoyment. Just across the room were a young couple who, carried away with their passion for each other, were virtually doing 'it' in their corner. Suddenly Mum spotted them and, pink with pleasure, drew herself up and stared. Even into her eighties she was still a beautiful woman, with a commanding presence. Suddenly, there fell upon the pub one of those silences that sometimes happen even in the most crowded bar. Into this silence rang my mother's voice. 'When I was their age,' she said in her cut-glass accent, 'I used to fuck like a rabbit.' The pub roared its approval and she had free whisky all night.

When my middle son was married I was asked to read at the ceremony and we chose Yeats's 'He Wishes for the Cloths of Heaven'. This is my favourite of all Yeats's poetry. In fact, I was so carried away with its beauty that I badly wanted to announce from the pulpit, 'Here is Yeats's beautiful poem "Cloths of Heaven". He wrote it for Maud Gonne who left him to marry John MacBride, one of the leaders of the 1916 Easter Rising in Dublin. This has always amazed me, as I would have thought that any woman worthy of the name would, upon hearing a poem of such beauty, instantly throw herself upon the floor with her legs in the air.' Luckily, my son dissuaded me.

Writing this book has brought back so many joyous memories. It has made me think of several friends with whom I have lost touch. So, would Nigel Lasson who introduced me to 'The Actress'; Willy Cooper (now, I am sure, Sir William Cooper, as he must have inherited the baronetcy by now), who drove one of my vans in the chapter 'London'; Sally, a nurse with whom I used to drink in The Nelson in Montpelier Square; Jacky Taylor, who starred as Lady Anne in the Berlin production of *Richard III*; and last, but very much not least, Jeremy 'Fucker' White, with whom I made so much dishonest money whilst at Sandhurst, please contact me care of my publishers, as I would so enjoy pouring strong drink down their throats.

THE FINAL WORD

As this book goes to press, I feel it might amuse to tell the tale of its title. My publishers and I have had great difficulty in deciding upon a name for the book. I wanted to call it *Fishing and Fucking*, but for obvious reasons this wasn't acceptable. My publisher then decided upon *Confessions of a Fly Fisherman*. I replied that there were only two words that I liked in that idea and they were 'of' and 'a'. I pointed out that 'confessions' denoted guilt and that I did not feel guilty about anything I had written. On the contrary, for the most part I was proud of my accomplishments including, and possibly especially, the threesome with the two lesbians in the London chapter. I also pointed out that I am not a fly fisherman, which is a singular and dedicated branch of angling, but an angler, and hugely enjoy the pursuit of all species of fish.

I then pushed forward the idea of *Philandering and Fishing – A Life with My Rod in My Hand*, but sadly my publishers did not like the *double entendre* and also said that large swathes of the population would not, nowadays, know the meaning of the word 'philandering', as it was too old-fashioned. Thus we were at an impasse until my editor and friend, Toby Buchan, came up with the present title, which proved highly acceptable to all of us.

As Chris Tarrant was writing the Foreword to the book I felt that it was important, and good manners, for him to be the first to know of this decision. I wrote the following email to him:

I have to say that, against my better judgement, I like it and it makes me laugh. Provided it sells the book I couldn't care less if it's called *How to Bugger Cats: A Dedicated Introduction to the Sport*, or some such.

EPILOGUE

I received the following reply from Chris:

It's a good title but *How to Bugger Cats* would be much better.